THE HUNTER, THE HAMMER, AND HEAVEN

ROBERT YOUNG PELTON

The Lyons Press

Guilford, Connecticut
An Imprint of the Globe Pequot Press

Cover design by Yann Keesing
Text design by Nancy Freeborn
Map design by Lily McCullough

The Lyons Press is an imprint of the Globe Pequot Press.

Printed in USA.

10 9 8 7 6 5 4 3 2 1

Library of Congress Cataloging-in-Publication Data is available on file.

CONTENTS

ACKNOWLEDGMENTS

In writing a book about war I have been lucky to meet people who believe passionately in bringing the truth to the rest of the world. I would like to thank Cobus Claassens, Neill Ellis, Cassie Nel, Margaret Novicki, Michael Grunberg, Max Watts, Rosemarie Gillespie, Rob Krott, Franies Ona, Omar, Khalid, Abu, Khampash, Aqil, and the hundreds of people who made the conscious decision to assist me when they could have simply ignored me. It is also important to say that many of people who gave me hospitality and refuge are no longer alive. This book can only be a minor record of their goals and ideas.

This book would not exist without the dogged determination of Jay McCullough and his team of Dave Schoolnik and Alicia Solis. Finally, nothing I create or do could compare with the joy of returning home to family, my daughters Claire and Lisa, along with my patient and understanding wife Linda.

INTRODUCTION

We live in a world of war. Few of us will ever experience its direct effects. Nevertheless it should be evident by now that after decades of unending conflicts, war has become the natural condition of some regions. Afghanistan, Sudan, Sierra Leone, Liberia, Somalia, Bougainville, Congo, and other areas have generations of inhabitants that have known only fear and fighting. In America we have been at war since our violent birth in the eighteenth century. We have had world wars, the "Korean War," the "Cold War," the "War on Drugs," the "War on Poverty," the "Vietnam War," the "Gulf War," and the "New War." To an outsider we seem to be a fat, happy nation that is uncomfortable with being at peace. Now that war has come to us, it may be important to learn more about the root causes of conflict and peace. I write a book titled *The World's Most Dangerous Places*—an annually updated guide that seeks to lay out the players and problems in twenty to thirty countries embroiled in conflict. Along the way I am struck by unusual places and people that seem to offer insight into the future of war and peace.

This book deals with three types of wars that at first seem based on three different energies—money, religion, and environment. It is only after careful examination of all sides that the complexities and answers appear. After visiting these regions a more profound message begins to emerge.

Sierra Leone, Chechnya, and Bougainville are three tiny and very different places that have each experienced a complete destruction of what we would consider civilization. They are to me the three incubators of future wars, where money, technology, and outside ambition are brought to bear against internal social forces. Where the values of culture, life, and land are unrelated to the concepts of money, military power, or privilege. In the last three years a new term has emerged deep in the fluorescent-lit offices of the Pentagon and in posh Beltway think tanks—a term that has made its way into a few brave PowerPoint presentations—*asymmetrical conflict between nonstate players.* David versus Goliath. Conflicts where there may be no clear victory. On September 11, 2001, the United States of America found itself plunged into exactly that kind of war.

The concepts of terrorism appear with brutal obviousness in all three regions in this book. Children with severed limbs in Sierra Leone, vacuum bombs used on Russian retirees in Grozny, starvation and concentration camps in Bougainville. Treachery, brutality, extreme violence, and extraordinary casualties among civilians are also hallmarks of these conflicts. These wars are best defined by understanding the players who are part of them: a South African mercenary, an American mujahid, a reclusive rebel leader, and a wealthy investor. From these people come ideas and perspectives on what is wrong with the world, what is right or wrong with people, and how things may work in the future.

"The Hunter" concerns Sierra Leone, a tiny state in West Africa that was the economic and philanthropic brainchild of abolitionists in England. The original impetus was to repatriate black mercenaries and former slaves who had gained their freedom by fighting for the British forces during the War for Independence in America. Black Africans volunteered (or were sent) from as far as London and Nova Scotia to settle in Sierra Leone. The idea failed miserably. Two hundred years later black mercenaries from South Africa brought a semblance of sanity to what can easily be described as the most nihilistic and cruel war since the Khmer Rouge destroyed Cambodia. I made a journey to explore the minds and lives of the various players of a ten-year war that began with a cruel Liberian-sponsored rabble and ended as the outside world then granted political respectability to the most sadistic rebel movement in recent history. The country of Sierra Leone is now an odd, postapocalyptic world populated by mercenaries, mystical hunters, carpetbaggers, colonialists, and Samaritans.

In "The Hammer" I venture into a new war against terrorism—not ours, but Russia's. Although America has not had a war on its soil since the attack on Hawaii on December 7, 1941, the rest of the world is not so lucky. The events of September 11, 2001, in New York, Pennsylvania, and

Virginia bear a frightening similarity to the events that occurred around September 13, 1999, in Russia. A series of apartment bombs in Russia and Dagestan sponsored by persons unknown killed hundreds of innocent civilians. The outcry fueled by the new hard-line government was justification to begin a "war against terrorism." A month later, more than 150,000 Russian troops were sent to annihilate a small group of rebels in breakaway Chechnya. Now, more than two years later, between five to twenty Russian soldiers die each day on average inside Chechnya—with no foreseeable solution in sight. It will never be known how many civilians have died. This is a journey along the muj trail, a unique inside account of the world of mujahideen, and a glimpse of life inside Chechnya with the rebels under the Russian Hammer.

In "Heaven" I enter the paradise of Bougainville in the South Pacific. The story seems simple. The tiny island of Bougainville was slowly being dug up by the world's largest mining company. The island is the ancestral home of a unique black-skinned people who believe they are the descendants of Solomon. Then a new kind of mercenary firm was hired to crush a small group of natives who had shut down the largest single income earner in Papua New Guinea. They fought back with World War II–era Japanese swords, slingshots, and homemade shotguns. When the government blockaded their island in an attempt to starve them to death, the rebels responded by abandoning their white-collar lifestyles and two-story houses to live off the land. In a remarkable turn of events, even the most ferocious mercenaries—the same soldiers of fortune who had ended the rebels' dominance in Sierra Leone in just eighteen months—were sent home. The people of Bougainville believed that the war brought them their own piece of heaven as a small group of unapproachable rebels created their new country, called Me'ekamui, or the holy land.

Three stories, three countries, three causes, three wars, three worlds gone mad. Pack your gear; you're going on three strange journeys.

— ROBERT YOUNG PELTON
REDONDO BEACH, CALIFORNIA
OCTOBER 2001

THE HUNTER

The Hunter

THE HUNTER

THE HUNTER

Cobus and I were skimming through bliss: leaning back, relaxing on the rigid gray inflatable speedboat as we sped across the warm South Atlantic chop. A short fiberglass fishing pole was jammed in a holder in the rear in hope of catching a giant silver tarpon. It was all quite intoxicating. The spray from the blood-warm water, the drone of the twin 90s, and the equatorial African sun were lulling me into a drowsy stupor. Behind us were the sawtooth brown thatched huts of the Turtle Islands. The afternoon thunderheads framed the splayed coconut palms and white beaches like a tropical postcard. As we soared over the shallow water, flying fish squirted frantically from the green glass water and skipped out of sight. Cobus and I were headed across the bay toward the dark emerald hills of Freetown for cold beer and maybe some barbecued pepper chicken on Lumley Beach. Sierra Leone didn't get better than this.

Cobus Claassens, my South African–born host, had lived here since 1995. He'd invited me to stay with him and offered to show me around the jungles, islands, and beaches, as well as meet the people and players of Sierra Leone. He even offered to take me fishing at his secret spot.

As we left the shelter of the low-lying Turtle Islands and started the long journey toward shore, Cobus snapped me out of my reverie and pointed ahead. He squinted into the distance and pointed at two small specks on the horizon. I was pretty sure he said "Pirates."

I didn't come here to go fishing, I came here for the war: a ten-year period of terror that seemed to have little hope of resolution. Considering Sierra Leone was ranked by the UN as the poorest and the worst country in the world—number 162 out of 162 countries—the tiny West African nation would seem to have little to offer. But Sierra Leone had everything a country needed: minerals, forests, industrious people, and fish. The mountains, rain forest, beaches, and wildlife would even make this country an ideal spot for a vacation. The people spoke softly, laughed easily, held few grudges; even in the rawest displays of anger they refrained from attacking each other physically. There was really no reason for Sierra Leone to be at war, but it had been for the last ten years, and intermittently since it had been chosen as a peaceful haven for slaves freed by the British during the American Revolution.

I'd intended to fly directly into firefights on mercenary-flown gunships. I'd already made contacts to sneak off for meetings with the rebels in the jungle, and fully expected to push the limits of survival in this brutal land of seemingly perpetual warfare. Before I left, my desk was littered with reports of piracy, massacres, kidnapping, shelling, and mayhem. It made it hard to choose where to start or what to avoid. But I was delayed by a head-on motorcycle accident in Peru and postponed my visit for a month. In the space of those four weeks the war had suddenly exhausted its fury like a passing thundercloud, and the sun was beginning to peek through. Other forces and events had also intervened. There were the vicious air and artillery attacks on the rebels by neighboring Guinea, the coagulating effect of twelve thousand heavily armed UN peacekeepers fanning out across the countryside, and the ominous sight of six hundred British soldiers with full on-force protection roaming the streets of Freetown. The implementation of tough UN sanctions against rebel supporter Charles Taylor in Liberia and the incarceration of megalomaniacal leader Foday Sankoh had suddenly persuaded, inspired, and impoverished the rebel leaders into crying uncle.

On top of that, the rainy season was coming, the money for diamonds had stopped, and the rebels were faced with the very real prospect of not lasting through the wet season. All these events had brought about peace or, as some locals would describe it, the absence of war. The rebels suddenly viewed politics, peaceful business pursuits, and free handouts from aid groups as the most sensible path to survival, and perhaps riches. So when I stepped off the helicopter in Freetown I was visiting a very different Sierra Leone than the one I had expected.

Peace and the rainy season had brought a somnambulance and verdancy. The knife-edge tension that usually haunts a war zone was gone. The UN soldiers dozed at their sandbagged checkpoints. On Lumley Beach the fish belly white skin and smudged tattoos of the off-duty British soldiers contrasted with the sleek black bodies of local girls. Even the constant thunder of UN transport helicopters behind the beach at the Mammy Yoko Hotel was just a minor disruption to the volleyball games below.

This wasn't hell on earth. Peacetime in Sierra Leone was looking damn close to paradise. But make no mistake, the reminders of war were still very much in evidence. More than half of the 4.9 million people here remained displaced, up to 100,000 people had been killed, and an alarming 10,000 locals had had their hands, ears, or other body parts hacked off. Despite peace on the lips of combatants, Sierra Leone was just nervously staggering out from under ten years of warfare. When *Médicins Sans Frontières,* Doctors Without Borders, did a survey of residents of Freetown, they found that 99 percent had experienced starvation, 90 percent witnessed people being wounded or killed, and half had lost someone close to them. Seven percent had experienced amputation, 54 percent had seen torture, 32 percent had seen amputations, and 16 percent had been tortured. Even outsiders had paid the price for adventuring into this country. In the last twenty-four months the toll of foreign victims included five hundred UN troops kidnapped, seventeen peacekeepers killed, eleven crack British troops nabbed, and three foreign war correspondents brutally gunned down. So what was I doing fishing?

"Fishing," said Cobus as he broke open the airport Scotch I'd brought him as thanks for staying in his house, "is the future of this country." His logic was simple. "With the two-hundred-mile economic zone, there is as much ocean as there is land in Sierra Leone. People forget that when the rebels controlled the diamond areas, the only source of income to the government was from fishing."

Cobus was a youthful man, thirty-six, and looked like he would be a good runner. He had reddish brown hair, a twinkle in his eye, and a friendly, laid-back demeanor that belied his former profession in Sierra Leone. He appeared soft, smooth, and unweathered on the outside. On the inside was a lifetime of experiences in wasted blown-to-hell no-man's-lands filled with senseless death, cruelty, and lost causes. He had come here in 1995 as a mercenary to kill people for Executive Outcomes, a company that provided military expertise and weapons for clients who could foot the bill. There was nothing wrong or amoral about EO's former task here. Anarchy reigned in Sierra Leone, the future for the tiny coup-led government was dim, and the South African mercenaries were Sierra Leone's last hope.

But we talked about fishing for now. Big ships, big nets, government-sized fishing. The kind of fishing that would provide enough income to pay salaries, keep the lights on, and turn the rusty wheels of government. Even short term, if the wealth of fish was managed properly it could yield an easy twenty-seven million dollars a year, and it would be a renewable, sustainable resource.

"Everyone has diamond fever in Sierra Leone," said Cobus as he enjoyed his first sip of whiskey, "but try to show me how that has benefited the people. You can't eat diamonds." But even this simple idea and renewable resource were at risk now. Because of the war and the lack of infrastructure, pirates and poachers came from all over the world to drop their massive nets in Sierra Leone's aquatic breeding areas. They simply plundered the seas and vanished. Many would off-load their catch on factory ships just over the horizon, continuing unmolested for weeks. Entire tuna fleets followed the lucrative tuna schools into Sierra Leone's waters, made their valuable haul, and disappeared with their frozen cargo. The difference between pirates and poachers? Pirates were unregistered boats that came in to steal fish and even link up with local traders to smuggle cargo; poachers were registered boats that fished in forbidden or controlled regions. Together, they virtually stole ten to twenty-five million dollars' worth of Sierra Leone marine resources every year.

Some of Cobus's acquaintances might describe him as a dreamer, maybe even a schemer. Not in a dishonest way, but in a way that kept everyone happy and got the job done. You had to be that way to survive in Sierra Leone, a country where people can starve to death or become fat and wealthy by picking diamonds up off the ground. If you hold fast to Western morals, everything you own will be taken, conned, or stolen outright. People have to adapt here, learn the rules, take risks, and still be prepared for terrible consequences if they fail. A lifetime of work can burn to the ground in a few minutes if you don't know the rules. You have to think big, dream big, act big. That's how children became rebel colonels, 27-year old captains became president, and mercenaries could become angels.

I visited the tall bullet-scarred government building to meet with Okeri Adams, the minister of agriculture and marine resources, who had the numbers on everything Sierra Leone produced, from cassava to diamonds. He agreed with Cobus's estimates and explained how the government made its money.

They expected more than fourteen million dollars in fishing fees the following year and almost twenty-four million when things had had a chance to "quiet down." They allowed a limit of 150 commercial ships to fish, but only 40 to 60 managed to pay the fee of between twenty thousand dollars and sixty thousand dollars per ship, per year, to fish off the coast of Sierra Leone. Adams expected that fishing would be the number two or number three provider of income for the country in the near future.

"People come and go with ideas and schemes," he said. "There is currently a proposal to provide a fleet of patrol boats in exchange for the exclusive rights to fish, there are people hawking fishing licenses on the Internet, and there is even a two-hundred-million-dollar World Bank proposal to revive and protect the fishing industry. We would like to see some action before we do anything."

The current action was a "maritime surveillance program" comprising a rusting navy patrol boat with only one of its four engines operating, a smiling skipper, and a lot of good intentions. And Cobus Claassens. Adams explained the unusual arrangement they had with Cobus. "He came to me with the idea of providing security and monitoring, and I said let's see your boat first and we'll talk." If the poaching could be stopped, then the pirates and poachers would be forced to pay money to the government to fish. So Cobus came up with a plan to save the country. It wasn't the first time.

Cobus started patrolling the seas of Sierra Leone in December 1999. He bought his first boat and he was given a provisional letter. They drew up a contract, then the government issued a tender for the Marine Control and Surveillance contract and Cobus won, complete with a letter from the government confirming his new status. But somehow, in the time it took to receive the letter and the time it took to approve the contract, the paper-work magically disappeared inside the Ministry of Marine Resources. It appeared that the navy of Sierra Leone had offered to handle maritime security with the only boat allotted to it, the same craft that limped along with three of its four engines broken. I asked whether bribery was involved. Cobus's answer was a rueful shrug, but the question remained: Why was a perfectly capable, transparent operation never granted the necessary paper-work? Perhaps it was because Cobus was making a huge dent in the poach-ing business. In the half year that he was on watch, he busted forty-five vessels. Perhaps the Chinese and Korean fishing companies found it cheaper to pay someone to shut him down than pay the fees, or even the fines. How much would such an operation be worth? "Let's just say that in seven months we brought in four hundred fifty thousand dollars to the govern-ment, so you do the math," was all that Cobus was willing to say.

Mohammed Fouad Shariff, deputy director of Sierra Leone's fisheries, told me that what Sierra Leone really needed was a fleet of larger offshore boats that would patrol longer and farther. "We need ships that can carry a crew of twenty-four and stay out for weeks at a time. We can do the inshore ones with canoes."

I met with the skipper of the navy patrol boat, who apologized for not having a boat to skipper. "It has some malfunctions," he offered, before admitting what Cobus had told me about its engines. The fisheries people spoke grandly of plans and programs, but when I asked them who was out patrolling today and inspecting, they said, "No one."

This is not to say that they didn't care about the future of fishing or about Sierra Leone. I learned much as they shuffled me slowly down the bureaucratic food chain, until I finally ended up in the office of the woman who handled statistics. She explained the specifics: "The Inshore Exclusion Zone, or IEZ, is a sensitive area ranging from three to eight miles from the shore. This is an ecologically important area created to protect estuaries and nutrient-rich areas used by fish and crustaceans for breeding." She gave me a wad of paper that said there were about twenty thousand to thirty thou-sand fishermen in about seven thousand canoes who caught about 70 per-cent of the fish consumed by locals in the narrow IEZ shore. Local fishermen could ply their trade in traditional vessels, and with appropriate nets and methods. But the large, life-ending trawlers were forbidden from fishing in this area. On paper at least.

Then there was also the two-hundred-mile Economic Zone, an area designed to provide income to the government from the fishing activity within that area. Sierra Leone was 200 miles wide and about 150 ships were considered the maximum allowed, but only about seven to eight registered fishing companies operated up to 60 ships. Permits to fish cost between twenty thousand and fifty thousand dollars per year, depending on the size and type of fish involved. Ships larger than 250 gross registered tons could pay up to seventy thousand dollars per season. This was a major source of income for a country that was functionally bankrupt. Officially, about thirty million dollars' worth of fish were caught in 1998. At the same time, only sixty-six million dollars' worth of diamonds were officially exported in 1998 and only thirty-one million in 1999. The government made only 2 percent to 3 percent in taxes from either resource in addition to the fees, but it showed how fishing stacked up next to diamonds.

The word *future* was never linked to diamonds. As Cobus pointed out, "Diamonds are not a renewable resource. Once the diamonds are mined, it is over. It is too easy for diamonds to be handled in an unethical way." Diamonds had also been the reason for Sierra Leone's trouble and the main fuel behind the war. They were at the core of corruption, and they continued to create a carpetbagger mentality in the country. It was apparent that most white people who came to Sierra Leone quietly caught diamond fever.

It was supposed to be quite easy. The government charged a tiny 2 or 3 percent tax on any diamonds that were mined and exported from Sierra Leone. Miners were to register the diamonds, have them assessed, and pay a fraction of their worth. But even this modest tax didn't work. The Diamond High Council in Antwerp estimated that in 1998 the official export of diamonds from Sierra Leone was a pathetic 8,500 carats, but buyers had actually registered Sierra Leone as the source country for 770,000 carats in the same year. The discrepancy indicated the scale of the diamond-smuggling business. More disturbing was the fact that Liberia, whose mines could only produce between 100,000 and 150,000 carats in a good year, had been "exporting" an average of 6 million carats a year, worth about three hundred million dollars. The prevailing estimate was that two hundred to three hundred million dollars' worth of diamonds were smuggled out of Sierra Leone every year. So who was making the money from the diamonds?

The U.S. government estimated that the RUF rebels had made between thirty and one hundred twenty-five million dollars a year from the sale of diamonds mined in Sierra Leone. Captured documents from rebel leader Foday Sankoh's house in Freetown spelled out the arrangement that kept the RUF in business. Ten percent of RUF diamonds went to Sankoh, 10 percent went to RUF's number two leader Sam "Mosquito" Bockarie, and 30 percent was used to buy weapons and ammo. The remaining 50 percent went to Charles Taylor, the president of Liberia. How had such wealth created such desperate poverty?

Sierra Leone was created by and for dreamers. Its inception was a fantasy: a place created to repatriate African slaves who had fought with the British against the Americans in the Revolutionary War; a well-meaning but inadequate response to centuries of enslavement, murder, and abuse by Europeans.

Even the name Sierra Leone was a fabrication. The natives had called it Romarong, but the hilly coastline was renamed by Pedro de Cintra in 1467 as Tierra Leoa or Sera Leoja because the sound of thunder that came from the hills reminded him of the roaring of lions. The present-day locals told me that it was named for the hills, which they said were shaped like crouching lions, but there are no such hills.

When the Portuguese first ventured ashore their interest was black gold, or slaves. They needed cheap labor for sugar plantations on the newly discovered islands of Madeira and São Tomé, and there were thousands of healthy black males available from local traders. If they couldn't be bothered to pay for slaves and had weapons, they just rounded up the slaves themselves. They established a few agricultural sites in Sierra Leone to replenish their ships but made few attempts to colonize or explore the area. It was simply a place for pillaging raw resources. By the mid-1700s twelve million Africans had been sold to foreigners.

The economy of Virginia was based on slavery during the Revolutionary War. The British commander in chief, Sir Henry Clinton, issued the Philipsburg proclamation in 1775, which offered land, protection, and free-

dom to any Negro who deserted the rebel cause. Two thousand slaves opted to fight with the British. In 1783 the British and their supporters had to leave the United States, and George Washington demanded the return of the slaves who had fought with the British.

Blacks made up 10 percent of the forty thousand loyalists who sailed to Nova Scotia, then a British colony. Others made their way back to England. The goal of finding a new homeland for these former slaves was not entirely charitable; as the *General Gazetteer*, a London publication put it,

> The streets of London happened to be infested by a number of negroes recently dismissed from the army and navy, into which they had found their way during the American war. A committee was formed for the relief of the

poor blacks, the affairs of which were chiefly conducted by those excellent
men Granville Sharp, Jonas Hanway, and Dr. Smeathman.

The British had failed to provide the land they promised in America and
began a movement that tried to redress this wrong by creating a homeland
for slaves who wished to return to Africa. In 1787 two Englishmen,
Smeathman and Sharpe, bought twenty square miles from the Temme chief
Naimbamma, the king of what was to be called Sierra Leone. The well-
meaning English sent four hundred black settlers and sixty Europeans on
the *Nautilus* on May 9, 1787. By the time the second group arrived a few
months later, most of the original group was dead. In November 1789 the
colony was virtually wiped out after an attack by an African chief. In 1790
the colony of Sierra Leone was established under a mercantile structure
called the St. George's Bay Company, which would later become the Sierra
Leone Company. A group of investors owned the region and were responsible for making a profit during the thirty-one-year charter starting on July
1, 1791.

But back in Canada more black Loyalists had been left stranded, and
they sent a representative to London to petition the government for their
land. Instead, the representative struck a deal with a business group that
promised land in exchange for settling in Sierra Leone. On January 15,
1792, nearly twelve hundred black Loyalists set sail from Halifax in fifteen
ships bound for Sierra Leone.

Freetown was also to be populated by the "Poor Blacks" of England,
"Chestnuts"—Jamaican Maroons—living in Canada, and slaves taken from
slave traders who had no way of surviving. The displaced and repatriated
black settlers spoke a Caribbean-type pidgin English called Krio, since in
many cases they had long forgotten their mother tongues.

The directors of the Sierra Leone Company were to give each settler
forty-five acres in an area to be called Granville. One hundred Europeans
and 1,136 blacks arrived in March 1792. Sixty had already died in the
crossing. When they arrived the directors reduced the promised forty-five
acres of land to four acres. A supply ship failed to arrive and starvation
ensued. The rains and fevers came in May, killing eight hundred. They
finally persuaded the local king to let the settlers live near the freshwater

springs. One Sunday morning in April 1794, a French squadron attacked and burned the boats and buildings of Freetown, destroyed Granville, and captured two ships. As a result, only two or three weeks' worth of provisions were left and famine began again.

In 1800 the implementation of a ground tax caused a revolt: 550 Jamaican Maroons put down the rebels, but then forty war canoes full of Temme tribesmen attacked Freetown. After fighting off the tribesmen, the settlers and Maroons of Granville built defenses around Freetown. Another Temme uprising occurred in 1803. The attackers came from Port Loko and were led by a dancing, screaming, and drumming *grigri*, or female witch doctor. Life has never been simple or predictable here.

Britain finally abolished the slave trade in 1807, and Sierra Leone became a Crown colony in 1808. It was to be a place where "Christianity, civilization, and commerce" would be demonstrated. The slaves liberated by the British were soon sent to Sierra Leone. In 1819, 1,222 soldiers and their families came from a West Indian regiment that had been recently disbanded in Jamaica. By 1820 the population of the entire country was 12,509. Despite the abolition of slavery, slavers still traded humans from the interior and from places like Sherbro Island, now part of Sierra Leone.

The history of Sierra Leone sheds light on the country's current problems. It was created for the sole purpose of commerce and was populated by well-meaning but ultimately destructive Europeans, a teeming mass of divisive tribes, invaders, struggling settlers, and avaricious opportunists. All lived with the full expectation that everything they had worked for would be plundered by warfare or otherwise destroyed. Sierra Leone never became a land of hope, rather, a feral dumping ground for the world's unwanted.

When Sir Richard Francis Burton visited in 1861 he didn't seem that impressed. After three trips to the country he'd written eighty pages of observations, few of them positive. He started off with a quote taken from a Captain Chamier's *Life of Sailor:*

> I have traveled east, I have traveled west, north, and south, ascended mountains, dived in mines, but I never knew and never heard mention of so villainous or iniquitous a place as Sierra Leone.

Probably to reflect his own displeasure at being posted to West Africa, Burton wrote:

> Men come out from Europe with the fairest prospect, if beyond middle age, of dying soon. Insurance offices object to insure. No one intends to stay longer than two years, and even those two are one long misery.

At the time of Burton's visit in 1861, there were seventeen chiefs and two hundred minor tribes in Sierra Leone. One hundred languages were spoken in the streets of Freetown, a city of seventeen thousand people. The unusual mix included black Nova Scotians, Maroons, Sherbro Bulloms, and even Methodists of the Lady Huntingdonian subsect.

Sierra Leone existed more or less as a quiet backwater country until 1930, when the first diamond was discovered. By 1935 DeBeers had signed a ninety-nine year contract to hold the exclusive mining rights, and Sierra Leone quickly became a major producer of high-grade diamonds. Two years later it was exporting one million carats.

In 1955 the government abandoned the national agreement with DeBeers, left their monopoly in an area of only 450 square miles, and created the Alluvial Diamond Scheme to allow locals to mine and buy diamonds. Because the diamonds were in shallow alluvial deposits, seventy-five thousand illegal diamond miners descended on the Kono district in the space of a year. Most of the mining and buying licenses were held by Shia Lebanese, who had immigrated at the turn of the century. The illicit diamond trading market was run by Lebanese and Mandingo, traders who used Liberia as a base of operations. DeBeers actually set up a buying office in Monrovia to purchase these smuggled diamonds, along with the small amount mined in Liberia.

Siaka Stevens became president of Sierra Leone in 1957 and nationalized the DeBeers contract into the National Diamond Mining Company, which was under his direct control and the control and his Lebanese adviser, Jamil Said Mohammed. By 1960 the diamond output of Sierra Leone was two million carats. The country of Sierra Leone was given independence by Britain in 1961 with a positive bank balance. In 1968 noncommissioned army officers took power and installed Siaka Stevens as the winner of the 1967 presidential elections. Stevens declared a one-party state after winning the violent and very-much rigged 1977 elections. But something had changed.

By 1980 legal diamond exports had dropped to 595,000 carats, and in 1988 a mere 48,000 carats. In 1984 the government-run diamond company was sold to a private company run by Jamil Said Mohammed. Just one year later, eighty-year-old Siaka Stevens stepped down to retire. The new leader, Joseph Momoh, retained Jamil to run the diamond business. In an odd coincidence, the leader of the Amal militia and now Speaker of the House in Lebanon, Nabih Berri, was born in Sierra Leone and was a boyhood friend of Jamil Said Mohammed. Diamonds were magically vanishing.

As the country's resources were pillaged, the economy declined, and an ominous underground had developed by the mid-1980s. Libya's Muamar Qadaffi sponsored students who wished to study in Libya, and there they absorbed a revolutionary Muslim fervor. These groups were banned in 1985, but it merely forced them underground. Between 1987 and 1988 up to fifty Sierra Leoneans were trained in Libya in guerrilla and terrorist skills. Among them was Foday Sankoh, a former army corporal and wandering photographer who had been jailed in 1971 for plotting a coup against Siaka Stevens.

Another man who went to Libya was Charles Taylor. On Christmas Eve 1989 Libyan-trained and Burkinabé-supported Taylor attacked President Samual Doe, who had survived thirty-six coup attempts in his short rule. Operating out of the Ivory Coast, Taylor quickly aligned ethnic groups within Liberia for or against the government.

In 1990 the Economic Community of West African States (ECOWAS) created a military force made up of troops primarily from Nigeria but also from Sierra Leone, Guinea, Ghana, and Gambia to fight against Taylor using Freetown as a base of operations. In return, Taylor repeatedly threatened to attack Sierra Leone. When Foday Sankoh and his small band of men attacked Sierra Leone from Liberia in March 1991, the circumstances were oddly similar to the events that had turned Liberia into an anarchistic hell thirteen months earlier. It was no coincidence. Taylor and Sankoh had met in Libya in the late 1980s and had agreed to work together.

A new constitution brought in a multiparty system in 1991 and installed Ahmad Tejan Kabbah, a sixty-four-year-old Muslim lawyer and former UN employee as president. Within two weeks a military junta once again took power.

The Revolutionary United Front began in late March 1991 when a group of about one hundred Liberian mercenaries and Burkinabé soldiers crossed the Mano River into Sierra Leone and began raping and pillaging in Kailahun. President Charles Taylor of Liberia acted as their banker and arms provider. They were led by Foday Sankoh and included two other Sierra Leoneans trained in Libya. The rest were hired guns from Burkina Faso.

Their first military actions were more criminal than strategic. President Kabbah's slogan was "Give a Hand for Peace." The rebels sent a message to the government in faraway Freetown that things were going to change by cutting off hands—something that had never been done in this land. They also magnified their effect by frightening villagers, press-ganging fighters, and demanding diamonds to be sold to Charles Taylor in exchange for weapons and supplies. In the minds of RUF rebels no longer would a small, privileged group make millions from the diamond fields. The group's initial goal was to overthrow then-president Joseph Saidu Momah and end the rule of a small, corrupt group of privileged people. What had begun as an intellectually driven revolt to restore equity spun off into anarchy as the intellectual founders were purged and killed by Sankoh, who was described by a UN worker as charismatic but evil. "If you met Sankoh you would think he is the shining light of Africa. But when you look at what he does, you wonder."

The rebels used a number of tactics to sow terror amongst the population. Some were direct copies of Charles Taylor's brutal tactics in Liberia, but they were more horrific here. Villagers were rounded up and sorted into two categories; the quick and the dead. Those who could be press-ganged as fighters or camp followers were dragged away. Those who were considered disposable were cruelly mutilated. Their hands were cut off to stop them from marking ballots, their neck muscles were slashed to make them bow down, and cruel and unspeakable deaths were meted out as others looked on so that the word would spread. Using terror in a manner that would make Mao and Stalin proud, the rebels announced their attacks beforehand to frighten villagers away. The rebels quickly controlled the south and east of Sierra Leone with little resistance.

In a frightened, hurried response to this new threat, Momah quadrupled the size of the already strained and underpaid military and overstretched his budget. Soon the soldiers were not getting paid and in some cases not even fed or clothed. Shoes were considered a major improvement in military morale. Momah, who had overthrown Siaka Stevens earlier, was in turn overthrown by six army officers. In May 1992, a very small group of disgruntled soldiers, which included Captain Valentine Strasser, a 27-year-old paymaster from the Eastern front, went to discuss their grievances. Thinking he was about to be shot, Momoh fled out the back door and the baffled group of junior officers put Strasser in charge.

The problems facing Strasser weren't clear-cut. Government soldiers would fight with the rebels at night and be back on base during the day. It was estimated that 20 percent of the Sierra Leonean military wasn't loyal to the government. The junta forces fought not only the rebels, but sometimes the rural militia called the Kamajors, and even each other. *Kamajor* is a Mendé word for "hunter," and as a militia the Kamajors often protected their villages from pillaging and looting by both the rebels and soldiers. Strasser, intimately acquainted with the problems and incompetence of the Sierra Leone army and the dim prospects of defeating the rebels, decided to look outside the country for military help. He contacted a Guernsey based group called Gurkha Security Guards to train his army. GSG in turn hired Lieutenant Colonel Robert MacKenzie.

MacKenzie had been born in 1948 and joined the U.S. military in 1966 as an infantryman after finishing high school in San Diego. He was wounded in Vietnam during the battle of Mother's Day Hill on May 19, 1967. He was declared 70 percent disabled after a year of recovery from his bullet wound. In 1970 he went to Rhodesia and joined the Rhodesian Special Air Service, where he earned the Bronze Cross and the Silver Cross, resigning in 1980 as a captain and squadron commander.

He then joined the South African Defence Force (SADF) as a special forces major. In 1985 he came back to the States. He worked with REN-AMO in Mozambique to gain the release of seven Western hostages, trained troops in El Salvador, fought in Bosnia and Croatia, and wrote some forty articles for *Soldier of Fortune* magazine. In February 1995 he was hired by Nick Bell and Mike Borlace of Gurkha Security Guards. MacKenzie was to lead a group of sixty Gurkhas who'd been hired to train the Sierra Leonean army. Strasser's top military man was Fort Benning–trained Major Abu Tarawali.

The series of mistakes that led to MacKenzie's death on February 23, 1995, were typical of events in Sierra Leone. Pressured by rebel advances, the army chief of staff ordered MacKenzie to make a direct attack on the rebels in the Malal Hills area. This was a major change from the training mission, but MacKenzie accepted the mission. He went with two groups of as-yet-untrained Sierra Leonean soldiers. The first group was led by MacKenzie, Lieutenant Andy Myers, and Tarawali. There were only six Gurkhas; the rest were Sierra Leone Commando Unit (SLCU) troops. MacKenzie had planned an air strike to begin the operation at eight in the morning, but the Nigerian pilots bombed the wrong hill. The bombing alerted the rebels that something was up. MacKenzie was at the head of the column when he was ambushed. Tarawali was killed by the first volley; four SLCU troops were wounded. A Gurkha behind the lead group was wounded, and his five companions started to carry him out. MacKenzie was hit twice in the leg and once in the back. Myers stayed to give him assistance. At that point the troops fled, leaving Tarawali's body where they dropped it in their haste to retreat. Rumors quickly circulated that the rebels mutilated MacKenzie and ate his heart. This was the first time that mercenaries, flesh-eating rebels, and the world's youngest ruler hit the mainstream press. Something very evil was happening inside Sierra Leone.

The Gurkhas pulled out and the RUF rebels were only thirty kilometers outside of Freetown. Strasser needed more help fast. Strasser's last hope was a South African mercenary company named Executive Outcomes who quickly came up with a fee of $1.2 million a month. An odd source would foot the bill for the mercenaries: the International Monetary Fund (IMF). With a little lobbying from EO's reps, the IMF determined that hiring EO was the only way Sierra Leone would be able to carry on as a functioning democracy and pay its bills.

When Cobus came to the country with the mercenary group Executive Outcomes, he was a thirty-year-old major fresh out of the South

African parachute battalion, or Parabats. He needed a job, so he became head of EO's forty-man fire-force team. He and a dozen or so *Afrikaaners* fought alongside "the O's"; the Ovambo and Ovahimbo, fierce tribesmen from the border between Namibia and Angola who used their extraordinary tracking skills to hunt men. Many Portuguese-speaking soldiers from Angola, now naturalized South Africans, were also in the EO team.

EO got to work in April 1995 just outside Freetown. The monthlong operation they'd planned only took nine days. The rebels quickly retreated 126 kilometers into the interior to regroup. At the time EO denied taking part in military actions and said they were there to provide training for the Sierra Leone army. EO was supplied from South Africa by two American Airlines Boeing 727s, the longest supply line in the history of African war.

Within eighteen months the mercenaries of EO had pushed the rebels out of Sierra Leone and to the peace table. In January 1996, Strasser's main military man, Julius Maada Bio, made his move. He promoted himself from captain to brigadier general, held a gun to Strasser's head, and frog-marched Strasser to a waiting helicopter. Strasser got the point and left. In a cruel twist, when Strasser called the director of a very large diamond company who had benefitted from his largesse to retrieve the twenty-four million dollars he had stashed on his behalf, the Belgian said coldly, "What money?" Strasser was twenty-nine years old.

When elections were called for February 25 and 26, the RUF began a campaign of terror to prevent villagers from voting. In Moyamba district the RUF decapitated twenty-two farmers and cut off the hands of five others to dissuade people from registering for the election. Ahmad Tejan Kabbah was elected as president, but on March 7 the rebels marched into one village and amputated more than fifty hands from men and women who had voted. In the north and in Bo, the rebels branded the words NO ELECTION on villagers' backs. Things were falling apart quickly.

On March 25 Julius Maada Bio met with Foday Sankoh in Yamoussoukro, Ivory Coast, to discuss peace. Sankoh's deal breaker was the removal of Executive Outcomes. Rebel leader Sankoh told Maada Bio, "We are tired of being in the forest."

Four days later, on March 29, Maada Bio paved the way for the democratically elected Ahmad Tejan Kabbah to return to power. In exchange for peace, Foday Sankoh was to be in charge of all the diamonds mined and sold in Sierra Leone.

Part of the November 1996 Abuja peace deal that came later stated that the mercenaries would have to leave. It was a deal breaker proposed by the head of the rebels. To everyone's surprise, then-exiled President Kabbah agreed. By the time EO left on January 31, 1997, in accordance with the 1996 peace agreement, there was a little matter of nineteen million dollars still left unpaid. Of the 285 EO personnel in country, a hundred stayed behind and formed LifeGuard in May 1997. LifeGuard had been operating unofficially since 1996, guarding businesses and property liberated by EO. On May 25, 1997, less than a hundred days after Executive Outcomes left, soldiers attacked the Freetown jail and released six hundred criminals, Major Johnny Paul Koroma among them. They created the Armed Forces Revolutionary Council and invited the RUF to share power. What ensued was complete lawlessness and financial chaos.

Sierra Leone was to have an odd savior. Rakesh Saxena, a New Delhi–born businessman who moved to Vancouver on an investment visa, wanted to get in on the bottom floor, so when things looked desperate in Sierra Leone he sent his people to negotiate diamond and rutile mining concessions with President Kabbah. His representatives were in Freetown negotiating mineral leases with the government when the rebels attacked. The representatives escaped, but Rakesh Saxena had his own ideas on how to save Sierra Leone. He asked a Canadian mercenary what it would cost to put together an army, but that price was too high, so in mid 1997 Saxena went shopping and came across Sandline International, a mercenary group based in London. After Tim Spicer, Sandline's chief, flew to Vancouver, Saxena commissioned a study to figure out what it would take to oust Johnny Paul Korama's rebel army and reinstall Kabbah. The December 1997 plan that Sandline came up with would cost ten million dollars. It would arm ECOMOG and train and arm the local hunters who called themselves the Kamajors. In December 1997 and January 1998, Sandline International sent in a small group of men and hired Cobus to work on the operation.

At the time Cobus was working for LifeGuard guarding the rutile mine so he leaped at the chance to interrupt his boredom. Although he was a player in a bigger game, Cobus downplayed the whole event. "Sandline was just seven guys who got a million and a half dollars to support Saxena's bid to retake Freetown. In exchange, Saxena would get all kinds of mining concessions from the government." The only problem was that Saxena was a fugitive—he was fighting extradition to Thailand to stand trial for embezzling almost half a billion dollars from his former employer, a Thai bank. Although Sandline had carefully created a contract with the exiled Kabbah government, Kabbah was in turn relying on Saxena's money to pay Sandline.

Cobus remembered going into Freetown from neighboring Conakry in Guinea almost every day to check out specific assets, such as the location of an RUF helicopter gunship. His travels included passage through RUF checkpoints using an alias. At the first checkpoint, a rebel yelled out, "Hey, Major Cobus!" At another checkpoint he was arrested, interrogated, and even taken to coup leader Johnny Paul Koroma's house. Despite such brushes with death and the fact that any sense of surprise had been lost, he continued traveling in and out of rebel-held Freetown on his security guard's pay.

The other part of the job consisted of Sandline buying and delivering thirty-five tons of AK-47s, ammunition, and RPGs for the Kamajors even though technically a loose embargo against shipping weapons to Sierra Leone was in place.

Cobus recalled, "We stayed near Lungi airport in a hotel for six weeks of planning and preparations. This was phase one. During later stages our force would grow, and we would eventually attack key points in the city as part of the overall plan to release Freetown from the junta's grip. We were just a few guys, mainly from LifeGuard Security, and a helicopter crew. The Sandline deal fell through partially because the Nigerians took things into their own hands before we were ready. The ECOMOG commander, General Khobe, was a brave fucker, and he warned the RUF not to mess with his Nigerian troops deployed outside Freetown. He said, 'If you try anything I'll come in and get you.' They did, and a Nigerian soldier was shot at a checkpoint, so in February 1998 ECOMOG just up and attacked Freetown. It took the Nigerians three days and the RUF ran. Once Freetown was back in ECOMOG hands, that meant the government could return. The Sandline helicopter operation did a magnificent job supporting the Nigerian offensive. The crew often flew a heavily laden Mi-17 transport helicopter into the face of an armed Mi-24 gunship deployed by the junta. Our doctor also treated General Khobe when he was wounded during the battle."

Essentially the gig was over, because the government didn't need Sandline anymore. Sandline insists that their contract was never canceled but admits that Saxena's money stopped flowing, even though Sandline execs flew to Vancouver to demand payment. Saxena never got concessions, and his second payment of $3.5 million never arrived. He was finally arrested in a Vancouver airport when he was found carrying the passport of a dead Serb and was considered a flight risk. Seventy-year-old Kabbah returned to power, and a tenuous peace treaty was signed in July 1999.

A Sandline insider has a different view: "Bollocks! Sandline was around fifteen to eighteen guys—some ex-Delta and ex-SAS personnel. Some 'behind the lines' working with the Kamajors in the field at great personal risk, others planning HQ alongside ECOMOG at Lungi, medical support team, and yet more personnel flying helicopters. The initial one and a half million not only paid for our men but also covered the cost of equipment including radios for the government and the infamous shipment of weapons to the Nigerians. We never achieved our full impact because Saxena welched on the deal. The Nigerians used our op plan, and we finally sent Kabbah a letter saying we were withdrawing due to nonpayment."

The intervention of mercenaries, the shipment of weapons, and the fact that a fugitive under house arrest in faraway Vancouver was backing the plan didn't seem like a strange idea.

Cobus stayed behind with the core group of mercenaries who had morphed into the security firm called LifeGuard. Cobus and his ex-EO friends worked for the same people but now guarded the rutile mine near Bonthe, the diamond mine in Kono, and an Italian dam project in Bumbuna. Cobus was fired from that job when he had a falling out with the local LifeGuard manager.

He then worked with a U.S. contractor who provided firepower with Russian helicopters. They helped the U.S. embassy pull nationals out of Liberia when it fell apart in 1998 and supported ECOMOG troops as they fought the junta rebel alliance.

In any event, there was no one to hold the rebels back and on January 6, 1999, they attacked Freetown. The atrocities started in earnest.

Unorganized hordes of rebels waving guns and rocket-propelled grenades (RPGs) and rogue government soldiers invaded in an operation called No Living Thing. This well-named invasion forced President Kabbah to escape to nearby Conakry in Guinea. The rebels' policy of raping, looting, burning, maiming, and killing people was not an outgrowth of their violence; rather, it was the carefully planned core. The rebels of the Revolutionary United Front, or RUF, yelled for the people to come out of their houses and sing for them. Once outside, they hacked the civilians' limbs off and laughed as the amputees staggered around with bloody fleshy stumps where their hands had been. Child soldiers, high on ganja and injected cocaine, burned out the eyes of little girls with melted trash liners, and then stabbed and hacked the screaming children to death with machetes for fun. They tortured people, burned them to death, and dismembered them, then left their bloated bodies to rot in the hot streets. Homes were burned, stores were looted, and people were terrorized. Freetown residents covered their windows with mattresses and hid in their houses for weeks. There was no darker, more violent, more hopeless place on earth than Freetown in January 1999.

When I visited, vendors were selling videotapes of those dark days on the streets. The rogue soldiers and rebels had virtually played to the amateur video cameras capturing the horror. They rounded up citizens, selected some at random, and shoved them into the street. Then the rebels casually pumped bullets into their victims, even as the victims stared straight up at their killers. The civilians had an odd sense of acceptance. No one struggled as they were led to their deaths or as they bled silently to death in the jungle.

Freetown was the evil center of the rebels' hatred because the corrupt, the rich, and the hated lived there. But the rebels had long forgotten how to measure the enforcement of terror. Victimizing the innocent became the rule, not the exception.

The only barrier to total control was a surprisingly ineffective group of Nigerian peacekeepers under the banner of ECOMOG, the military arm of the Economic Community of West African States. Although the Nigerians had no legal mandate to restore Kabbah to power, they had stationed between forty-five hundred and five thousand Nigerian troops in Sierra Leone by as late as June 1997. Nigeria rounded up nine hundred of these ECOMOG troops and tried to oust Koroma and the RUF from Freetown. They bombed and used naval guns against the military, causing significant damage and civilian casualties. It was estimated that more than seven hundred Nigerians died during the January 1999 RUF offensive on Freetown. The official Nigerian reply to the number of casualties was "God knows." The rest of the world wouldn't lift a finger to stop the outrageous horror.

Cobus told me about another time he tried to save Sierra Leone. This time fish would save the country. "Kabbah and his government came to us in the dark days, mid-1999 after the rebels had re-invaded Freetown in January. The world was focused on the Balkans and no one would come to the rescue of this small West African country," he said. "President Kabbah knew we had saved Sierra Leone before and we could do it again. This time it wouldn't cost over a million a month like back in the EO days.

"The plan was simple: We were advised by a consultant that we could raise six million dollars if we could sell the exclusive fishing rights for Sierra Leone. We would use that income to finance our plan to restore President Kabbah to power. The Sierra Leone cabinet, still in exile, agreed to the deal. The British and Americans blessed the plan in secret, and Kabbah said, 'Just end this war.'"

Cobus's plan was to attack the rebels and finish them off in six months. It would be based around serious air power: helicopter gunships fitted with thermal imaging sights and side-firing guns. A forty-man special forces group would focus on killing the rebel commanders and destroying their headquarters in a plan not unlike the Americans' Phoenix program.

"We would focus on the leaders: put a price of ten thousand dollars on each commander's head and have their own fighters bring them in dead or alive. We were also going to use psychology against them. We would only fight at night using blacked-out gunships flying in on night vision, music, and psy-ops from loudspeakers. The FLIR (forward looking, infra red) technology illuminates body heat so no matter where the rebels ran they would glow in the dark through our scopes. We would pop them off one at a time and where they least expected it. At night in their camps, rebels would wake up with their comrades exploding into sprays of blood. They would never sleep. We knew the mind of the rebels. It would be Ju Ju . . . six million dollars' worth of Ju Ju.

"We knew we could fuck up the rebels, and we could do it cheap and fast. The first option was $180,000 a month. Hardware would be separate. This would include a composite battalion group of local troops trained and commanded and supported by us. The second option was $420,000 a month with more sophisticated aspects tied to the battle plan. It also meant we weren't tied to the Sierra Leone army, and that would have meant fewer casualties.

"I negotiated the mandate to sell the country's fishing rights and hired a South African consultant. We quickly learned that nobody would pay to fish in a country that was in chaos. We found only one Russian investor, who agreed to put in $2.2 million. We were given the rights for thirty days and after two weeks we realized it couldn't be done."

Cobus knew that this could have been his finest hour: the culmination of years of combat experience, planning, and the combined skills of a tight-knit group of South Africans and locals. More important it was a chance to do something right, something good.

"The war would have been over in three months," he said. "Do you know how many lives would have been saved?" But the lives weren't saved, and the war continued killing, wounding, displacing, and destroying Sierra Leone until the week before I arrived to stay with Cobus.

As a way of saying thanks for his part in ousting the rebels, the government of Sierra Leone gave Cobus the exclusive right to conduct marine security and monitoring on the premise that he was experienced and was willing to purchase a small patrol vessel and donate it to this cause. In his previous career as a mercenary Cobus had been there to protect not only the president but also the people of Sierra Leone. He also learned some of the tricks of the trade during those days. Sometimes he was paid, sometimes he wasn't. He didn't plan on getting into pirate hunting, but as he put it with a smile, "Those early days were different from what we do now.

"A group of RUF rebels was hiding out in the coastal flats north of the capital. They had stolen a number of speedboats, were heavily armed, and caused havoc among local fishing and trading vessels. They worked out of the coastal flats north of Freetown attacking sampans plying trade between

Guinea and Sierra Leone. We lured them into attacking what they per-ceived to be a regular sampan loaded with goods. The sampan was loaded with sandbags to absorb bullets, and each man was armed with an AK or an RPG-7. Soon two speedboats approached from the coast. Our own boats were lying off about three miles away and saw their approach on radar. The rest was, as they say, a piece of cake. We gave them a very nasty surprise. They were pirates intent on robbing the sampan. They were swiftly taken out with AK-47 and machine-gun fire, and an RPG-7 in the fuel tank finished the job."

But Cobus was quick to remind me, "Those were the old days." Oh yes, I forgot, peace had come to Sierra Leone.

These days he had a kinder, gentler approach to maritime surveillance. On Cobus's own initiative and money, he purchased two fast boats and armed them with his leftover arsenal from the war. He'd even brought in an Aquila ultralight plane for aerial surveillance and security, and was trying to figure out if he could mount an RPK machine gun below his seat as a deter-rent to any ships that thought they could slink away without penalty. We drove the yellow ultralight down the hill through town together, as friends kept unsuspecting pedestrians from walking into the three whirling pro-peller blades. When he got to the beach, he set up the plane.

I wedged behind Cobus in the frail aluminum frame. It felt absolutely normal to zip down the beach and into the air at fifty miles per hour. The contrast between the beauty and ugliness was more pronounced in the air. The light tan beach created a series of Ivory scallops that bordered the blue ocean and green shore. As we banked over the city, we could see a cancer-ous growth of rusted tin roofs as tumbling down the hills to the ocean. There the sand was a metallic black brown, the water a sickly gray green. There was one tall building downtown. The streets attempted to maintain a grid but quickly devolved into a jumble of capillary vessels teeming with people and beat-up cars.

The slums could climb only so high on the hills of Freetown; then they gave way to single homes carved out into estates. The higher the house, the larger and more ostentatious it tended to be. Some mansions sat unfinished with rebar sticking out like a picked skeleton. Up ahead was the Hastings Airfield where the UN kept its equipment.

There were rows of generators, white five-ton trucks, armored troop carriers—all the equipment necessary to maintain a self-contained peacekeeping mission. From the air the rows of white vehicles look like a new-car lot except these were the tools of war, or peacekeeping as it was called there. Down below were a giant Mi-26 helicopter and a smaller Mi-8. Off to one side a jumble of armored troop carriers had lost the crisp white orderliness common to UN property. I found out later that they had been stolen, stripped, and then returned by the RUF rebels. They seemed Africanized, like the country. Destroyed, stripped, and barely functioning, they tried to maintain a sense of Western order, color, and shape but finally gave up.

We landed on the runway and taxied into one of the empty hangers. It was cool in the shade but workmen were busy removing the slat windows that let the air in, sealing them up with Plexiglas. They were installing air-conditioning; it was frigid in one of the sealed-up rooms. The UN must have been coming here; when the power went out, as it often did, the room would be as hot as a furnace and completely unusable.

A group of Pakistani generals who were inspecting the hangar for their deployment came over. They were fascinated by the small plane. Cobus gave them a tour. He explained that it was cheap, easy to fly, needed no base, was perfect for Africa, and could be fixed by local mechanics. The Pakistanis were bringing in thousands of troops, Cobra gunships, and support aircraft to assist in the peacekeeping.

Cobus and I talked about his plans and past as we waited for a lift from his driver in the shade of the hangar. Cobus had figured he could enlarge his security business. He'd employed about six hundred people, and although it wasn't turning a profit he'd figured he could survive by running a privateer marine security and splitting the fines and bounties on pirate ships with the government: It would have been a simple arrangement, but it somehow went awry.

Freetown was filling up with the sounds of loud Westerners who were here to make a buck. My ears were assaulted by a Californian yelling at someone to get some local papers as I sat in the tiny English-style Crown Bakery. The large man, dressed in a touristy safari suit, looked at the vendor's selection of Freetown papers and shooed him away in disgust. It was Nick Karras.

The headlines proclaimed that he was suing a small paper, *For Di People*, for defamation because they insisted that Karras was related to a number of criminal acts in other countries.

"Apparently they got the wrong Nick Karras," he said after introducing himself. "Karras is a Greek American who operates out of London."

Karras's efforts to become a diamond dealer were covered with embarrassingly accurate detail by writer John Richardson in *Esquire* magazine in his article "The Opportunist." Richardson accompanied Karras in his efforts to secure a diamond export license. Karras was more than candid with the writer on his opinions and tips on doing business in Africa. He had chartered private jets, handed out radios as gifts, and bragged his way into diamond export license number 000001. It cost him fifty thousand dollars, and he was in town to make sure he got full benefit from it.

Karras had a curious habit of always traveling with a gaggle of bodyguards. His former bodyguards were more than candid about him. His new bodyguards looked like lost tourists, with their long hair and colorful brand-new adventure gear. One had a broken nose and carried a fair-sized can of pepper spray on his belt.

Karras told me he was being profiled by a big magazine, and that film director Ron Howard wanted to do the story of his life. I don't know why he wanted to impress me. He wrote his numbers on a card and handed it to me. A waitress came to take my order. He rudely rebuffed her. He clearly enjoyed his reputation, but everyone wanted to know why he'd been here for so long; the word on the street was that he had yet to make a major deal.

I decided to travel around the uneasy countryside while Cobus made arrangements for another trip. A few weeks before it would have meant braving the roads, whose checkpoints consisted of a small piece of string, a cluster of kids in ragged T-shirts, and a bristling collection of rusty, battered automatic weapons. The checkpoints were a way to make money here, and passage was a very arbitrary process that required negotiating skills, money, and gifts. If you used too many of your resources you'd never make it to the next checkpoint, or the one after that. There was also no chain of command, no one to appeal to if your new hosts wanted to have a little cocaine-induced fun, and no one to come looking for you if you disappeared in the overgrown bush that surrounded the red dirt roads.

The checkpoints were usually manned by stoned children, pugnacious teenagers, and zombielike adults. In places like Rogberi junction there had been rotting corpses with thin blades of green grass growing through the white bones and blackened skins. On May 24, 2000, 52-year-old Kurt Schork and 32-year-old AP camerman Miguel Gil Moreno do Mora were gunned down in a short, violent ambush. Foreigners were kidnapped regularly, and entire towns encircled and besieged. There were enough stories to make travel by helicopter seem the perfect choice.

The UN was very helpful to visiting writers and journalists, and provided transportation around the country so that the journalists would cover their various efforts at peacekeeping and rehabilitation. With a quick letter, a homemade press pass, some paperwork, and a handshake, you had an entire fleet of helicopters at your disposal. Despite this the UN got very little good press—mostly stories of high-minded aspirations being ground down by third-world realities.

Like Cobus, the UN had a plan to save Sierra Leone. Although Cobus figured it would cost six million dollars to wipe out the rebels, the UN had a larger view and a much stronger military stance. They had already deployed seventeen thousand foreign troops and civilian employees, a fleet of aircraft, trucks, cars, troop carriers, helicopters, water trucks, and copy machines in their half-a-billion-dollar-a-year plan to save Sierra Leone.

On October 22, of 1999, the UN created UNAMSIL, the United Nations Mission in Sierra Leone. The UN doesn't do anything without a snappy acronym. Their mandate was to implement the Lomé peace accord. As more and more UN soldiers and aid workers were kidnapped or killed by the RUF, the UN expanded and modified their mandate. The official diplomatic language had started with such bland instructions as "cooperate with the Government of Sierra Leone and the other parties to the Peace Agreement in the implementation of the Agreement" devolved into blunt language and specific goals, such as:

- To provide security at key locations and Government buildings, in particular in Freetown, important intersections and major airports, including Lungi airport
- To facilitate the free flow of people, goods and humanitarian assistance along specified thoroughfares

- To provide security in and at all sites of the disarmament, demobilization and reintegration programme

- To coordinate with and assist, the Sierra Leone law enforcement authorities in the discharge of their responsibilities

- To guard weapons, ammunition and other military equipment collected from ex-combatants and to assists in their subsequent disposal or destruction

The Council authorized UNAMSIL to take the necessary action to fulfill those additional tasks, and affirmed that, in the discharge of its mandate, UNAMSIL may take the necessary action to ensure the security and freedom of movement of its personnel and, within its capabilities and areas of deployment, to afford protection to civilians under imminent threat of physical violence, taking into account the responsibilities of the Government of Sierra Leone.

The UN was authorized to spend half a billion dollars a year to maintain 17,500 military personnel, including 260 military observers and 60 civilian police personnel—more money than Sierra Leone's gross domestic product and thirty times the Sierra Leonean government's budget. What the world got for this was mountains of statistics, press releases, interviews, and dog-and-pony shows. Success was never absolute here, only incremental.

The UN has become a cottage industry for many poor nations. They didn't spend their money inside the country, but let the spillover create instant new economies. Most of the troops that filled the peacekeeping roles in Sierra Leone came from equally poor countries. These troops were Bangladeshi, Pakistani, and Ghanaian. The UN paid the provider country $988 for each soldier, a clothing allowance of $98, and $5 for ammunition for training purposes. Other perks included compensation for transportation, leave pay, food, and housing of a caliber higher than their normal home base. This made it unattractive for first-world countries to contribute troops, because they had to make up the shortfall. In the case of third-world countries, it was a very profitable venture, since the country kept the difference between the UN salary and the local wage.

A soldier in Sierra Leone made an average of 120,000 leones, or $55 a month. Nigerian soldiers made around $150 a month. Civilian employees of the UN made professional-grade salaries that were comparable to what they would be paid in Europe or the United States, and as first-world bureaucrats they lived like pashas. They had to pay their own rent, usually in the few well-to-do neighborhoods at inflated prices: Rent for a house in a nice part of Sierra Leone started at $1,500 a month. The average annual income for a local was $130.

The UN's purpose was clear. They were there to stop the fighting, disarm the rebels, and introduce a measure of stability until the country returned to relative normality. The only flaw was that they were acting on behalf of a local government that caught the next plane out whenever gunshots were heard, and worked with both sides to create a democratic government.

The UN's operating style was also clear. The UN had already rented the best luxury hotel in Sierra Leone. The glacial pace and staggering expenditure of the UN were evident when I approached the grounds of their headquarters, the bullet-scarred Mammy Yoko Hotel. It had a perfect location overlooking Lumley Beach, nicely landscaped grounds, and high walls to ensure that the residents were isolated from anything that might occur.

Outside, a man painted the cement sidewalk UN blue at a pace that was painful to watch. It was hard to imagine why this chunk of sidewalk should be painted that always-out-of-place unsky blue, but someone thought it was necessary. The parking lot outside the hotel contained rows and rows of new Toyota Land Cruisers, Toyota Four Runners, shuttle buses, and Land Rover Defenders. And as if to put a fine, sharp point on the inequity, there were two brand-new, perfectly polished Mercedes S320s with the license plates UNAMSIL 1 and UNAMSIL 2 parked across from the main entrance, adding a very posh touch.

The contrast became even more marked when I walked inside the Mammy Yoko, which had been completely trashed by the rebels, the refurbished to an industrial level of comfort by Roger Crooks, an American who collected a reported two million dollars a year in rent from the UN.

The locals liked the UN. They spent money and clogged the streets, the bars, and beaches with their clean white SUVs. They supported an army of prostitutes, drug users, and petty scam artists. Corruption was part and parcel of the UN's presence, clearly visible as mountains of clearly labeled equipment, western supplies, canned goods, and military hardware that had been stolen or sold by UN employees in the day-to-day operations. Corn-flakes, juice, rice, and other food supplies appeared in Lebanese shops around town, sometimes selling for less than cost. Ghanaian-supplied UN troops ate beans while their officers shipped materials on UN helicopters to be sold in Freetown.

There was also an entrepreneurial spirit here. The Nigerians in the UN and ECOMOG brought in marijuana and cocaine and made a tidy profit. *Jamba,* or marijuana, had formerly been common but now there was cocaine, a hunger that was created when the RUF injected fighters before battle. Drugs hadn't been a major part of life here, but now they were com-mon on the streets. One "matchstick,"—a tiny, thin-rolled stick of smok-able cocaine—cost less than a dollar. "Dairy milk," or small, folded packets of heavily cut cocaine cost twenty-five dollars. Marijuana, often sold by Nigerian soldiers, ran between fifty cents and four dollars for a small three-by-one-inch folded plastic parcel. But overall, there was more good to blame on the UN than bad. People had a sense of security, and the peace process was progressing.

I went to meet the UN press officer, Margaret Novicki, a large, happy American woman who wore an earth-mother-style dress. The UN work-ers were packed two or three to each room. The bathrooms were used to store file cabinets. Everyone had new computers, printers, faxes, and phones; there was a general bustle and hustle. Whenever the phone rang in her small hotel room/office—which was a lot—Margaret rubbed her head and wrung her hands. To give me a selection of activities, she rattled off a list of scheduled events, like a travel agent suggesting tours between ciga-rettes, phone calls and interruptions. Disarmaments were promised soon, as well as the recovery of kidnapped child soldiers and camp followers and a neat little program that turned "swords into plowshares." All types of rebels were apparently waiting to hand over weapons just as soon as the local dis-armament committee built camps. She asked me where I wanted to start.

"How about the Kamajors?" I said.

She rolled her eyes. Margaret wasn't a fan of the Kamajor leader Hinga Norman, because he was always making some outlandish statement in the daily papers and because the Kamajors were reticent about disarmament.

She explained that the weapons handed in by the rebels and the CDF were then given to the government of Sierra Leone. Everybody was ready to disarm but the disarmament camps weren't ready because the construction of the camps was a local affair. She said that they could disarm the entire country in a couple of weeks. A child's drawing on the wall of her office said MY MOM THE ANGEL. There was also the photo of an eighteen-month-old girl amputee that had appeared in almost every article and Web story about the amputees.

Margaret saw a lot of journalists. Tony Loyd from the *Sunday Times* had just left the day before but was smashed and injured.

"He was in a terrible car accident in which his guide was killed," she said. With all the checkpoints stopping people for money, I wondered if locals were putting nails in the road to cause accidents. Tony had been robbed as he lay there stunned.

Margaret also thought that peace was here to stay. "The leadership of the RUF is young and they have their life in front of them. I don't think Foday Sankoh will ever see the light of day." Still, longer-term outlook was less favorable. "Nothing has changed in this place in twenty years. The governments here are totally corrupt. They built this hotel—and others—hoping they would get the OAU summit in 1980 that ended up being held in Lagos."

Just then she was distracted by an email from UN headquarters in New York. She groaned as she picked up the phone. "Do I really have to write this report?" She hung up, unsuccessful in her plea for mercy. "Headquarters is the bane of my existence."

She said that one unfortunate change to Sierra Leone was the advent of crime. Sierra Leonean army soldiers had robbed the houses of some of the UN staff; one UN employee was robbed at three in the morning by seven men armed with AK-47s—"trained by the Brits," she injected with sarcasm. "We are just here to assist. The government is supposed to deploy in the country. The Brits have their own agenda. It seems at odds with our mission, but we get along fine with the Brits."

I asked her if she thought the UN presence distorted the local economy.

She looked are me blankly. "They've never had it so good," she said. Her rent was fourteen hundred dollars a month for a simple flat. Next door lived a group of Kamajors who didn't take kindly to her comments about Hinga Norman, so she asked for a group of Nigerian soldiers with guns to protect her. It was peacekeeping and low-intensity conflict on a micro level.

Margaret had to bend a few rules and bark a few orders and make a number of phone calls, but she got me on a helicopter the next day.

All the UN flights went in and out of Freetown. It was a bizarre change of scene from the luxury of the Mammy Yoko Hotel to the stripped hopelessness of the countryside. The routine soon became familiar: botched paperwork, delays, the body odor of the Russian pilots, the sweat-drenching heat as you got ready for takeoff, the smell of kerosene, the preflight check in Russian, the turbine backfire sound as the auxiliary power was shut down. Then the tentative judder as the long wheel shocks of the helicopter decompressed and the slow climb from the red dirt and crushed gravel of the Mammy Yoko hotel landing pad into the cooler air above.

From above Freetown was a mix of lush suburbs, a scabby office center, and a rust-colored maze of slums. Derelict ships sat rolled over and half submerged in the harbor. The serpentine maze of mangroves, mudflats, and tiny *pam pams* gave way to vistas of overgrown coconut palm plantations. The only vehicles on the roads were the occasional white UN convoy or single white Land Rover—brilliant white contrasted with the red strips of dirt roads and green jungle.

The effects of war were easy to see. Some of the houses were stripped of their tin roofs. The gray cinder-block walls underneath revealed signs of looting—stripped doors and window frames, burned interiors, weeds growing through the floor. Other areas were pristine. The only incongruous structures and patterns visible from the air were the many reflective beige holes. At first they looked like shell craters. I learned later that they were actually diamond digs around rivers or on flat lands once traversed by rivers. It was the rainy season, and they had filled with muddy water. Diamond mining was an entrepreneurial activity that continued to corrupt and inflame greed.

We landed in Bo, a center for diamond mining and buying. Like the Klondike, the stores had shovels, pans, and mining supplies. At the other end of the business spectrum were the tiny diamond buying shops, all with

Lebanese names and big diamonds painted crudely on the signs and doors.

As I wandered through the town taking pictures, a man came by to lecture me for not paying a small boy for his photograph. "After all, you will make a lot of money with these photographs when you go back," he said. "You must pay the boy something."

I explained that I was simply taking pictures. Another local came over and chastised the man for being so inhospitable. I left them to their heated discussion. That was when I was accosted by the delegation.

It took about eight men to explain my transgression. Apparently, I'd taken a photograph of the sign outside their building. I couldn't remember which building or sign. I was amused by the entire event and asked them if I was to be shot, imprisoned, or beheaded for the offense. Caught in their own bluffing game, they stammered with a peculiar form of colonial legalese, "Is it not *true* that you took a *photograph* of our *headquarters?*" Once again I asked if I was to be summarily executed or simply flogged. I was enjoying myself. They were trying to figure out whether I was insane or just too cheap to give them "small small"—a payment for their troubles. While we were at a verbal standoff two fiftyish Americans came up to see what all the fuss was about. One had graying blond hair held in a tired ponytail; the other was dark and had a toupee that fit poorly. Lou, the dark-haired one, fired the first volley by rattling off all the important people he knew. To bolster my case, he pulled a series of tattered damp business cards out of his crushed wallet as de facto evidence. The Africans seemed particularly unimpressed. Soon the Americans' enthusiastic rebuttal of the Africans' accusations had taken over the event, and once again I'd become an amused bystander. Greg, the blonde, made small talk with me between harangues. It turned out that we had a mutual contact in Sebastian Junger, who'd come by to do an article on Sierra Leone and suggested I look up Greg if I was in the country. Greg was laid back about the event, while Lou gesticulated wildly and continued to launch tirades against the tiny lynch mob blocking my path.

While Lou went after the older leader, a younger bespectacled member of the group made his formal appeal. "It has been reported that you photographed the front of the government building," he said in all seriousness. "We have *evidence* and we can provide *testimony* that you *photographed the sign.*"

"Do you want to shoot me, put me in prison for twenty years or burn me alive?"

"No we do not want this but you have broken the rules." The discussion had veered past logic into psychological warfare. "What if you were a spy or a mercenary for the rebels?"

"Then I would be a very stupid spy wouldn't I?" They'd run out of accusations, so I continued my offensive. "So you mean to tell me that a visitor can expect to be assaulted and accused on the street? You should be happy that people are here to visit your town."

Finally we came to an impasse. Every time they brought up my crime I asked whether I'd be executed or jailed. Without a consensus, they started to mumble amongst themselves as the first drops of a rainstorm came down. I wandered off with the Americans into the tiniest, darkest café they could find. The Lebanese owner and his wife got us Fantas and a lunch of greasy chicken and dry rice. It was hot, there was no electricity, and we watched the rain through the cheap plastic beads in the doorway.

Lou had had a bad day. Some guy said that Lou owed him money and tried to steal all his equipment. He finally sorted it out at the Bureau of Mines. Then he was physically attacked by one of his friends. Then he bumped into the goons who'd given me a hard time on the street. It had been a bad day all around. Lou had been an aircraft mechanic in the air force. He rattled off his rank and unit. "I came here for gold and diamonds," Lou began. "I fought all over this continent in nine wars. I came here in 1989. I never planned on staying here but I got involved in a Congo mining deal. I used to keep a diary, then I realized it could get me killed, so I burned it." Greg Lyell and Louis Supera looked and acted very American in this odd place. Greg said he was fifty-five, Lou was fifty-six. Despite being residents for several years, they both looked sweaty and uncomfortable in the heat. Although I'd let the photography incident slide, Lou was still pissed off.

"These people will fuck you. It doesn't matter how you treat them. When the rebels came into Freetown and went after the Lebanese, their houseboys pointed out everything in the houses to the rebels. You can be their best friend for fourteen years and if you fuck up once they forget the years and fuck you."

Greg came here in 1994. I asked him when he'd last gone back. He laughed and intimated a darker reason for his being in this far-flung region. "I can't go back."

I was fascinated by Lou's toupee. Greg sported a graying ponytail and had about him the happy karma of a good ole' boy. Neither of them fit in here. Most expatriates simply get their hair cut short to deal with the heat.

In contrast to Greg's happy ambivalence, Lou was an angry man. He communicated with a series of rants buttressed by vague hints about his ability to throw his weight around. Greg was quiet while Lou ranted. "There are only two kinds of people in this country: liars and thieves. Valentine Strasser gave Serge twenty-four million dollars in diamonds. Serge ran Rex Diamonds and promised to look after Strasser's money for him. When Strasser was kicked out by his military man, Maada Bio, he called Serge up and said, 'Where's my money?' Serge said, 'What money?' They tried to kill him in London. He went there to study law and ended up a bouncer in the Midlands. Now he's a drunk and a basket case and living with his mother. He walks around here like a zombie without a penny to his name. Johnny Paul Koromo wasn't any better. The NPRC used to jail everybody and beat them up for their diamonds. Everybody fucks up. Someday I'll probably end up six feet under."

Lou and Greg told me about their businesses. Lou liked gold; Greg was here for diamonds. Greg picked up a Fanta cap and said, "I can find one diamond and make a fortune."

Lou mimicked Greg and picked up his own Fanta cap "Yeah, but you gotta dig up a ton of gravel to find it. If I dig up a ton of gravel I can find all I want of these"—he waved the orange cap. "You can open one pit and make a lot of money or you can open a bunch of pits and make nothing. One guy scraped the soil off of one plot and there they were, diamonds. Then the people found out, ran in, and started grabbing them all."

Lou had gold export license number nine. "People come here and get diamond fever and forget all about gold. They throw away the gold. This may be the richest country in the world. Where you find diamonds you find gold. But where you find gold you won't necessarily find diamonds. Diamonds run in lines like waves on the ocean. Back in 1989 I took out nine tons of gold. Most of the gold is alluvial. Around the dam in Bambuna they have nugget gold. The Italians came here to excavate for the dam and found so much gold they never finished the dam." Lou had an angry, cinematic view of things.

"In 1991 they chopped the first hands off. Why did it take Britain nine years to come in? DeBeers paid $230 million for the Branch Energy kimberlite concession, the last beautiful fucking diamonds. Then the diamonds started showing up in London. This is what I was told."

Greg liked working the riverbeds for alluvial diamonds, but it was dangerous. "The best place to mine is in the rivers, but they can come up [in groups of] twenty-five to forty and kill you. It is very difficult to make a living here. Down here the stones are not that good. We couldn't get up north because of the rebels. You don't go up there unless you have big balls. We were asked to go up there and work, but if you work with the rebels, after the war they come and kill you. If you have a Liberian passport they assume you are working with the rebels. General Pamper, the head of the Nigerian army, took home 450 carats. They had three thousand Nigerian soldiers in Kono.

"A half carat in good shape and good crystal goes for $180. Two pyramids back to back is the ideal shape. The worst shape is flat. The ideal situation is to mine them, cut them, and sell them. We really don't have the ideal situation here. Hell, we don't even have a situation."

Lou added his story. "I did business in every country in Africa. Every country has its problems. I came here because it's a nice peaceful country. The rebels didn't mess with many white people. The only guy that had a hard time was the Sabena manager and his beautiful blond wife. Us Americans have staying power. I left with an AK, three magazines, and three land mines. I tried to get a job with the UN in security. The guy said, 'I checked you out with a few people and sorry . . . the UN doesn't have enough body bags'." Lou was developing a knack for overstatement.

"When the shit hit the fan on May 25, 1997, I got caught on the streets. I had a sat phone and so I called the embassy to let them know what was going on. I said there was a coup going on. They said, 'What coup?' Suddenly you could hear RPGs in the city. They wouldn't let me in the embassy building. They asked me to update the situation. They evacuated about four thousand people, mostly Sierra Leoneans with U.S. passports. Ever see the Vietnam War? They had jets coming in bombing the city. When the coup happened it was the army. The rebels didn't come into the city until the next year. The fighting was between the loyal and disloyal troops. Five or six guys showed up at the door of the government building. Momah heard the shooting and just left."

Greg was amused with Lou's tough talk. "Someday we will make it rich here," he said. "In diamonds."

Lou corrected him, "In gold."

"In diamonds"

"In gold," Lou said, and pointed to my notepad computer. "You don't have enough memory in that thing to write all our stories. This was a beautiful country before the Lebanese fucked it up. What bankrupted the country was when they had the OAU. They bought twenty-four new Mercedes, built twenty-four new villas, and an entire hotel.

"After Siaka Stevens had spent all the country's money, Stevens went to Shell to ask them to drill for oil. They said no. They had two chances to stop this war, when the mercenaries were here and when the Americans were here, evacuating people with that airplane, [referring to a C–130 Puff gunship], there were rebels everywhere."

"The Americans pulled out on May 3. I sat there and laughed my ass off. The hovercrafts came right up the beach, across the road, and every rebel in town came out to watch. They evacuated everyone out of the Mammy Yoko. They could have stayed and taken care of them right then and there."

Greg added to the story. "I have a bad case of CRS in this country— Can't Remember Shit. No movies. No news. Corruption in this town is terrible. People want it all—now. Everybody is making money now. Roger Crooks, the owner of the Mammy Yoko Hotel, either you hate him or you love him. He makes forty thousand dollars a month from the UN. A house you used to pay forty five hundred dollars a year for, you pay forty five hundred dollars a month for now.

"Back in the old days when the rebels were ringing Freetown, things were bad. Strasser took all the bars off the beach. They only chopped off 450 hands. That's all. Then they went after the Lebanese. Gas was thirty dollars a gallon, rice was eighty dollars a bag. A father held a gun to the head of his daughter and said if you rape her I will kill her." Greg chuckled oddly as though he were telling a fishing story.

"I buy diamonds. As a diamond dealer I am obligated to buy diamonds from a supposedly licensed diamond miner. You never ask to see a license. It's pretty simple. You pay five thousand leones for a miner's book. You write down what you want and what you don't want. You don't want 99 percent of what you see here. The people who run the mines and are supposed to regulate diamond sales are the crookedest motherfuckers on the face of the earth. One time I brought them a carat and they switched it for a lesser diamond. If you have a diamond-shaped stone that's clean and white you can get one hundred dollars a carat. 'Mackels' or double-decka they call them. There are five basic diamond shapes. It's a pretty simple business. If you find a good diamond here you don't tell anyone. You could end up dead.

"Usually people carry diamonds in their mouth. They come out full of spit. I work with a Russian named Victor. We buy diamonds for our partner Nick Karras. He came here and sued the newspapers. He got the first exporter's license. Here, money talks.

"We buy the bigger diamonds in Kenema. Victor paid about eighteen thousand, about one thousand a carat—and got two round diamonds out of it. They spent three hundred thousand dollars and bought a lot of diamonds. Karras makes money, but only if you buy and cut it. Then you can make 100 percent on your money."

Greg told me that he was from West Virginia, and that he was a vet. "I was in Vietnam. It wasn't *Apocalpyse Now*." He'd been in prison for "stuff."

"I learned the gem business in prison," he said.

I mentioned that he didn't look like a man in his mid-fifties. His response: "Two things have kept me this way: all the formaldehyde in the beer I drank in Vietnam, and all the cocaine I took when I discovered there were drugs in the world."

Greg admired a young girl who stood two feet away and stared at him with that dull, bemused look that the women had here. Greg pointed at her as if she were miles away.

"See that girl there? She is fifteen and will fuck you like a thirty-year-old. I used to be an officer in the KKK and I have a black girlfriend. I never paid for a woman here. These girls will fuck you before they will kiss you." In 1994 there were two hundred cases of AIDS here. Then there were a lot. ECOMOG and the UN brought AIDS here."

As they left Lou said, "One year we'll make more money than we could make in a lifetime."

Greg checked the tiny bill for the two Fantas and chicken and smiled. "Hey man, we're broke. We're miners."

Western sensibilities and ideals eroded away quickly here. Corruption was a way of life, but it wasn't an evil thing. In some places it is called patronage. No different than the king handing out parcels of land to officers who fought in the war. No different than tipping a waiter or sending a gift to a business client.

The way things worked in Sierra Leone was easy. It was all about "now" and "me." It could be the "small small" demanded at the airport, or it could be the diamond concessions handed out to mercenaries to pay a debt of gratitude.

Rulers had little incentive to struggle along on the tiny official salary they were paid. The real money was in business deals, up-front money, patronage money, money that could ensure a preferred existence. Every ruler needed to hedge against the day that a younger, more aggressive man would surely push him out. But there was no money inside Sierra Leone. It came from outsiders infected with dreams of riches.

The talk in the bars of Freetown was about what people were going to do now that peace had unexpectedly come to this troubled land. The gunships weren't gunning, the fighters weren't fighting, the rebels weren't rebelling.

When I went to Alex's, one of the main expat hangouts in Freetown, I found that peace was making the mercenaries very nervous and strangely reflective. They drank their beer with the cans stacked two or three high in the fist.

Kasi was a gunship pilot. He looked like a young Santa Claus with his curly hair, stocky build, and deep laugh. Whenever he visited the two main hangouts in town, Alex's and Paddy's, he often found business cards with Lebanese names that strangers had tucked into his shirt pocket.

English was his second language, Afrikaans his first. He had stories of growing up being picked on by the British kids. He called them *salpil*, or salt pricks. Kasi was a Boer, a descendant of Dutch German settlers who came to live in South Africa, a people known for their toughness, resilience, and above all, pragmatism. He was part of Jesa Air, a group that flew two Hind gunships for the government of Sierra Leone. And although he had hundreds of hours in the South African air force, with eighty to one hundred hours of logged combat flying per tour, he was sitting and waiting, not flying.

The last action they had seen was when they took out the West Side Boys, a group of ex-army thugs who had kidnapped a group of British soldiers on patrol. The Brits then sent in the SAS to rescue them, but didn't finish off the "West Side Niggaz"—as they liked to call themselves. The British had left a few loose ends and looked the other way while the South Africans "sorted them out."

"I remember them trying to hide under sheets of corrugated tin, thinking it would protect them. We just wiped them all out. God will forgive me. I think," Kasi said. He crossed himself, looked up, then laughed.

"In the old days we would fly out twenty miles and blow the shit out of people and be back on the beach that afternoon having a beer. That's what was so great about this country. But you know, Robert, I go to work now and I see the gunships with the eighty-millimeter rockets and the machine guns and I stop and I say to myself, 'fuck, Kasi, it's peace.' "

Peacetime is not the normal state of affairs for a mercenary. Contracts are ended; phone calls are made, tickets back to South Africa are purchased.

Cobus was also an Afrikaaner and could trace his lineage to the first group of Dutch that landed in South Africa. They were Boers, farmers who came up against the British when they ordered the farmers to stop reinforcing their garrison in South Africa. The British had been undefeated in their Zulu War of 1879, as well as the Second Sudan War (1896–1898). But the Boer War (1899–1902) saw the invention of a form of guerrilla warfare that rendered the British army's size, technology, and firepower useless. It took four hundred thousand British soldiers to fight fewer than fifty-two thousand Boers, many of them boys. The war began on October 11, 1899, mainly because the British wanted the gold reserves in the Transvaal. The Boers invented the "commando" group, hit-and-run attacks, snipers, and ambushes: all the elements of guerrilla warfare that remain in vogue. The British were unable to defeat the entire Boer nation by attacking small groups of Boers, so they started to burn farms and put women and children in concentration camps, an action some say Hitler studied and copied. More than twenty-five thousand women and children died from dysentery, measles, and enteric fever. The Boers realized that they could still fight, but if they did, their race would be wiped out. They finally surrendered in 1902.

The war took thirty-one months. The Union of South Africa was created in May 1910. South Africa was a land of three peoples: the British, the Afrikaaners, and the blacks. When the Russians began to meddle in Africa, the South Africans realized exactly what was happening and began attacking the Soviet-supported insurgency groups at their bases. They fought dirty and they fought hard. When apartheid ended there were a lot of very tough, very seasoned Boer commandos with very little economic future.

When fighting men were needed for wars in Africa, recruits came from an army that had been fighting for almost two decades.

Among them was the most feared man in Sierra Leone. I met him at a mixer at the British High Commission. He was very quiet, very polite, with an elegant demeanor that let everyone around him relax and trust him. Neill Ellis was a South African who'd been raised in Rhodesia. Some said he was the world's most experienced helicopter pilot. Others ground their teeth at the description and attributed it to Neill's reputation for just being friendly to journalists.

To be fair, Neill made no claims. When I brought up his reputation, he apologized for having flown only twenty-five hundred hours since leaving the South African air force. He reminded me that most if not all of those hours were in combat or under direct fire. Although Cobus was proud to have been a mercenary, he was careful to use the word *mercenary*. In contrast, Neill liked to say that he was a private military corporation. He told visitors that his office was a Russian-built Mi-24 gunship. Neill was part of a Jesa Air the company which provided the air wing for Sierra Leone's army. Technically you could describe him as an employee, a pilot, or even an adviser—until you see the deadly tool that he operated with Cassie Nel, the other South African pilot.

Everyone who did peacekeeping or military work in Sierra Leone agreed that the only thing that truly struck fear into the heart of the rebels was the pounding turbine of Neill's Mi-24. He was deadly accurate, calm, and professional as he methodically fired eighty-millimeter rockets from pods on either side of the ungainly green and tan camouflaged helicopter. Neill had come here to fly transport helicopters for Executive Outcomes and then stayed. Now he had a nice contract, a house, and a business. Jesa Air was a mini United Nations with partners from Ethiopia, Fiji, South Africa, Rhodesia, and the United Kingdom.

The sleek Pumas of the South African air force used to be the tools of Neill's trade. His coolness under fire and ability to sort out tight situations made him a legend. Now his workhorses were the Russian-made helicopters found in every war in the third world: the twenty-passenger Mi-8, the Mi-17 transport and sometimes gunship, the leviathan Mi-26 that could lift sixty tons. Last but not least was the narrow, googly-eyed, hump-backed Mi-24 gunship, which flew in low and sported rocket pods mounted on stubby winglets, a nose-mounted Gatling gun, and as many machine guns as they could fire out the windows on either side.

Neill was paid six thousand dollars a month, good money for an African helo pilot but not a lot by European standards. He used to get two thousand dollars an hour. Prices for his "office equipment" were going up, and labor was undercutting his good living. "The Russians are screwing up this business. They only charge two thousand dollars a month and then lease their helis for a lot less than they cost to buy. The prices of helicopters are going up. Mi-17s used to go for under a million and now the prices are climbing. Mi-24s could be bought for a million and a half, but now they go for two and a half million."

We went to Lumley Beach for a drink and some pepper chicken. His Mitsubishi Montero had a smashed windshield. I assumed a bullet had caused the damage, but it had in fact been from an argument with his girlfriend, who saw him kissing another woman a few days ago.

A warm wind came up off the ocean and rustled the fronds on the palm trees. We sat on cheap plastic chairs shoved into the sand in an area that was lit with bare bulbs strung from poles. Loud reggae music played under a palm-thatched dance floor as hawkers stood quietly in the darkness outside a small string fence that marked the borders of the restaurant, trying to attract our attention.

Neill said he was too old at fifty-one to do other flying. He was short and compact and seemed to move and talk with a deliberate economy. His speech was soft and disarming, like a college professor or a doctor, and he needed some coaxing to tell his story. Throughout our conversation he put on his glasses and took them off as if he was trying to ignore them. If you were looking for a cartoon version of a mercenary, he would be a disappointment.

In more than twenty years of combat flying he had never been shot down. He said he'd had some flesh wounds and that his helicopter had been forced down, "It's very hard to shoot down a helicopter," he told me. Some said he would crack up one day and that would be the end, but Neill had a different view of things.

"African wars are fun. You can live like this, go to work in the morning, do your job a few minutes outside Freetown, and be back on the beach in the afternoon having cold beer and pepper chicken."

As I transcribed his words I wondered how well they would be received by the Western press. Wars aren't fun; people don't choose wars based on how enjoyable they are. But he was making a subtle point: The war in Sierra Leone wasn't a real war; it was a source of income. Those who lived here and knew Sierra Leone had a certain cold cynicism for the uncaring world that kept the war going. Neill was even convinced that the Nigerian ECOMOG soldiers had tried to destabilize things to keep their business interests going.

But with peace and the UN here, there wasn't much of a future for Neill. Now that the British were here they didn't want him flying with an all-white crew, even though Neill's partners and maintenance crew were black Ethiopians.

"So they put a Sierra Leonean in the front gunner's pod," he said, and chuckled. "You know, just like the first Americans in space." He was alluding to the chimpanzees that were initially substituted for astronauts.

He had a bit of time left on his contract and could move on, but he'd found a place he loved. To him, Sierra Leone was home. Neill had a Sierra Leonean girlfriend and was putting another local girl through college in America. I asked him which place in Africa was his favorite. He looked at me with surprise.

"I haven't seen much of Africa. It was hard for a South African to get around, you know. I have been to Angola and Mozambique, but only when I was being shot at."

Neill was slipping in information and descriptive images that reinforced his legend. He was legendary among South African mercenaries as a calm, trustworthy pilot who could be relied on to show up at the end of a tough mission or to "sort things out" when things went crazy. But he never really told war stories; he liked to nibble around the edges and let you imagine the bigger picture.

Neill flew with the South African Defense Forces, which supported the infamous 32 Buffalo Battalion inside Angola. They would fly their Pumas thirty miles into enemy territory inside Angola and just wait. "We couldn't use our lights or electricity. But we would sit there with our beer and half a bottle of whisky. That was rations enough." They also flew men in and out under just about any conditions. "Angola was intense. I flew Alouettes, and one time we had fifty-seven holes in our helicopter. And an Alouette is a small helicopter."

After he left the military he went fishing for a year, then he tried farming. He wanted to make a go of it but his wife said he was crazy and eventually told him to fuck off. He got a call from a pilot friend who asked him if he wanted to go to Bosnia, so he went with six other pilots, two of them still on active duty with the South African air force. "Bosnia was a bit of a cock-up. There was no support, no medical, no fallback. When you get out of your comfort zone you reassess why you are there. The two air force guys quit, and since they had a deal that if one quit they all quit, they left.

"When we flew for the Muslims in Gorazde we had to fly over two front lines every time we went in. Because it was encircled, the Serbs knew exactly when we were coming, and they knew when we were leaving. That meant we had to be shot at for at least six minutes every time we flew in supplies. Thankfully, it's hard to shoot down a helicopter."

Neill was also active in Zaire during the last days of Mobutu. Mobutu paid him fifteen thousand dollars a month but Neill didn't have fond memories. "This mercenary stuff is shit. You need to work for a reputable firm like EO or Sandline. You never want to go in on your own. Mobutu promised me that if things went to hell he would come and get me. One day I woke up and heard all these 727s taking off from the airport in Kinshasa. He was gone. The city went very quiet and then the shooting started."

Neill and his crew tried to escape with a Frenchman who flew for the local airline. They passed through a number of checkpoints by letting the Frenchman do all the talking; Neil just nodded. When they got to the last one the soldiers let the French pilot go and said, "You, you are South African mercenaries."

"They made us strip and the soldiers made us get dressed again, but without our shoes. Then they told us to walk into the bushes with our hands over our heads. We got a few yards out and then they started shooting. We ran and then the locals starting firing on the checkpoint. That distracted them long enough for us to escape. We walked out barefoot."

He came to Sierra Leone with Executive Outcomes flying transport helicopters and stayed behind when Sandline left. As a token of their appreciation and to plant the seed of future deals, Sandline gave him the Mi-17 transport helicopter, and he founded Jesa Air. The name comes from the initials of the crews: J for Johan Joubert, a South African; E for Neill Ellis; S for Sindaba, their Ethiopian partner; and A for Alphonso Marafano, better known as Alphonso Marijuana because his real Fijian name is unpronounceable. Sixty-year-old Fred Marafano was the first black man badged into the SAS, was in on the Princess Gate attack, and was known for doing "James Bond stuff." Fred was described as crazy by his fellow mercs, a term of endearment tinged with concern. At the time, Fred was off working with film director Michael Mann in Zambia and Mozambique, doing security on a film about Muhammad Ali.

It was nearing "pumpkin time"—the midnight curfew. I figured we should head out, but Neill said that we could leave at twenty minutes to and make it back in time. "The Nigerians were bastards about the curfew but the UN soldiers don't really care. You slip them a few bucks and it's solved. The UN is fucking this place up. It is a big moneymaking machine. They just reduced the Guineans' fuel ration in half because they were selling diesel to the RUF."

But Neill liked it here. "In South Africa it's too civilized. Here, if a cop tells you to slow down you can just drive on. Nobody hassles you. You are free here." Neill wanted to be a Sierra Leonean but he'd never heard back after the first citizenship interview. He said their constitution had racist laws. Where was his home? "Here. This is home."

Home was not a happy place. Although the peacekeepers were deployed and there was little fighting, deep undercurrents could ripple to the surface at any time.

The rural rebel group was led by entrepreneurial commanders who had little ideology and even less structure. Foday Sankoh sat in Pademba Road Prison in Freetown, but many speculated that he had yet to play his final card because he was armed and supported by Charles Taylor in Liberia. On the surface ECOMOG was a U.S.-backed Nigerian force that came to defend the democratically elected government against the slightly socialist, Libyan-backed rebels. But when an Indian peacekeeping force and its commander quit in disgust, it ripped open an ugly scene. Not only was the UN completely disorganized, but the Nigerians were actively colluding with the rebels.

The Indian commander also accused the Nigerians of profiteering and described Brigadier General Maxwell Khobe as the "Ten Million Dollar Man," after the old TV series starring Lee Majors. It was alleged that Khobe was simply paid ten million to allow the RUF to continue diamond mining unmolested.

"Now the Guineans, Nigerians, and others with the UN all have their scams. The big guys are focused on diamonds and gold, the little guys are into the little stuff. The PX brings in everything tax-free. I remember flying out the looted goods the ECOMOG soldiers brought out of Freetown. They had cargo planes taking out vehicles, luxury goods, and TV sets."

I asked Neill if peace had come to Sierra Leone.

"The RUF is finished. In just two weeks they melted away. They even accuse the UN of harassing them. They showed up and told them to leave their HQ, and the RUF complained of harassment. The UN was unprepared for how quickly things happened. This war is over for now. The big guys have made their money, and now they want to get into politics.

"The spokesman for the RUF was a math teacher. When he was asked if he would return to teaching, he said no, he had decided to go into politics. Why? 'Because that is where the money is.'"

✦   ✦   ✦

Despite its violent history, the South Africans liked Sierra Leone. It was a vast contrast to the, poisoned Africa they knew. Apartheid had been a way to control the blacks, who were receptive to the communist message of the ANC. South Africa was, in the apartheid years, attacked from all sides—Angola, Mozambique, and Namibia. So they resorted to guerrilla warfare and commando groups operating inside enemy territory with an aggressive African-style approach. They were intelligence-rich but strategy-poor, moved rapidly, employed simple tactics, and had a take-no-prisoners policy—the mind set of the hunter. Understand and track down prey, he in wait, and kill him. The rest would sort itself out. Groups like the 32 Battalion or Buffalo Battalion were made up primarily of black Angolans and Namibian trackers who went deep behind enemy lines to disrupt and destroy much larger enemy units. They were the remnants of the FNLA who had been defeated in Angola by the communist forces. The FNLA's mercenary leaders were arrested and tried, and some were executed in 1975. They used the Cape buffalo as their symbol because it is the most dangerous, unpredictable animal in Africa, and also because the nineteenth-century black Americans who'd fought in the U.S. cavalry were called Buffalo soldiers by the Indians, for their curly black hair.

Some operations required a two hundred-kilometer hike to get to the insertion point, but the 32 Battalion usually flew in Puma helicopters, hiked in, conducted operations, and then hiked out to a extraction point from which the helicopters took them to their base. They would stay in their area of operations for around three months fighting the communists. As a result, the 32 Battalion killed more enemies and received more medals than any other group in the South African Defense Force.

Cobus spent thirteen months in the 32 Battalion. "They chose the reckless ones. It was not by physical qualifications; they wanted the crazy ones. They would hire a baby officer to go in to go with a group that had five hundred years of combined combat experience."

Cobus thought the special forces guys were a bit timid compared to the hard, native tactics of 32 Battalion. "The 32 guys said 'I want to have fun' and were plunged straight into the shit. Thirty-two had the most combat experience. When I was in 32 Battalion as an FAC and officer I was in charge of a recon, but I always wore my Parabat beret and considered myself above the 32."

Cobus's commander taught him how to cut the liner out of his sleeping bag and then roll up his cans of food into a tight roll. He'd carry this and his AK for weeks in the dry bush of Angola. "You carried water, ammunition, the clothes on your back, and that's it. Nothing to clatter in the bush. You stop for the day roll out your blanket and there is your food." Cobus still sleeps under his liner.

Ultimately the government betrayed the 32 Battalion. They fought far from home and family and won their battles—but they lost the war when the ANC became the government of South Africa. The South African army was downsized after twenty years of combat, and thousands of highly trained, highly experienced soldiers were forced into the private sector.

Peace had made the normal activity of drinking dull. It had once been almost dashing to enjoy a night out in a war zone. Now everyone was just sitting around in a third-world country, and not a very glamorous one at that.

If you wanted to learn anything about Sierra Leone, the best classroom was Paddy's Bar. To get to Paddy's on the Aberdeen peninsula in Freetown, you had to snake through the UNAMSIL checkpoint made from white fifty-gallon fuel drums and wave at the blue-helmeted Nigerians. Paddy's was a large open beer hall that remained open even during the rebel occupation of Freetown. There were two main bars. The one next to the dance floor was popular with locals, while the square bar near the door was usually lined on three sides by white faces, and on the fourth by thin, young local girls who dressed like Destiny's Child and spoke Krio. If they'd gone to school, the Krio sounded like quaintly accented English. If not, it was imcomprehensible.

On weekends the bar was full. Locals usually didn't drink or smoke; they had no money. They came to dance to the painfully sibilant music with a Western beat.

Nick Karras was there and, yup, over by the bar were his ex-SAS bodyguards, wearing their out-of-place adventurewear. They wanted to rent Cobus's boat for a day. Peacetime boredom was getting to them, too.

Explorer Sir Richard Burton was right about West Africa: It grinds the white man down. The white faces of the expats hunched around the bar had that peculiar look that comes with Africa: a permanent, slowly con-

sumed drink in one hand, a burning cigarette in the other. They were permanently untanned serial drunkards at night, uncomfortable and sweaty
during the day. Out of place with their short-cropped graying hair, storklike
slouches, faded blue shirts, and beer bellies balancing a flat butt with pasty
stick legs. In contrast, the locals glistened in their blackness. They men were
chiseled, bright eyed, and laughing. The women were fine featured, high
hipped, and boisterous. The only catch was that you didn't see a lot of old
people. The average life span was less than forty years. The expats seemed
almost morose and sordid as they wallowed in their loneliness and gossip.

The South Africans were easy to spot in Sierra Leone. They didn't have
the tired expat look. They were healthy, laughed loudly, drank rapidly with
two or three beer cans to a fist, and could be found at most bars until pumpkin time. They spoke mostly in English, but broke into Afrikaans when talking among themselves. The word *fookin* was liberally interspersed in the
hard, gutteral Afrikaans. Unlike the thinly veiled altruism of the aid workers
and expats, the South Africans freely admitted they were here for the
money, whether as businessmen, mercenaries, miners, pilots or "consultants."

Although the location changed, the activities were always the same—
barbecue, drinks, and gossip. One night was Paddy's, the next night was
Alex's, or maybe a beach bar for a bit of variety, or private parties on the
weekends to get away from the regular routine. One night there was a big
party for an NGO, or non governmental organization. Outside, the white
SUVs blocked both sides of the road. The aid workers were a little different from the ordinary expats. They were younger, smaller, sported ponytails,
and long hair, and generally looked like college students of the 1970s. The
French were usually the ones with the longest hair, the Brits the shortest,
the Americans the tallest, and the NGOs who dealt with food and aid
seemed to be thinner. Their uniform was a T-shirt, loose pants, and sandals,
with a mandatory piece of local handicraft to accessorize.

The South Africans stuck out here as well. They stood in a loose group
and talked and laughed loudly. They were too beefy, too tanned to fit into
this crowd. There was a definite distance between the NGOs and the former mercenaries, and, in fact, the French NGOs were under direct orders
not to talk to the South Africans. Newcomers got intense stares from the
plain-looking NGO women, but they made no overtures.

Fritz, a towering, wide South African, kept to himself and just watched. He was a former paratrooper turned medic who was currently working as a guard at Sierra Rutile's vast mine complex in the south. He'd made two hundred dollars a month as a sergeant in the paratroopers before signing with the mercenaries. He neither drank nor smoked and made polite conversation with me. A flush-faced Aussie NGO walked over to make small talk.

"Hey mate, where you from?"

Fritz answered obliquely, "A Southern Hemisphere country."

The Aussie was taken aback but figured it out quickly. Fritz explained the routine. "They discover I am a South African, they assume I am a mercenary, and, depending on how much the NGO has had to drink, they either backtrack quickly or make their distaste for mercenaries very plain."

The dozen or so South Africans in Sierra Leone were the remnants of the 160 or so South Africans who first came here for Executive Outcomes in May 1995. They fought for twenty-one months, and then about a third of them stayed behind to guard mining installations and a hydroelectric project at Bumbuna. A smaller contingent remained as part of Southern Cross, Cobus's company, or as gunship pilots for the Sierra Leone army.

Fritz was a gentle giant. Once he felt me out, he shared his views about Africa and war. He didn't apologize for apartheid or even his opinions. He said apartheid had begun when the blacks starting believing in communism. "They were illiterate and susceptible to propaganda so we had to separate them. As soon as the ANC was voted in, two million South Africans fucked off." Fritz spent his time in the South African army fighting black insurgents. I asked him if there would be peace in Sierra Leone.

He cast a glance that only a man who has spent his entire life fighting wars in Africa could give. "In Africa, peace or war, it is all the same. Fighting breaks out, peace breaks out. In peacetime you fight crime, in war you fight low-intensity insurgency. What is the difference? In 1993 in the townships we shot hundreds of them. Now they are shooting each other. What does it matter?"

But there was something else to his bitter tone. "This country is a mess. When all hell broke loose in Sierra Leone, the NGOs, the people, the army, they all ran away. We were the only ones who stood and fought."

I drifted over to talk to a tall American NGO who was with a food distribution group. He told me it took a while for the world community to react to the events in Sierra Leone. Although the atrocities and the fighting began in 1991, the UN didn't really make a stand until 1999 when it became painfully obvious that the war was simply about control of diamonds and making certain people rich. By then seventy-five thousand to one hundred thousand people had died and two million people were refugees. Six years previously EO had already shown that a small group of well-trained troops could defeat the same rebels, but foreign opinions about mercenaries allowed the bloodshed to continue after EO left. Now the UN was here indefinitely, spending half a billion dollars a year to do the same thing EO charged thirty-five million dollars to do in twenty-one months.

The NGO said that the British were here because the movie *Cry Freetown* had had a big impact on the aid groups. It was shot by local cameraman Sorious Samara during the January 1999 invasion and occupation of Freetown by the rebels. *Cry Freetown* featured footage of RUF atrocities, executions, and maimings. The footage was considered too graphic to be aired, but even with very limited violence, the film rubbed the Western world's nose in the horror.

The aid worker didn't have a high opinion of the UN. Although Sierra Leone was the UN's largest and most expensive peacekeeping project, he said it wasn't a prize posting for UN workers. "They tend to get their weaker members." He was also critical of his own field: "There is lot of corruption in the NGO business as well. People sell off tons of food and we know that isn't healthy."

He predicted problems as they downsized for peace. "They are already informing the refugees in the camps that they will only provide food to the elderly and the young. The rest must go back to their homes. We are worried about riots. The people have gotten used to free handouts."

I pointed out his T-shirt, which said, IF VEGETARIANS EAT VEGETABLES, THEN WHAT DO HUMANITARIANS EAT?

He laughed, "It's hard not to become cynical here." He was happy to be leaving soon. He was going to Mazar-I-Sharif in northwest Afghanistan. "A much nicer place," he said.

✦   ✦   ✦

I'd driven past a sign on the way to Paddy's Bar many times. It said AMPUTEE CAMP, and although I'm not squeamish, I felt I had to wait for the right moment to visit the camp, a moment when I could focus and properly consider what I would see. A discussion with British peacekeepers had unsettled me. I'd gone with them to deliver a piano to a home for the blind. The children were dressed in yellow and posed for photographs as a British soldier leaned uncomfortably on the piano for the benefit of the British military video camera. It was a photo op to show the folks back home that the boys overseas were doing a splendid job. They chatted and joked with the children, but there was an uncomfortable feeling about the need to videotape the event in such a calculated manner. I asked an officer about the amputee camp. "Sure," he said, "you can do that, like every journo. You can go over there and shake all the stumps you want."

Marie Koroma was the star of the show because she was the youngest amputee to survive. Amnesty International, Human Rights Watch, the UN—everyone had jumped on this story, and it was visually stunning. She'd been wounded at thirteen months old, although some stories reported that it had happened when she was three months old.

A tall, thin man walked up behind me, grabbed my camera pack, and shouldered it with a smile. There was something wrong, though. He was holding his hand up to greet me but he had no hand. As he shouldered my bag I realized he was missing not one but two hands—he had only thin wrists that terminated with a tuck of brown skin.

There was something unsettling about seeing the mutilated bodies; it was as if their missing parts were hiding, or fooling you somehow. The man offered to show me around the amputee camp as another young man began the azzam, or call to prayer. According to Muslim tradition he was supposed to cup his right hand over his ear to keep pitch, but with his stump pushed against his ear it looked like he had shoved his hand inside his head. Five feet away, a man with no ears listened. He nodded to me and waved his stump.

The people here had not only suffered terribly, but would continue to suffer until they died. Even though there were 226 amputees here, more than two thousand family members lived in the camp, which resembled a minislum. The amputees could no longer support themselves, and the families acted as protection from thieves. If it was hard enough to survive this country in perfect health, it would be virtually impossible to survive without hands or legs, or arms or ears.

My guide pulled a pack of smokes from his right front pocket, took out a cigarette, lit it, and put away the pack in one smooth move. Gibrill Sessay, forty-three, smoked his cigarette by using two wrists to hold it.

"We have had many, many, many, many journalists," he said. "Many famous people. Kofi Annan, Madeline Albright, even Mary the human rights lady from the UN. They are so many. But they never bring money." He thought it was good that journalists came here to interview the victims. His story was typical.

"In 1996 I was a contractor in mining. The rebels drove us from Kono and my whole family was in the bush for four months. Then on April the second we heard that ECOMOG had taken over Kono. We were on the way toward the ECOMOG line when the rebels ambushed us. Their first words were, 'Where are your diamonds?' I had put my diamonds in a bottle and buried them in a swamp. I had thirty-six pieces but I would have given him the diamonds to save my hands.

"My hands were cut off by the soldiers that aligned themselves with the RUF. They took me over to a cross stick and cut off my hands. When they amputee you, they tell you to go to President Kabbah and ask for a hand.

"You see, I knew the man that amputated me, Staff Sergeant Al Haji Bayoh. He lives in Kono. He is in the bush now. He was my friend for more than twenty years. He used to borrow my generators to drain his diamond pits. It was probably just jealousy. The RUF was always looking for diamonds to buy ammunition; that's why they captured all the diamond areas and settled there. He amputated nine of us. Three of us are here. My wife was raped and killed. They stabbed her to death. I don't really know why.

"I have forgiven the man that cut my hand off. If he comes and apologizes I will have to forgive him. For now I need money to do business."

The people around us carried their prosthetics and practiced using hooks, wheelchairs, and plastic feet. Gibrill didn't want prosthetic hands. "There is not much you can do with hands," he said.

"All of us are still waiting for repatriation. We are not happy. We live a miserable life. The government has not focused on our situation here. We are living on the handouts of Muslim and Christian organizations. We support the peace agreement. We need them to come here and apologize to us. We would tell them, we are your brothers and sisters. No one has come here from the RUF. Those who have committed the crimes will not come here."

Ishmail Daramy from Kono was a driver. He described the events of June 26, 1996. "I went to see my brother, who lived in Kenema. The RUF Komo Kay Group arrested me, took me to their base, and cut off my hands. I ran after them begging them to kill me. I didn't want to live in this world but I had my wife and children. They did not accept to kill me. That day and night I walked about fifty miles, then I got a vehicle on the highway. I made it to the hospital at about ten o'clock that night. They cut the people so that the people will run away; the people cannot handle the idea of amputation. Most of the people were from the diamond area."

Ishmail wasn't so forgiving. "I would like war crimes for the people who cut the people to stand on trial before the people of Sierra Leone. That guy who said we should forgive them,"—he snorted angrily—"look at me, I am living on handouts. I am suffering. Now who can support me? I support the war crimes. The man who cut off my hands was a friend of twenty-five years. He was not crazy, he was wicked. Most people in this camp want the people to be punished.

"If I can see the person who amputated me in prison I can be happy. But if I see this man with a good job, good house, and happy family I will want revenge. I am forty-two years old. Let the RUF explain the reason for the amputations. We are miners, farmers, we know nothing about politics. Maybe I can be useful inside the community now that I am just a funny-man. People are laughing at me because I am begging every day just to eat. They are fed up with me. Why are we to be everlastingly punished?"

Cobus remembered May 1995. "We were put on a plane in Pretoria and no one knew where we were going. We knew we were going to some hot spot in Africa. On board they finally told us. There were eighty of us in-country at any one time. We were rotated out so on the first flight there were about 120 of us. I had signed up to fight, it didn't really matter why or against whom. We were the elite of South Africa's fighting machine but we had no future in peacetime. War was the only life we knew. If you were in Executive Outcomes there was no safety net. EO was getting twelve to fourteen thousand dollars per man and spending $3,000. It was business, I suppose. There is none of the fun when you fight for money. In the army there was an esprit de corps, but in EO it was just money. A couple of guys came a few weeks before as an advance party. When we arrived they hid us in the garages next to Cockerill base. The rebels were right outside the city, four clicks from the army training grounds. There were thousands of rebels living in zinc-tin huts hidden in the trees. Our first job was to capture that base. Three days before we captured the base we drove into an ambush."

Henri had the distinction of being the first man to go down in EO's first action with the rebels. Henri was still here five years later, running the Cobus's Southern Cross office in Bo. He met me at the helicopter landing pad, looking thin and tired. I figured he was around sixty, but I learned later that he had just turned forty. He had a glass eye to replace the one he lost in combat back in 1995 and was on crutches because he'd broken a foot falling from a ladder.

As we pulled into the office I noticed a small child sitting on the cinder block fence. I started to point out the dangerous predicament when I noticed that the child was really a baby chimpanzee.

"Oh, that's Alice," he said. Alice liked to drink coffee out of a tiny cup, but only after Henri had blown on it to make sure it was cool enough. Alice had been in bad shape when they bought her from a local. They fixed a molar abscess that would have killed her. The surgery gave Alice a crooked smile.

As expected, all the promises and arrangements made by Chief Norman and his advance man had come to naught. No one was aware of my arrival. So as Alice skipped around the room Henri called up the local Kamajor commander and we got down to business: For two hundred dollars I could have my own Kamajor army for the entire day.

Henri and I meet later at the only expat bar in town, the Happy Cottage. The room was illuminated with one blue light. Rain hammered on the rusty corrugated roof, forcing me to strain to hear Henri. With his graying beard, bald head, and brown glass eye, he resembled an oracle. Henri spoke with a thick Afrikaans accent and a slow, careful, and gentle delivery. Even the often used adjective *fookin* was more a simple grammatical place marker than a curse.

"I was Koevoet-Crowbar—a police force in armored columns. Our job was to track down and eliminate insurgents coming over the border from Angola. Koevoet operated out of bases in south west Africa just south of the Angolan border. We drove Casspir armored cars, large armored fighting vans with gun ports for machine guns and assault rifles. They worked with the Ovambo trackers, mostly young kids trained as goat herders. Their job was to find 'terrs' and kill them.

"If you go back in history to Namibia, we did most of the killing. I was in the big South African operation in Angola. We were only three thousand but we did 60 percent of the killing. Our success was because of the trackers. I was a policeman in South Africa and my father was a policeman before me.

"I joined EO as a trainer for the big Angolan job. Executive Outcomes had been hired by the government of Dos Santos to push back the UNITA rebels.

"Then one day the guys from EO came to us and said, 'Things have changed a little, boys. We're going to have to do a bit of fighting.' As soon as they heard that, a lot of guys up and quit. Some guys stayed another month and just before we had to fight they buggered off.

"I came to Sierra Leone in May of 1995. One of our first jobs was to clear the road to Makeni.

"The rebels ambushed us eight times in a day. It was our third ambush of the day. The rebels weren't that good at fighting but they knew how to ambush. They would let you have it with fucking everything at once. Every time they hit us we would attack them, and Cobus would track them down into the bush and sort them out. They were not used to being hunted. We would engage from the front and the blacks would go around and get them from the back. Fucking marvelous.

"I lost my right eye on our first major operation. They ambushed us in a zigzag ambush. Rebels would line both sides of the road spaced at intervals and let us have it with everything they had at once. The noise was incredible.

"There were nine of us on the road. The first BMP (a Russian armored troop transport) lost a track when the driver turned. Our driver stalled when we were hit by the RPG. The thirty-millimeter cannon was jammed. There were only nine of us with AKs and 150 rebels, so everyone must do his bit.

"The piece of the RPG that hit the turret was small." Henri held up his little finger and measured off the first segment. "The rest hit my battle jacket. I thought it was a scratch at first then I realized I was hurt, but I had no choice. The RPG hit the turret on our BMP and splattered. There was blood, but I just continued with the job. The round knocked out my eye and shredded my battle jacket.

"I was manning the 14.5 cannon. I was going to give them some gas but the gun jammed. I went through fourteen magazines of AK ammunition, then we ran out. When we stopped shooting they came in for the kill. There were nine of us on the road, with our BMPs missing tracks. It was fucking close enough, ja?

"They gave us quite a surprise. Usually they hide, give you a surprise, let you have it with fucking everything and if it gets too hot, they run away. They were quite fucking brave that day.

"Cobus was fuckin' Double Charlie that day...Calm and Collected. Cobus came from behind with his group and wiped them all out. Cobus was fucking brilliant."

Henri paused to take a sip of his beer. Bob Marley's "Buffalo Soldier" was playing on the jukebox and the rain pounded the tin roof harder. I had to strain to hear Henri over the din of the raindrops.

"Ja, in Cobus's squad there was a guy hit in the leg and the arm. We sorted them out. The rebels got a big hiding after that. They knew the South Africans were there. They were fighting against something, ja?" Henri continued to stare into the darkness.

Men in combat develop a bond deeper than money, longer than memory, and tighter than family. Cobus thought back on that time. "We fought like no other unit of men ever could have. It was an extreme feeling of commanding guys that were prescient, fantastically professional, and very brave. I felt the enemy did not have a chance, even that early in the campaign, and I was right. I had serious doubts about our senior command even then, and had already decided during that first contact to tune them out and concentrate on my immediate job. That got me into trouble with them, but they couldn't fire me—I was delivering the goods.

"The overwhelming majority of the people in this game are pros and will not dream of stepping over the line in the real sense of the word. Our Hollywood image falls far short of the reality. If you want to attain your objectives and stay alive there is only room for the professionals. Most guys are very particular who they work with and for.

"I was hired from friends among the senior EO people. I signed up in May 1995. In those days I took home around R4500 in the army and was offered R11000 by EO ($3,150 in those days). My first impression was that they were slick and corporate, unlike the army. Later I felt they spent too much on the corporate side and too little on the boys in the bush. Still, I admire them, am proud of having served with them, and am grateful because they gave me my start in my next career.

"After eighteen months of operation we had reached the Liberian border southeast of Bo. The rebels fled into the refugee camps inside Guinea. There was a series of recon in force. This big assault was planned with Nigerian Alpha jets and the Kamajors. Our gunship pilots did a strike on the rebel base and wounded Foday Sankoh and killed two of his commanders. Sankoh was later nabbed in Nigeria on a diamonds-for-weapons sting. At that point we realized that the war was over. It was published in the press. For the first time the people of Sierra Leone realized there were no organized rebels in their country. We moved into the peace mode for six months.

"Mercenaries in Africa are never a comforting thought. The word was out that white mercenaries had defeated the rebels. Fabricated and exaggerated accusations of human rights abuses, fuel-air bombs, slaughtering of innocent civilians crept into the media now that they were able to actually visit the country, after the fact. It was odd that few, if any, wrote about the most brutal rebels in recent history being defeated. To the press the word mercenary had an ugly ring to it: a cartoonish, B-movie aura that didn't sync with the cool professionalism of these career soldiers."

The mercenaries came to Sierra Leone to train the country's ragtag army—a process described candidly by a former merc as "concentrating on the top 10 percent and forgetting about the rest." Ultimately the local army was more of a hindrance than a help. Many times the mercenaries fired on the army for mortaring their camp. Often the South Africans would discipline the troops in their own way, putting their exercise room to good use. Ultimately they ignored the army and did their own thing. Later, to provide backup, they worked with the Kamajors.

The Kamajors were one of those wartime phenomena that are formed under pressure and emerge in a strange, mutated, but valuable form. The Kamajors ignored the conventional training but proved to be aggressive, brave, and determined fighters because they were bulletproof and sometimes invisible.

Kamajor means hunter, but to be a hunter here you needed special skills because the jungle animals of Sierra Leone are scarce and timid. A hunter entered a secret society that conferred on him the responsibility of defending his village. The tribal hunters were formed into more official militia groups in the early 1990s and adopted the more respectable moniker of CDF, or Civil Defense Forces. They were essentially a militia recruited outside the normal military that was loyal to the government of Kabbah. Their leader, Sam Hinga Norman, was wisely installed as deputy minister of defense. Because the Freetown-based military had had a hand in most of the eight coups and countercoups since independence, the Kamajors were a stabilizing force, and were the only groups that fought against the rebels when the army refused to leave the main roads or towns.

Sandline sought to arm and train the Kamajors in order to oust the military and rebel junta from Freetown. But that wasn't my main area of interest; I wanted to know about their mystical powers. Kamajors said they could not only deflect bullets, they could become invisible. So I decided to interview Sam Hinga Norman, their chief. Norman regularly caused paroxysms of pain to the UN and outside groups with his bellicose statements. In one local paper, Chief Norman was asked to explain why he was talking tough in a climate of peace. "Because I am tough!" he said.

Chief (Captain Retired) Sam Hinga Norman, Deputy Minister of Defense, was like most of the politicians around here: large, happy, and ready to drop everything for an interview. A gaggle of tired country folk waited in the cheap wood-paneled waiting room outside his office. Despite having no appointment, I was ushered straight in. He wore one of those faux

Chinese-African dictator leisure suits that did its best to hide his round politician's belly, and he welcomed each of my questions. Norman was born in Mongere in 1940. He didn't know his birthday so he said, "write down January first."

I'd seen his face in dozens of Freetown newspapers, mostly talking peace and talking tough at the same time. Even though the Kamajors and CDF had pledged to disarm, he didn't think the peace would last. "We view the rebels as politically adventurous against the democratic government." He added that they were "a group that will never adhere to democratic principles."

After a few minor pleasantries I got right to it. "How will the warrior culture of the Kamajors survive in peacetime?"

"Ah, that is what we are all wondering, this is on all our minds," he said in the enigmatic and vacuous manner of African politicians.

Norman was sitting pretty. Peace required that all the rebels and Kamajors disarm. On the surface, this seemed fine with Norman, but the CDF had adopted a "you go first" attitude with the rebels in the countryside.

The Kamajors weren't the only militia faction of the CDF, but they were the largest, with about ten thousand members.

They came from the Mendé tribe and evolved directly from the secret societies of Sierra Leone and the tradition of hunting with mystical powers. The young men were initiated into the mystic skills of hunting and fighting by an elder and then charged with defending his village. In the south and the east the Kamajors were Mendé but other groups were created along similar lines: the Donsos, Arekonos, Tamaborohs, Alunka, Kapras, and Gbethies. The Organized Body of Hunters was the most recent group—formed in Freetown during the January 6, 1999 crisis—but the Kamajors was the only group that had seen major successes against the RUF rebels.

Norman explained that "the Kamajors began in 1993 after the rebels had been fighting for two years. We were not paid. We stood up with traditional weapons: the cutlass, the shotgun, spears, and even sticks to defend our villages. I met with the authorities and told them the best way to fight the rebels would be with a militia. Traditional Kamajors are hunters—men who prepare themselves with herbs to find food. In 1994 a few Mendé chiefdoms selected men between eighteen and twenty-four and initiated them into the secrets. There are three elements in this secret: the Bible, the Koran, and the herbs. It doesn't take more than seven days, and in that time you learn the rules of war. If you break the rules you must go back for reprotection.

"We refuse to wear a uniform because our enemies have tricked us by wearing our uniforms and then attacking us. We wear armaments made from natural bark. Initially we did not have tactics because we were bold enough because of our beliefs. When the enemy shoots two or three times and nothing happens then he realizes this is a Kamajor and he runs away."

I asked what happened when journalists or skeptics demanded to see proof of this invincibility.

"It is not 100 percent foolproof, just like your defenses. Don't you have radar, bulletproofing, jamming systems that sometimes fail? Don't your soldiers also believe that their helmets, gunships, and armaments will protect them, but often don't?"

It is hard to argue mysticism versus logic, but it was an okay response to nonbelievers. I asked him about the Kamajors' work with the mercenaries.

"EO did very well for Sierra Leone. At that time it was very rough. Whatever name you call them, they would only fight for the recognized government. EO has stood out there and fought. We have soft feelings for these people. We fought with them, they ate with us, slept with us. They never beat people, they never took their wealth."

I asked him about the UN.

"What they do cannot be measured. The UN must have a rule for what they are doing. Are they here to stop the suffering? To stop the war? All we want the UN to do is tell the people with weapons that they are not going to fight anymore. Put the message out there on every radio station. The presence of one platoon of the UN is enough. When there is a man with a gun and a man without a gun, who are you going to be afraid of? The RUF will not have the interest of defending the government. The military is unstable. The CDF is the eyes and the ears of the government, an auxiliary to government forces.

"The army did not just jump and become bad. The army was entitled to a salary and the logistics to fight with. The soldier fighting on the ground did not get his food; everything the soldier wanted he did not have. So the man who he was protecting had food and he took that food. The Kamajors were not paid, they shared food. They gave them bulgur and they went into bush.

"The people that are here have seen strange things. Children under ten have been exposed to some languages and blue films. Some of them have been injected with drugs to make them fight.

"What do all these people want that come here? The NGOs, the Brits? These people come here for something?"

He excused himself abruptly. He had an upset stomach from traveling upcountry, something he apparently had no protection against.

When he returned, he continued, "I am appealing to the fighters, if Sierra Leone goes bad it is their own suffering that will go on forever . . ." His head lowered in mid-sentence and—*poof*—he was asleep. I waited for him to finish, but the chief had disappeared.

Back in Bo, the truck driver and I stopped at various homes, businesses, and apartments to pick up the Kamajors. The driver would stop and shout, and then men in basketball shorts, faded T-shirts and grubby clothes would jump on the back of the truck, all carrying weapons and plastic bags. The first sign that this might not have been a crack fighting force was the hardened mud shoved into the barrels of their guns, which ranged from rusty AKs to battered FNs, and even corroded shotguns with worm-eaten stocks. Most of these weapons appeared completely inoperable, but that didn't dampen the Kamajors' enthusiasm. They sang and chanted as our armed party of a dozen men blew right through the UN checkpoint and headed into the woods.

When we found a suitable place to stop, the men jumped down and reached into their plastic bags for the mystic uniforms of the Kamajors: stained T-shirts with Koranic versus written in faded blood, barkskin vests and hats, chains, tiny bundles that went underneath the bark cloth, and various-sized hornlike amulets with hair tails. They finished dressing and assembled in front of me. The first thing I noticed was the smell. It was enough of a protection in itself. The Kamajors couldn't wash their uniforms because it would require them to seek re-protection. The small colorful cloth bundles sewn onto their clothes contained "secret" items.

Rumor had it that these were the livers and hearts of their dead opponents, and the smell that rose up from them supported this theory. They also were bells, mirrors, and colorful decorations and carried a variety of special talismans.

All fighters in Africa have war names. The commander's was Tiger Face. He took me through his magic arsenal. The horn-shaped cloth device with the animal tail was his most powerful. This was a Controller.

"What if you leave it in your pocket by mistake?" I asked in a pathetic attempt at humor.

Tiger Face pointed to the back of his *boj*, or hat, where there was a smaller Controller that made the bullets go over his head if the enemy shot from behind.

He explained that his Controller was bigger than everyone else's because it could control rocket-propelled grenades, or RPGs, as well as bullets. Ah, I should have guessed that. I tried to calculate the dimensions required for our missile defense system in my head but was interrupted.

"We also have an RPG Bat," said Tiger Face. This was a paddle with a mirror that would actually return the missiles to the enemy. The men around us confirmed that there was such a thing and that yes, the man with the RPG Bat had never been hit by an RPG. Of course, it would be hard to get a testimonial from someone whose RPG bat suddenly failed on him.

The Kamajors sensed my disbelief, but they continued. "It is normal for white men who don't understand these things to be skeptical. You too wear bulletproof vests, helmets, believe in stealth, jam radar, and employ all manner of devices that do not always work." I remembered reading an article about how stealth bombers can be detected by simply measuring the change in cellular phone transmissions. Or better yet, by people simply watching on the ground. We continued with the show and tell.

"Some fighters wear mirrors trimmed with wool cloth. These show the direction of the enemy." Unfortunately, the thin boy who demonstrated the mirror didn't realize it was a piece of glass with nonreflective backing. But there I went, being a disbeliever again. He pointed to a grubby sack around another fighter's neck. "Here is a pouch that is called Silent Gun—it will silence the enemy's weapon so that he cannot fire," Tiger Face explained patiently.

I remembered to note that this device was similar in function to the Cut Off, which would also shut down any hostile weapons. But I forgot to ask for a finer distinction as I tried to keep up with Tiger Face's version of *Jane's, All the World's Magic Charms*. There was a snakeskin belt with a small buckle mirror that would foil bullets. I couldn't tell whether it stopped or deflected them. I asked if the mirror might actually return the bullets to the person who fired them. Tiger Face smiled. I was learning fast. Next he showed me a leather armband that tightened when the enemy was near.

"What's it called?" I asked. "Sphincter?" The sad joke passed without a giggle.

"No," Tiger Face explained patiently that this was called a Notice Band. He demonstrated by padding through the bush. Suddenly he mimicked the feeling of the animal skin tightening and looked all agog with his eyes bugged out.

We discussed the concept of cowrie shell necklaces that worked only against snakebite, shirts that were bulletproof, and magic potions that made soldiers invincible.

Before Kamajors went into battle they drank a special potion. The contents were secret, but it got them into a methlike lather; they no longer had to eat or sleep. They also washed their face in this mixture and wrote Arabic scripture on their arms with it. From that point on they had to go straight to battle. If they touched a woman, they had to go through the whole procedure again.

Soon it was time to demonstrate the Kamajors' fighting skills. The group chose a volunteer to attack and dispersed into the bush. The men crept silently through the bush as Tiger Face proudly held his industrial-sized controller up high. I was going to point out that it wasn't quite high enough to cover the men in the back, but he had to have known this.

"Gentlemen, advance," he said. They stalked. Then, "Gentlemen, attack."

Naturally, our single enemy fell to the Kamajors' sustained attack. They were quite polite with their inquiry: "You sir! What you doing here?" But then he was dispatched in typical African fashion and the Kamajors danced and sang in a circle around the body. He was then tortured, and I guessed he would then be the donor of certain key organs.

They staged an ambush as an encore and once again the unwitting were arrested and summarily tortured. No matter what sham military procedure was demonstrated, it always ended with the victim's interrogation or torture. Over and over again, the victim's only reply was, "Ah doan know nothing man, ah doan know nothing man."

I tried to take a few photographs and noticed that the Kamajors held their weapons over their heads and sideways.

"No. No," I said. "Look down the barrel of the gun and aim at me."

In one coordinated motion they squinted painfully and held the guns above their heads.

No one really volunteered to show off their bullet dodging or bulletproofing powers. I didn't know if this is because their guns didn't work or they hadn't checked the charge on their "Cut Offs." Or could it be that their Cut Offs had shut down their own weapons? I'll never know, because one of the Kamajors lost his watch in a valiant attack and the others went to help him find it.

On the way back to Bo, a local policeman had constructed his own checkpoint directly in front of the UN checkpoint. The UN had a white BMP troop carrier with cannon; the policeman's checkpoint was, well, a string with little dangly bits hanging off it. At the sight of our heavily armed group rumbling down the road, he dropped the string in a hurry and forced a weak wave as we coasted by.

The Kamajors were singing fighting songs. The only word I recognized in the Mendé chant tune was *fuck,* repeated in every verse. The young fighters hung off the truck as they sported their stars-and-stripes bandannas, garage sale assault weapons, and GI Joe outfits. As we blasted down the road a loud *thump, thump* tapped the roof of the cab and rolled back to the platform. The fighters jumped, weapons at the ready.

"Mango attack," I yelled. They stared at me, wide-eyed.

War here was about hunting and terror. Surviving. Fighting fear. Using fear. Stalking men, trapping men, using terror to drive people away from diamond rich areas. Using fear to disable your enemy before he even saw you. It was not a war a Western army would understand or even win.

Cobus explained, "If you had a six-hour firefight in any other war you would have terrible casualties. Here we would have a two-hour firefight and have no casualties.

"The original Kamajors were serious. They would have five bullets for a year. During the fighting, things changed. You could pay five dollars, spit on a chicken, and presto you would be a Kamajor. The Kamajor group we fought with thought the only way they could get killed was if the enemy put them in a pit and poured acid on them. So they spent their time looking for pits and forty-five-gallon drums full of acid. They never did figure out how many pits and how much acid would be needed to kill them all."

Despite the mystic nature of the Kamajors, their role was simple. They hunted to feed their villages. When threatened by predators, they hunted them. I was starting to understand the basics here. The Kamajors were hunters. The mercenaries were hunters. The gunship pilots were hunters.

The rebels were predators. The Nigerians were predators. The UN were predators.

In the middle were thousands of skittish locals darting and fleeing to avoid the terror. Ultimately, the hunters would move on, and the predators would fill their bellies.

Back in Freetown it was time to party in a large house on the hill, just up the street from ex-dictator Johnny Paul Koroma's home. There was an official and unofficial social structure. The British army wasn't allowed to consort with "South African mercenaries," even though they weren't mercenaries, but they worked closely with South African pilots, who were mercenaries. There were also a number of UN military observers—MILOBS in UN jargon—security guards, and expats. There were coolers of beer—Heineken, Beck's, Tuborg, and Star. There was a weak attempt at a buffet, but plenty of meat was on the barbecue. Music was irrelevant. The party was about drinking. Newly arrived South Africans, MILOBS from New Zealand, and Britain, and a host of British army types strolled in. The official party dress was outlandish British-style safari jackets trimmed in Day-Glo faux leopard skin topped off by a large safari hat with colorful puggarees, like mercenary pimps who were ready to party. Sam, the Kiwi SAS MILOBS, was jumping around wearing his heavy, fully functional black utility vest complete with Sykes-Fairburn commando knife. Local beauties showed up along with a scattering of NGO women, who were attractive and ready to party. There was a certain easy edge and camaraderie that made each one different and fun.

The talk tonight centered on Rocco, the South African and former Parabat, and Sam the SAS commando. They'd decided to set a world record by jumping out of Neill's Russian gunship at ten thousand feet and had landed on the golf course and beach below. It was clear violation of just about every personnel and equipment rule but everyone celebrated in the sheer coolness of it all.

There was talk about diamond mining. The South Africans were given concessions as a way of saying thank you. All they had to do was mine them. Sam danced with his dog Rambo. He was quitting his UN job and military career to become a partner in a diamond venture. He needed to raise money, purchase equipment, hire people, and arrange the necessary security.

A year before there had been twenty-four ex-EO mercenaries. Now the number had thinned. The talk shifted among rugby, war, hunting, and diamonds. Neill talked about fighting SWAPO in Namibia; Kasi talked about the fuck-up in Papua New Guinea when he went there to fight with Sandline against the rebels in Bougainville. The South Africans shuttled back and forth between South Africa and Sierra Leone. When the *harmattan* comes from the Sahara and the winglets and the turbine blades of the gunships develop a fine tan dust, then it is too hot in Sierra Leone. People are irritable, the sky is hazy, Sierra Leone becomes an ugly place. It is time to go hunting.

There was a hunting story about a private ranch in South Africa. The guide took an Israeli sniper to a private ranch to hunt for the first time. The sniper would only kill the animal if he ate the meat, but according to his religion the animal had to be cut and bled while the heart was still beating. That meant he could not use a heart shot but a tight, almost impossible behind-the-cranium shot. He took aim at five hundred meters through the shimmering heat of the South African veldt, compensated for wind and distance, and squeezed slowly. Crack. One shot. The tiny .22-caliber bullet severed the spinal cord. Impressed with the sniper's cool accuracy, the guide asked if he had ever hunted before. "You mean animals? Never."

Despite her world-weary tone and cynicism, Margaret Novicki of the UN press office did her job well. She cornered me as I walked down the halls of the Mammy Yoko. "I have a special trip. Do you want to be on it?" The

UN had received permission to pick up some child soldiers who were being released by the RUF in Kailahun, a remote, rebel-held corner of eastern Sierra Leone.

The area had been under RUF control since the war started in 1991. It was shaped like a parrot's beak that jutted into Liberia and Guinea, and it made the UN nervous.

A year before, more than two hundred UN peacekeepers were surrounded by RUF rebels. The peacekeepers were on their way to monitor a disarmament, demobilization, and reintegration that had been set up as part of the July 1999 peace agreement. Foday Sankoh, the RUF leader, had the group's full blessings, but the local RUF commander refused to let the UN pass. Although it seemed like an arbitrary decision on the part of three hundred rebels, it was really just a test to see whether the UN would fight back. The peacekeepers meekly handed their weapons over. Later, an additional group of eleven kidnapped military observers was released into the beleaguered camp. The UN troops were running out of food. The UN abandoned diplomatic efforts in July 2000 and launched rescue Operation Kukri, with Indian troops, gunships, and an SAS contingent in a Chinook helicopter. The UN troops broke out under fire. The gunships strafed and rocketed the rebels as they chased after the UN column. The convoy made it to the town of Pendembu and was airlifted to a location seventy miles away. Seven were wounded; one died from his injuries.

I was going with a small group of UN and NGO people to collect fifty-nine children who had been kidnapped by the RUF and were being returned for "reintegration" as part of the peace process. They were part of almost a thousand children whom the RUF had disgorged from the jungles and camps back into society. Most were kidnapped years ago and had been fighters, camp followers, and "wives."

I sat in the Mammy Yoko heliport, just past the bar and the pools. The terminal was a collection of temporary square Cogim buildings set in a flat, rock-covered field. Our flight was scheduled to leave at 7 A.M., when the morning was still cool, but as usual there were papers to fill out, arguments over reservations, phone calls, consultations before everyone could get on. Zambian troops were arriving with newly bought boom boxes and extra baggage. Truckloads of UN toilet paper were loaded onto helicopters. The usual scene.

The mix of Russian and African body odor inside the terminal was pungent. A cluster of Russian Mi-17 and Mi-8 helicopters sat outside. Half were military versions with titanium bullet deflectors and hard point for mounting bombs and rockets. The others looked worn and dirty in their temporary white paint jobs.

The helicopters were Ukrainian and Russian military and billed at a profit to the UN. The shirtless, beer-bellied pilots worked on replacing a wheel. Inside, the grouchy flight director pushed paper and made people fill out their forms. A small erasable marker board on the wall listed the seven flights around the country. Even the hotel landing pad had a three-letter airport designation—MMY, for Mammy Yoko. Passengers traveling with weapons were asked to remove the magazines and clear the chambers before boarding. The Russians delivered hurried safety briefings before departure. But then the flight to collect the children was delayed while we waited for approval to land. Bituin Gonzales from the UN Child Protection group was worried about the state of the children. She kept in touch with the office with her tiny cellular phone. The office stayed in touch with the Ghanaian UN commander in Kailahun, who in turn kept in touch by radio with UN negotiators who were with the rebels.

The Ghanaians were now negotiating permission to deploy half a company as security. The local RUF commander had approved the idea, but he needed to get confirmation from his commander before he agreed. The last time he'd made a decision on his own, he was slapped by the senior RUF commander. Bituin said in her Filipino accent, "I know you are a soldier, but this time could you pray for us?"

Since this was the UN and we were going into the heart of RUF rebel territory, we weren't just flying in and flying out. First, a ground unit of armored troop carriers, soldiers, and trucks would be deployed to secure the landing spot. Then two Mi-24 gunships would fly over the area to provide air cover. After we landed, a massive Mi-26 transport helicopter would to scoop up the children and fly them to the enclave of Daru, where they would be put into camps that had been set up to receive them. The UN seemed a little twitchy on this trip. *Overkill* would be an understatement. Instead of just driving the five hours from Daru and picking the children up, tens of thousands of dollars would be spent on logistics, troops, transport, helicopters, pilots, fuel, and resources to meet five dozen kids. The Mi-26 transport helicopter seated seventy-two, but it had a lease rate of twelve thousand dollars an hour and would burn three thousand five hundred pounds of fuel on the hour-long trip between Daru and Kailahun.

And of course, the UN had decided to stage a little ceremony to make it oh-so-official. After she hung up the phone for the twentieth time, Bituin said, "Tonight I will get drunk if this goes well. I am so used to things going smoothly."

There were also people from Save the Children, UNICEF, and members of the National Child Protection Committee including the Ministry of Social Welfare, with the RUF there to monitor and observe.

There were more problems than just permission. Tom Sandy, the RUF commander, was demanding food. The UN was only prepared to provide food for the children. Bituin said, "They will demand food for the children, but how do you know if it's for the kids? You don't want to offer them rice in exchange for children. We think there should be a balance. If you pay them money or give them food there will be a price on their heads."

There were also some tougher decisions to make. Not all the children were fighters or had been kidnapped. Ten to 30 percent of them simply wanted to get out, and looked at the magical repatriation as a way to get free education.

Finally all the arrangements were made and everyone loaded onto the helicopter. It was an hour and a half flight due east to Kailahun. The countryside was flat and denuded, and turned gradually into a series of granitic mounds. They were smooth humpbacks of bare black granite, most with green mossy tops and sheer cliff faces. They were the cores of large mountain ranges that had worn down and the source of much of Sierra Leone's mineral wealth as they were washed into the meandering rivers below by eons of rainfall. I saw a small town below. We hovered in random circles, waiting for the gunships to appear. It seemed that our delay in getting permission had thrown off a finely tuned plan. The two white Mi-24 gunships arrived early and then had to return to Kenema to refuel. Our pilots were under orders not to land unless the gunships were there. You could almost feel the extra electricity in the air as the radios and cell phones sprang to life. Inside the shuddering, deafening helicopters, we had to communicate with handwritten notes. The first suggestion was to return the hour and a half back to Freetown and restage. The pilot noted that we would run out of fuel and end up landing in the river. The next proposal was to hover and wait for the much faster gunships to reappear. But further calculations forced us to fly to Daru to refuel.

On the way, we flew over the multiclored primary rain forest. Each tree tried to splay its upper canopy over the others to grab enough light to survive. Not many areas of tropical forest were left in Sierra Leone, but there was still a primitive feel to the jungle in this remote corner. There were also the telltale signs of diamond mining in the form of round beige scars. Some of the best diamonds in the world came from this area.

We landed in the enclave of Daru, a town the rebels had never taken. Two Mi-26 cargo helicopters were already on the ground. One was unloading cornflakes, milk, and juice while the other waited, its blades turning idly in anticipation. There is no such thing as fifteen minutes in the UN, only hours. It was now 2:23 P.M. and we'd left at noon. I wandered through the building-sized Russian helicopter on a tour from the pilot. The Mi-26 was the largest production helicopter ever made. It was 110 feet long, 26 feet high, and had eight 105-foot-long rotor blades powered by two eleven-thousand-horsepower turbine engines. It had the same power and capacity as a Boeing 737-200. It is hard to imagine 112,000 pounds (56 tons) of takeoff weight, 44,000 pounds (22 tons) of it in payload. The Mi-26 was first flown in December 1977 and could fly seventy-two fully equipped troops 500 miles at 183 miles per hour. Inside there were industrial-sized cranes, a cabin the size of a small aircraft, and a ramp so that trucks could drive straight in.

To see two pure white Mi-26s waiting in this godforsaken part of the world was memorable.

I grabbed some juice containers off a truck and sat inside our relatively small Mi-8. The UNICEF representative was a thin older Englishman who wore a floppy white hat and UNICEF T-shirt. We propped open the back of the transport helicopter to let the air in and chatted.

"I wouldn't call this postconflict Sierra Leone. We are all quite jumpy here. The rebels used terror to magnify their numbers and now they control a lot of nothing." He scanned everything that was going on around us, at the helicopters and the troops. "It takes a thousand times the power of good to combat the power of evil."

At last we got the word and went back into the air. When we arrived we could see a clearing below with armored personnel carriers and blue-helmeted soldiers in a ring around the space. We landed as close to the trees as we could. In the shadows I could see the slim, dark silhouettes of villagers watching us. The pilot shut down the power. We waited under the gaze of silent zombies.

Finally two battered and muddy six-wheel-drive army trucks pulled up. The children were under the tarp in the back. I peered in the back of one truck. The smell of body odor was overpowering. All I could see was scared white circles staring at me, wide-eyed and impassive. There were thirty children in the back of each truck. Like animals in a cave, they hesitated to come forward to the light. The UNICEF man coaxed them out slowly. The children were dressed in rags and faded T-shirts. The seams of their clothes were stitched up roughly with thread. They had bare scarred legs, callused feet, sores from skin diseases. They were hollow chested and terribly mute. They were lined up and photographed, and then a small ceremony took place. Tom Sandy, the RUF commander, made a rambling speech in Krio about peace. The aid organization thanked them for their help. No one mentioned what it was that made the girls or the boys cower behind them. There was only a handful of females. Most of the children were between ten and fifteen. One of the older children then made a long uncomfortable speech. The nervous Ghanaian soldiers watched the perimeter.

The village had the appearance of an ancient ruin. The trees and weeds were slowly erasing the hand of man; there was a sense of devolution from progress and technology to something feral and green.

The clearing started to vibrate with the distant rumble of a helicopter. Like the mother ship in the movie *Close Encounters,* the white Mi-26 Halo helicopter appeared over the trees and searched for a spot wide enough to land. The trees bent, the wash from the propellers forced everyone to turn away. Bits of houses, clothing, and paper became airborne, and then like a divine appearance the massive helicopter rested gently and shut down, the double blades tracing slow giant circles.

The children were sorted out according to a list, lined up again, and then released like pigeons as their name were called. They ran, arms and legs akimbo, into the giant white maw of the waiting helicopter. Each child disappeared into the big rock candy mountain with a look of glee. Once inside the barn-sized vehicle they sat in four long rows of red-vinyl-covered seats, eyes wide open, unable to speak.

Technology, half a billion dollars, and the combined efforts of the world's nations had descended upon this forgotten place to give a few terrified, emancipated children a fifteen-minute ride. Not so much for the children's benefit, or to be more efficient, but to show that the outside world cared.

I had another disturbing thought—something the UNICEF worker had told me back in Daru in the shade of the helicopter. "I hope these kids can return to normal life. Many of them have been fighting for ten years. They've never known a normal life. They say that once these kids have experienced warfare and killing they will never go back."

Port Loko was just another wasted, ravaged town outside of Freetown. I entered a compound where people were penned in by twelve-foot-high white stripped saplings woven into a basketlike shape and sharpened to a spear point. Inside, young men and a few women were sitting around.

I walked up to an unhappy-looking man wearing baggy jeans cut in the style of the 1980s and a clean shirt.

Mohamed Fofana or "Colonel Peacemaker" was thirty-five and had been fighting since he was twenty-four. He had come to the DDR—the Demobilization, Disarmament, and Reintegration camp—because he wanted to get a job. He was promised money in return for his weapon but had only received fourteen dollars so far; he was angry.

"How am I going to support my wife, my mother, and my four children?" he said. They were supposed to receive money while he trained, but they were just sitting and waiting. "I want to further my education overseas," he said. "I would like to go to Mississippi to become a truck driver."

While I pondered his fate, a British officer came over and asked me if

I would like to interview his commander, since he was here to inspect the camps. His superior was standing around looking uncomfortable, doing his English best to appear that he was in charge.

The young men in the pen just stared up at him from their perch on the logs. Another group saw my video camera; within seconds they had assembled and started to chant. Each man leaned his head in to get a better spot on the video, and soon they were chanting and jumping up and down in unison. They didn't really have a purpose, but with thirty hyped-up men jumping, chanting, and running around the enclosure, the British officers were not amused. Still, they did nothing but tried keep up the appearance that they were in charge. Then they left diplomatically in white, air-conditioned Toyotas.

I focused my attention back on Colonel Peacemaker. He had been captured and press-ganged by the RUF on April 23, 1991. He rattled off a number of battles he had participated in over the last ten years. He pointed to a couple of men sitting on the log. "I captured him and him," he said. The men looked up and watched us. "I was a battalion commander. No one can defeat the RUF." He looked at a British soldier and sneered. "I fought against the Gurkhas in the bush. You cannot bring the British to our country and fight in my own land. You cannot copy South Africa and win here. We captured four mercenaries in Kono and released them back." He delivered his answers in an arrogant, detached style. He also kept looking around while he talked. I asked him about the future.

"I don't have any money and I cannot go back to my village because the Kamajors have not disarmed. How can you expect me to fight a war and not have a job?"

"How did you get paid during the war?" I asked.

He looked at me. "We paid ourselves."

"How?"

"With weapons." He tired of our conversation and wandered away.

The man whom Colonel Peacemaker said he captured was a former Kamajor and member of the Civil Defense Forces. Sattie Bisessay now called himself the Captain of the UN Strikers football team. They'd started soccer teams to wile away the time. Both CDF and RUF played on the same teams. He came to the camp to enlist because the British were recruiting young men for the army. He guessed he would get fifty to sixty dollars a month in the army. The trades program only paid thirty dollars a month.

The U.S. Embassy funded classes here that taught reintegration. I could hear singing and chanting mixed with the energetic sounds of teachers yelling out phrases. Their goal was to take young people who had been ripped from their social structure and plunged into a nihilistic world of warfare and drugs and teach them how to go home and lead normal lives. The teachers showed their pupils social functions as basic as how to greet people. Their tone was motivational as the teachers hopped and whirled around in front of their nervous students. Here it was common for family members to fight against each other. Now that they were expected to reintegrate there would be many problems and much fear.

The teacher led the young men in chants and gospel-like exchanges.

"I . . . am . . . A . . . Sierra . . . Leonean." The teacher chanted, pointing to a blackboard. He pirouetted from the blackboard to the class and pointed again.

"You . . . are . . . the . . . youth . . . of . . . Sierra Leone! Not . . . a . . . so?" He spoke in Krio.

The students repeated dully and mechanically, "I . . . am . . . the . . . youth . . . of . . . Sierra Leone . . . Not a so?"

In another room the teacher asked the men to stand up and introduce themselves. The men got up shyly and announced their names. The class repeated each name in a primitive attempt to teach the basic tools of social interaction. Most of the students couldn't read or write. Many had never been in a school or in social system other than a ragged army. Many had previously used a gun or blunt violence to get their point across.

"What is the meaning of reintegration? Re . . . int . . . e . . . gra . . . tion. Not a so?" Another teacher yelled, "It mean for everyone come together."

Yet another teacher wrote on a presentation pad with a thick black marker TO UNITE. The students sat dumbfounded in their tiny desks.

"What is peace?" he asked. Some stared at their tiny notebooks. Some smiled at me, some stared angrily. Some hid their faces.

The teacher broke it down for them. "U . . . ni . . . ty. Not a so?" He paused. "That mean . . . we are of one accord . . . of one mind . . . not a so?" The students stared dully. Lunch would be soon.

In another class farther down the assembly line, the instructors led the people in song. The students clapped and giggled. They liked this. They were happy for now.

There was also a reintegration camp for the youngest members of the war. Some were orphans, some almost grown up; all were under eighteen. Carritas, the Catholic group, was trying to sort out this collection of mostly Muslim children. Unlike the adult fighters who may have been in camps for ten years, the children who were kidnapped by the RUF had endured less time in the bush; still, many had no memories of where they lived or their parents' whereabouts. They also harbored frightening images and emotions.

Leonard Bairoh, the assistant project officer, presented the standard preamble on flip charts, then we took a tour. He said that the children spoke or cried in their sleep. They were traumatized and would quickly resort to violence. They gave them each a physical and sent the injured ones to the hospital in Freetown for treatment. Festering bullet wounds and tropical infections were common, but most of the children had skin diseases and showed signs of malnutrition. Here they lived in round tents and were fed and cared for. A tiny child slipped his hand into mine as we walked around the camp. The orphans would be put into homes, and the others would be matched up eventually with their parents.

The children followed us around and when I stopped to take pictures they threw gang signs and posed. A two-year-old flashed a "V," the sign of Tupac Shakur. There were plenty of Tupac Shakur shirts, evidence of the odd cultural time shift found in every third world country. Images from ten years earlier were now in vogue. I asked why they liked Tupac. "Because he is a nigger," they replied, in the sense of a tough, bad black man. Most of them didn't even know that Tupac had been gunned down and murdered.

Eighty percent of these kids were fighters, and they had odd stories to tell. Some smoked marijuana, while others were injected with a liquid they couldn't name. The drug's purpose was to remove the children's fear during battle. One tried to describe the feeling of being injected or of smoking weed.

"It makes my head feel big. I no fear nutting. It make me fly. I feel very brave."

"Do you want to be a fighter again?" I asked.

"No, I want to go to school."

The goal was to place the children with families and lend them money to buy goods to sell. The families had to provide two meals a day. Many of the kids had been abused physically and sexually. Most of the young girls had provided menial labor and acted as wives. They were now expected to enter school and carry on where they left off before they became miniature killers and sex slaves. But most children seemed resilient and eager. It looked like a summer camp. Some used sticks to pull carts made of tins and pencil-mounted wheels. They played marbles, a violent form of tetherball, and stood around the muddy ground, waiting. Some threw rocks or just stared.

Isat Jalloh was sixteen and from Makeni. She had been captured in 1998 when she was thirteen. She was going to the market with her aunt when the rebels attacked. She said that when she was captured she was a virgin. She was marched to the bush and had to stay by the side of the road. She played with the hem of her skirt as she spoke. She was "vaginated" by a twenty-three-year-old man, who made her his wife, and who was later killed. He had three other wives and they wanted to punish her. She had a recurring dream: She was attacked by a man named "Black Black," but she took her revenge. She was happy when she had that dream.

Momoh Samura was fifteen. His war name was "Leftenant Johnny." He was captured in Nadeni while he was in school. They told him to walk with them or they would kill him. He was given weapons to fight with, but he wasn't very good. He became a domestic servant for his commander's wife, who was having a new baby. His conversation trailed off from a mumble to silence. The camp counselor egged him on. "Talk, talk bold," he said. Momoh continued. He operated an AK-47. Twice in Makeni, and in Rocuopa around Kambia. At first he was "having the fear" but later he was "not fearing anything." Do you fear anyone? "No sah." Were you a good fighter? "No sah. I was not used to the weapon. I don't know if I kill any-one. Sometimes I kill many. I don't remember anything. I just want to go back to school."

Lansana Kamara was fourteen years old and from Freetown. He'd been captured when he was eleven. They came to his school and took him away to Kabalah Kuenadougo, where he was trained. They taught him how to operate a submachine gun in a month and he became "Colonel Francis."

He always used *jamba* or marijuana when they went up to the war front, "Because I no be afraid. They give you a choice: Kill or be killed. If you drop your weapon they will shoot you."

He took part in a long list of battles: Kono, Mongor, Al–Kaliyah, Ife, Makeni, Kambia, Freetown, Lunsar. At Al–Kaliyah they were fighting heavy artillery.

"Did you kill many people?"

"Not face to face. When I fired my gun I closed my eyes."

"How do you feel now?"

"Better. I have free movement. I am not scared. They had jungle justice in the bush. I don't want to be a combat man anymore. I want to go to school. I need uniforms, books, a bicycle, and shoes. Look at dis, no shoes," he said, pointing at his muddy feet.

The children playing inside the walls of the camp were yelling, "Snap me, snap me." A group of children gathered around. They wanted to sing the rebel national anthem for me.

> *Ooh we fighting for save Sierra Leone*
> *Ooh we fighting for save our people*
> *Ooh we fighting for save Sierra Leone*
> *Ooh we fighting for save Sierra Leone*
> *Go!*
> *Go and tell the president Sierra Leone is my home*
> *Go and tell the president to see me no more*
> *We are fighting in the bush*
> *We fighting for the rights*
> *Every Sierra Leone fighting for Islam*

They then sang the Sierra Leone national anthem and recited the Lord's prayer. Many performed the face washing ritual associated with Islamic prayer. Whatever works, I guessed.

Ever mindful of good press hooks, the UN was busy turning "swords into plowshares." The reality of it was quite different. I went to a weapons collection program and saw a cluster of shipping containers with a pile of the most useless assortment of weapons I had ever seen. The five-foot-high pile of rusting pipes and worm-eaten stocks weren't even *shakaboulas*, or home-made shotguns. They had been dug up from underground and hastily assembled to collect disarmament money. Some were literally just pipes attached with string to crudely shaped stocks. Some looked like they may once have been serviceable, but most were equivalent to children's toys.

Nevertheless, two men dutifully sawed the barrels in half with power cutters in front of a large banner in the shade of a large mango tree. A bored Chinese military observer looked on from under the shade of a tree. There was a display of agricultural tools made from more serious gun barrels so I asked if they could make a souvenir, a plowshare from a sword as it were. They selected a nice AK from the locked containers, cut off the barrel, and laboriously heated and hammered the barrel into another shape.

One man pedaled a blower to heat coals while another hammered away to flatten and bend the barrel. After a while they handed me my souvenir, a mean-looking ax. Perfect for chopping off hands.

I was curious to see what was in the locked containers. There were 12.7-millimeter antitank guns, mortars, wooden-wheeled North Korean machine guns, AKs with cut-down stocks. There were plenty of weapons here, but they were so old that they might have been the dregs left over from the last failed disarmament. One of the UN observers admitted that the last time they disarmed the rebels, the weapons disappeared while in the care of the UN and were resold by the Nigerians.

They said they didn't have the key for the other containers, but what I saw versus what was actually being cut up and destroyed made me wonder if this collection of weapons was just waiting for buyers. When I returned later that day I found a lone Nigerian officer examining each container, now mysteriously unlocked. When I peered over his shoulder to see the weapons inside, he grinned, closed the door, and quickly disappeared.

The phone had been ringing in Cobus's house. A woman wanted to know where Cobus was. She said she would be around with some people. Later there was a knock on the steel door of Cobus's house. Punjuhim's chief of police led a procession of four diamond dealers from his hometown. They'd shown up twice before, but Cobus was always out. People here just showed up at the oddest hours. They made polite introductions and pulled out a folded white piece of paper that was tucked into a secret spot. The chief rolled out a small and varied collection of rough diamonds—a double-decker, a yellow clear, and some graphitelike stones. Even to the untrained eye they were junk, or so called passport diamonds because they traveled around without being sold. The biggest was three and a half carats, but its quality made it almost worthless except as a souvenir. They'd already sold the good stuff and were looking to unload the rest of their merchandise. Despite the poor quality of the diamonds it never paid to insult a customer. Cobus didn't buy diamonds. It was too easy to be set up and lose everything. He went through the process of making small talk and admiring the stones, and then offered to make an introduction to someone else who might buy the diamonds.

Cobus pulled out his battery-powered Tanita diamond scale and zeroed it out with a twenty-gram weight. He also had a color-corrected diamond light that illuminated flaws. What was transpiring here would be illegal if Cobus was to buy any goods—but this was just show and tell and an introduction to a legitimate diamond dealer. It was obvious that these folks hoped to find someone with a need for bush diamonds, someone who wanted to circumvent the normal process and smuggle them out of the country. They left with the name of a diamond buyer. On the way out the dealers took great pain to remember my name.

A few minutes later, another group showed up. This procession was from Bo and led by the woman who'd called earlier. She explained that the Kamajors were after them and they needed to move some diamonds quickly. When they spilled out the contents of their white packet, there was a definite glitter. This group wasn't dressed as well as the first, and they were downright nervous about me photographing their diamonds. They had some good octahedron stones. Not perfect, but something that looked very jewel-like with clear, crisp edges and few internal flaws. There was only two thousand to three thousand dollars in diamonds. Cobus thanked them, made a call to a diamond buyer, and they left.

He and I resumed talking about what happened after the two years of fighting that began when he came here in 1995.

"Once we pushed the RUF back into the bush after eighteen months,

Executive Outcomes was supposed to stay and train the Kamajors," Cobus said, "but nothing came of it. We were laid off instantly. Some of us were hired to guard the mines and the dam project at Bumbuna.

"We warned Kabbah that if EO left, the rebels would come back and there would be a coup in less than one hundred days. The coup happened ninety-six days later when Johnny Paul Koromo deposed Kabbah. That left us guarding the mines and the dam surrounded by thousands of rebels we had just finished defeating.

"LifeGuard was the same people that owned Executive Outcomes. Rutile is one of the three places in the world where they mine rutile. It's a strategic material used to make aerospace materials. It can even harden ceramics. The CIA used to own the mine through a front company but now they can get rutile from other places.

"The mine is near Bonthe, half an hour by helicopter. There is not much to do there. The rebels didn't know what to do with rutile but they would loot the equipment. When we got there the Americans had built two swimming pools that were abandoned, a bowling alley that was boarded up, and even an overgrown nine-hole golf course. There was not much to do so we used to work out and play golf. Every shot had to be a tee shot because of the high grass. Even though the clubs were right-handed and I was left-handed I became a scratch golfer. I had an eleven handicap. During the week it was practice, and on the weekend it was competition. When I went back to South Africa I played for the first time on a real golf course. The instructor couldn't believe I had never played on a real course.

"I was thin and wiry until I began lifting weights at Rutile. We used horse steroids to beef us up. I ended up weighing over eighty-eight kilos but my balls began to shrink to about the size of raisins."

Cobus and the mercenaries waited for a war while they worked as security guards. Isolated and surrounded by thousands of rebels in an uneasy peace, they held their ground. Sometimes it was fifteen mercenaries against more than a thousand rebels. Cobus had always thought that what Sierra Leone needed to begin rebuilding was security. He left LifeGuard and formed his own firm, Southern Cross Security. He underbid LifeGuard for the rutile mine contract, hired some of the same people, and managed to retain a business relationship with the owners of LifeGuard.

"By the end of February 2000, LifeGuard became Southern Cross and was in control of LifeGuard's former contracts. It was business and I learned fast. Southern Cross today is the largest and most professional security outfit in the country. We accept no military work of any kind, keep our noses clean, and service the country and our clients in a positive way. We employ close to five hundred Sierra Leoneans, from security officers, drivers, and radio operators all the way to management level."

Cobus was happy running his security company in Freetown. It protected NGOs, businesses, and individuals. It hadn't turned a profit yet, but there were new inquiries everyday, new clients, and hope. More and more foreigners showed up at Paddy's and Alex's to talk business. Things were looking up in Sierra Leone. These people knew that any business venture here needed security, especially in a place where people were focused on diamonds. With peace on the horizon and thousands of armed rebels and soldiers without jobs, crime was rapidly replacing warfare as the growth industry of the day. Cobus was selling the right service in the right place at the right time, and he knew he could make a difference. But Cobus was also going through a transformation. He'd come here to kill people; he was armed and prepared to land in a generic African cesspool to "sort things out." Now he used those skills to keep the peace and to allow businesses, aid organizations, and investors to conduct their business. He he'd also set his sights on a higher goal: tourism, and once again fish played a big part in it.

We were just seven degrees north of the equator. The coastline was flat, with fetid mangroves that led into dense secondary jungle. Farther inland were small hills and weathered mountains—nothing to really attract the backpacker or even the intrepid tourist. The government had setup a number of game parks and reserves, at least on the maps, but they were simply good intentions marked on old maps. Cobus knew that the real riches of Sierra Leone were under the ocean, and he knew that tourism—or the money generated by it—could help put Sierra Leone back on its feet. People would pay big dollars for catch-and-release fishing in a pristine environment.

He wanted me to go to see the secret spot where we would find "Big Silver."

We rolled the boat into the water and within the few minutes it took to get ready the warm, sunny day became a black maelstrom of horizontal rain, lightning, and large waves. We waited a piece for the storm to pass; then it was a perfect tropical day. I couldn't help but think that it was an exact mirror of the political situation here. The trip to the islands took us past the coastline and beaches south of Freetown. The scenery transformed into endless vistas of light golden beaches carved endless crescents, interrupted by rocky points set off by curtains of palms and anchored by the dark green forested mountains that rose rising behind them. Fresh water flowed from rivers, herons flew from the jungles, and there was not a soul in sight. It was the view that had greeted the Portuguese five hundred years ago. If you didn't know the horror within, you would assume this was somewhere in the Caribbean.

But there was no war, so we pulled the boat in closer, stripped down, and swam to shore. We explored Whale Beach, which was completely empty and pure Robinson Crusoe. Another dark squall was coming in, so we pushed into the bush and found crumbling traces of civilization—a smashed concrete bench, an overgrown road, a rusty metal bridge that had collapsed.

Two small boys collecting clams on the river flats ran away at the sight of our white faces. There was still fear in the jungle; it was time to leave. We walked along the beach in the soft tropical rain and then swam back to the boat.

Cobus made a sweeping gesture with his arm toward the beach and rocks. "This is where I want to build the base camp. From here we will take the boat out fishing to a satellite camp on the Turtle Islands." The idea of a remote thatched hut on a deserted island did have a magical appeal, even if I couldn't care less about fishing. It was more about that odd Western idea of exploring, of being the first, of turning 180 degrees without seeing another person. It was about adventure.

Our trip to the Turtles was bumpy and wet, a refreshing break from the tropical heat. The weather moved off the land in a series of giant rain tiaras that slid off the mountains, moved over the ocean, and plunged us into deep blackness. The rain and wind emptied upon us so hard that is was difficult to breathe. Finally, tired of its malevolence, the thunderhead drifted away, leaving sun and brightness.

The Turtle Islands were flat sandbars built up by silt from the river and the constant pounding of the Atlantic surf. Inside the protection of the islands was a vast, shallow nutrient-rich ocean.

Previous explorers had remarked on the native fisherman's pristine lifestyle and resistance to change here. In fact, these people, along with other slaves from Africa, could be found living the same lifestyle they had when they landed in the United States, where they were called Gullah, a contraction of the word Ngola or Angola. They can still be found on the Sea Islands of South Carolina. It was easy to understand why they were so firmly fixed in their idyllic lifestyle. The basics were close at hand: fish, coconuts, subsistence crops, and easy access to the mainland. Their dwellings were rustic and neat, constructed of stick frames tied together with grass rope and "mudded" into tiny two-and three-room houses topped off with thatch. Each village was carefully swept, the fishing nets were hung to dry, the cooking fires tended to.

As Cobus and I cruised the tiny islands, the villagers came out and ran along the shore, waving to us. They called out and laughed with excitement. We stopped a passing canoe and traded two beers for a large fish. They wanted to trade more: shirts, shoes, hats, whatever we had, but the sun was getting low and we had to make camp.

We landed on Buki next to two small houses that were built by a Frenchman who had married a local girl. In accordance with local custom, we checked in with the chief and discussed niceties. We made sure he got a beer and an invitation to dinner. In response, he offered to have his boys make a fire and cook our fish for us. There was evidence of a rebel attack on the houses. The RUF had commandeered a navy boat and some canoes and stripped the place down to the sinks and toilets. Even the lightbulbs were stolen. Four Western-looking rooms had only the concrete bed supports. The boys built a fire and made a salt and pepper seasoning by pounding it into a fine powder in a wooden pestle. We sat under the stars and enjoyed the large-scaled fish, called a Jumbo by the locals.

Cobus kept his AK leaned up against the wall as we talked about his dreams. They centered on the hunt for "Big Silver," *Megalops atlanticus*—the two-hundred-plus-pound tarpon that lived in abundance here. To be more exact, Cobus was fishing for a select group of fishermen who would spare no expense and brave any danger or discomfort to catch an International Game Fish Association–class tarpon on regular fly tackle. The race had been on to catch a man-sized record holder on tiny fly-fishing tackle ever since the first world-record tarpon was caught in 1958 at a paltry 125 pounds.

Cobus knew this was the place. He loved the sport and knew how to treat his guests right. He'd build a main base that would feature a casino and eco-tours and then take the serious fishermen out for some real fishing. Since 1991, fifteen world records for tarpon had been set in the area from the Sherbro River out to the islands. There was a perfect combination of temperature, depth, and nutrients, and absolutely no one was disrupting any part of the life cycle of this massive fish. Fishermen have such respect for tarpon that they are a strictly catch-and-release species.

It wasn't unusual to catch a three-hundred-plus-pounder, or to get an average of six strikes a day. There were also barracudas, snappers, groupers, jacks, sharks, and bream. The best fishing was from February to May, just before the rainy season.

Cobus thought he could also fly in people in his ultralight to see golden crescents of unpopulated beaches, flowering rain forest canopies, exotic birds, and uncataloged orchids. There were forests of odd granite domes and an escarpment 130 kilometers inland that divided the cooler five hundred-meter highlands from the lowlands with dramatic waterfalls. Farther inland were herds of elephants, pygmy hippos, monkeys, apes, and feral pigs. It was a world lost to ten years of war and awaiting rediscovery.

As I sat on the porch of one of the tiny houses with Cobus, the drum-roll of distant thunder and the crashing of the waves on the far side of the island gave his concept a sense of drama. The excitement in his voice and the new peace made the whole endeavor seem not only plausible, but also damn adventurous. Down below, the waves lapped gently at the sides of the boat, the palm fronds swished in the warm breeze, and we could hear the crackle of the fire and the soft chatter of the local fishermen. It was as peaceful as any place I'd ever been to. I asked him what Sierra Leone had been like when he first came here in 1995.

"Our job was simple: Kill the rebels. The way EO worked in Sierra Leone was straightforward. There was a company of eighty guys divided into two platoons of twenty men each. I was in charge of the fire force. Joss

Robler commanded all the vehicles. We were often surrounded, especially to the east. The rebels would hit us but they never expected us to respond by attacking instead of retreating. We would not only attack but also pick up their trail, track them, and hunt them down.

"We would gather intelligence, chopper in or drive to about five miles away, dismount, and then move in. We walked in formation on the shoulder, as we called it. That point-man stuff you see in the movies is bullshit. We never had a point man. The more weapons you can bring to bear to the front, the better it is. The line would walk abreast with the trackers until we got within half a click of a village. Then we would deploy mortars. The 32 Battalion was famous for their eighty-two millimeter mortar teams. We could drop a mortar into a rain barrel at a thousand meters.

"The choppers would go into a holding pattern just out of earshot, usually four to five thousand meters away, to prepare. There would be a platoon in front, myself in the middle, and a platoon behind. We would then stop and I would go back to the mortar position to mark the rebels' escape routes and work out the firing data on a 1 to 50,000 topo map. I would guess where the rebels would escape by looking at topography, the vegetation, the footpaths, and the river. If you had a guide you would ask him where the paths out from the village went. We would also target the shit paths that the villagers used every day to crap.

"I would post a reserve guard to protect the mortars and then go back up to my front. Then the moment someone yelled contact I would call in the gunship. We all would then turn our hats around to show the Day-Glo patches on the inside so the pilot could pick us up visually. Once we had contact, people went running. The pilot would come in and shoot at them with the Gatling. We would be forty to sixty meters away, sometimes less than five meters. The gunship would then swing by and come in over us.

"We believed in firepower. Where most armies carry one or two spare mags, we carried ten to twelve with a double mag in the weapon. On first contact, if it was a heavy stand, the soldiers would drop prone. They are trained to cover a narrow area in front of them. We fire at real or potential targets sweeping from right to left. You shoot at the enemy and where you think the enemy is hiding. Even when you can't see the enemy you keep shooting. We'd shoot straight through mud walls into bushes to kick up stones and chips. We worked in teams. You are number one and your number two is on your right. Your number two fires slower so you are covered when you change magazines. Our style is to shoot, observe, then yell, 'Changing mag.' That means dash down, crawl to the side a little, observe, and fire. Then you yell 'Buddy, Buddy, Advansar.' That's the signal for your buddy to get up and repeat. There is nothing that can stand against a line of South African infantry.

"When the fighting started it very quickly got haphazard. Shouting on the radio, tending the wounded, incoming mortar fire, and people firing all around you. In Angola the rebels would run backward and then split into smaller and smaller groups. Here the rebels just ran away. They would pick the nearest footpath and just run. If we had done our work we would be dropping mortars on them just as they hit the predetermined spot. Often we would sleep in the village to see if they came back. Our casualty rate was low compared to the rebels. We just massacred the shit out of them. It was basically a small group of well-trained guys against great masses of untrained rabble."

"Was it like hunting?" I asked.

Cobus thought a moment and said, "no, it was more like culling."

We were sitting under the stars when I smelled gasoline. Even though three of the local boys had cooked our dinner and were right in front of us, another one was trying to steal our empty gas containers from the boat ten yards below. Cobus racked his AK and said, "I will shoot anyone who steals from me." He told the boatman to sleep on the boat and to yell loudly if anyone came again, but not to run.

"Why?" the boatman asked.

"Because I will be shooting whoever is running."

After searching for the culprit, we found the yellow gas can abandoned in the bushes.

Cobus and I continued our conversation. I had learned that it wasn't unusual to go from a lighthearted mood to intense violence and back as fast as the thundershowers formed off the coast. I commented on the photo of the blond child next to Cobus's bed at home. He was married and had three children back in South Africa.

"I try to be a part of my boy's life," he said. "My wife is a trained nurse. She caught my eye and I married her." He paused and reflected. "She is a good soldier's wife."

Cobus had no sense of remorse or sadness, no sense of outrage, no post-traumatic stress syndrome. He had been in combat for almost twenty of his thirty-six years and had seen everything that the human animal can do to another human animal. He'd been witness to a bloodlust here that was even more horrific when you came to understand the gentle nature of these people, something that grew from the terrible things done to them in the name of terror.

"In 1994, before we got here, the RUF began deliberately mutilating and raping people. It's like Sankoh had read Mao's little red book on terror and only got half of it right. Even though you use terror to multiply the effect, a revolution is supposed to have the support of the people. He murdered and slaughtered innocent villagers to clear out the diamond areas. He then press-ganged young boys to fight or work, and raped and enslaved young girls for sex and menial labor.

"You could even see where the rebels had been when you flew over in the gunship. You would see women on the road, their legs splayed, the large pool of red around their heads showing that they'd had their throats cut. Atrocities were committed by all sides."

I asked Cobus if he participated in any atrocities.

"The people we dealt with didn't get anything they didn't deserve."

He thought for a moment, then tried to put the moral dilemma into perspective.

"There was a village just outside Kono that had been raided by the rebels. They were still sitting around a fire cooking when we snuck up on them. They had tied up all the men. It was tense. We could only line up four rebels from behind a banana tree. Then up walks this little kid. Most kids would scream or run away but this little kid comes around the corner and sees forty mean South Africans and he didn't bat an eyelash. He just took his mother's sleeve and walked her out of the way.

"There were seven rebels sitting around the fire. The villagers were trussed up and lined up like sausages. They were getting ready to rape one woman. We opened fire, killing six; one got away. The last rebel got up so fast that he stepped in a pot of boiling rice. By the time we got back, the bush telegraph had told everyone what had happened.

"The Kamajors found the last remaining rebel wandering around the bush with gangrene from the burns. Unfortunately, by the time I got to him he had been a guest of the Kamajors for around twenty-four hours. When I saw him he was missing most of his appendages. They had shoved a knife up his ass several times, he had a stump of a penis, and his lips, ears, nose, and tongue were missing. Death is a gift at that point.

"When we got back to the village the people were lined up and cheering. They knew what had happened before we even radioed back to headquarters. It took a while to realize that we were doing something good. We were the good guys, something that hadn't really struck home until that moment."

We turned in for the night. I lay on my back and stared up at the stars. We'd talked about a lot of things: how tough it was to actually cut off the cartilage of human ears, what happened to a person's bowels when he was gutshot out of spite, what little children could do to women in the midst of battle, how governments worked in Africa, and how paradise could slide into hell in the space of a heartbeat.

Cobus had come a long way, a reverse journey from darkness to light. From a hunter of men to a protector of nature. From mercenary to fisherman. From soldier to savior. A journey not many of us take. Maybe it was one of the beauties of Sierra Leone. Here darkness could pass as quickly into light as light could turn to darkness.

The next morning, after a walk to admire the breakers and chat with the fishermen, we started the journey back to Freetown. The weather was still and warm. My feeble attempt at to catch anything resembling a tarpon came to naught, so we left the shallows, gunned the 90s, and set a course on the GPS for Freetown via the Banana Islands. Cobus pointed out a spiked mast shimmering on the thin blue horizon, then another. "Twelve o'clock. Another one." He asks, "What do you want to do, Rob?"

Technically we were in a dilemma. Although Cobus called them pirates, I would have called them poachers. Yes, they were stealing, and if you did the math the eight-thousand-dollar-per-ton of shrimp they were netting outweighed anything a scabby *pam pam* loaded with pirates could snatch. And after all it was peacetime, so maybe their crime was more grave. Cobus didn't have permission to hunt these poachers; I was here on a tourist visa. But we both grinned when he whipped the boat toward the first ship and pulled back on the throttle. My weapon of choice today was a video camera, and Cobus had his reputation; the AK stayed in the compartment for now, loaded but not brandished.

The first ship suddenly wheeled around and headed in the opposite direction, toward Liberia. He hadn't put his net in yet. The lead boat wasn't so lucky. The thin outline quickly grew into a black three-hundred-ton trawler. As we flew toward a direct confrontation, Cobus described the procedure and what happened the last time they were fired on.

"Normally we sail in front of a ship that is poaching and use the loud hailer to tell him we are coming on board. If a ship doesn't want to stop, we fire warning shots and then we board it. Usually there is a ramp that they use to pull the nets up the back. We approach, shove the prow of the boat up the ramp, the boarding party jumps off and scales the ramp. On two occasions they shot back. We were attacked by Chinese vessels. We boarded them, gave the captain a bit of an education, and then locked him and his crew in the freezer for three hours. We became good friends with the crew afterward."

Although the first ship was steaming away, this ship didn't seem to notice us as we drew near. Finally we were on it like a mouse assaulting an office building. Our tiny, rigid inflatable was dwarfed by the two-hundred-foot long black ship. The battered, rusted hulk rose out of the water above us. Foul bilgewater pumped from its guts to the sound of a pained metallic groaning.

Normally, Cobus would have fired shots above the wheelhouse to alert the captain to his predicament, maybe even accidentally destroying the expensive radar equipment. The ship kept steaming forward, ignoring our tiny craft. The crew finally noticed us and stared over the side. The Chinese captain came out and waved limply. There was no confusion as to what they were doing here. The shoreline was only a few hundred yards away, and they'd even draped a green tarp over the ship's bow to conceal the name.

Their net lines were dragging deep below the surface. This probably wasn't the first or the last time their ship would be caught raping the oceans.

In case the captain was in doubt or became confused about our intentions, Cobus yelled, "Get the fuck out of here, you bastard!" Puzzled but relieved, the captain attended to getting the fuck out of there. There was little we could do but circle the ship as I videotaped it along with the GPS coordinates, the time of day, and the contents of the net. Suddenly, two barn-door-sized green spreaders leaped out of the ocean, followed by the net floats. They were strip-mining the sea.

"He is fishing for shrimp in their breeding ground," Cobus yelled. "The net goes down, churns up the bottom, and scrapes everything into the net. The mesh on the net is small enough to capture the inch-long shrimp that haven't even made it to maturity yet."

The men on deck now kept an eye on our buzzing, angry boat as they worked frantically to haul the net in. I could see that Cobus had to restrain himself from ramming the speedboat up the greasy loading ramp in the back and collecting his prize. It would have been an easy catch; fifteen thousand dollars if they were a registered ship, one hundred thousand dollars plus the sale of the boat if they were pirates. The end of the net appeared with a pink haul about the size of a bus. The few tons of baby shrimp inside would have turned into a much larger and more lucrative catch, but there would be no reckoning today.

As the captain steamed away toward Liberia, a native in a large wooden fishing canoe stood up and cheered for us.

POSTSCRIPT

When I showed the videotape of two unarmed men chasing off two poaching trawlers to Minister Okeri Adams, I asked him point-blank why Cobus's pirate hunter license had been lifted. Embarrassed into an answer, he smiled and said, "Soon, very soon." Three weeks later Cobus was issued his long lost letter. He is now back in business hunting pirates.

THE HAMMER
The Hammer
THE HAMMER
THE HAMMER

I'm a world assignments editor for BBC news and the line manager for
_____ in _____. I understand you've been asking his advice on going to
Chechnya. Our view, and that of the British Foreign Office and numerous
experienced and expert people in Moscow, is that it's mad to contemplate
a trip to Chechnya. Not only are there serious risks of the obvious kind
attendant upon any battlefield situation, but the risk of kidnapping for ransom is extremely high, not only in Chechnya, but also in the neighboring
republics of Ingushetia and Dagestan. (Some British Telecom engineers
working on a contract in Chechnya, and with the highest guarantees of
official protection, were kidnapped and beheaded a few months ago.) At
the moment we only approve visits by our people under the most carefully
researched and heavily guarded circumstances, and that means either the
Russian army or absolutely top-level guarantees from the Chechen authorities. We regard Chechnya as the most dangerous place in the world for
Western journalists to work.

Our strong advice is—keep away.

It is one thing to dream, another to plan, and quite another to make the
decisions that can result in your death. There are easier and more useful
ways to die than to visit someone else's war.

Getting into Chechnya wouldn't be easy. The British and American governments had told any journalists to leave Chechnya immediately, but
reports still came from the few desperate or crazed stringers who remained.

There were reports that chemical containers were being transported
into Chechnya from Russia. One of the largest assembled armies in mod-

ern times—150,000 Russian troops—was grinding toward the tiny breakaway republic. *Contractistya*, or Russian mercenaries, had been hired to fight alongside ragged conscripts. Russian politicians declared that the war would be over by Christmas, with the result that the terrorists and bandits would be wiped from the face of the earth. The Russian generals warned the politicians that they would not turn back even if they were ordered to.

I was preparing to enter not with the Russian military juggernaut but with the rebels, whom they were poised to smash. I contacted anyone I thought might help me get in and get out safely: journalists, aid groups, friends, think tanks. Most responded in disbelief, and as I made the preparations, the reports became grimmer. A Sipa photographer had been shot. The Russians were cluster-bombing the pass from Georgia to Chechnya every twenty-four hours. A French journalist had disappeared in an entryway I'd intended to use. The *New York Times* sent instructions to their person to get out, but they couldn't find her.

NTV broadcast an amateur video of an unshaven Frenchman standing in a dark room. A spokesman for the FSB—Russia's Federal Security Service and successor to the KGB—said that the man was French photographer Bruce Fleutiaux, and that gunmen had seized him when he tried to enter Chechnya.

Fleutiaux complained of being kept in a cold cellar, beaten regularly, and "treated like a dog." The FSB spokesman said that Fleutiaux's captors had made the tape and were demanding money for his release. It had subsequently made its way to the FSB.

"The FSB has released the film for Russian and foreign journalists to be cautious when going to the North Caucasus," the spokesman said. Fleutiaux was believed to have been seized by gunmen near the Georgia-Chechnya border when he tried to bypass Russian checkpoints and sneak into rebel-held portions of Chechnya.

"He went to Turkey, then to Georgia, where he got in touch with criminal gangs who have ties to Chechen gangs and tried to use this channel to get into Chechnya," Alexander Zdanovich, the head of FSB public relations department, told NTV. "The result is tragic. They did transfer him to Chechnya but only as a hostage."

Many kidnap victims were killed, often beheaded. Some had been mutilated. Survivors said that they had been tortured, starved, bought and sold, worked as slaves, or raped.

As winter set in and the bombing intensified, even the stringers left.

I became acquainted with Aqil when he contacted me to ask if I knew how to get into Chechnya. My curiosity piqued, our emails turned into phone calls, but he refused to elaborate over the phone. If I wanted to meet him, I would have to visit him at home in the suburb of Tempe, Arizona. The houses there were light colored and virtually indistinguishable from one another. Two-year-old sedans and pickups occupied the driveways. He shared his home with his wife and two children. They had a fish tank, suburban furniture, kids' toys, a TV, videotapes, newspapers, and an AK-47 leaning upright in the corner.

He was a polite young man with a stocky build, red hair, blue eyes, and a shy demeanor. As a devout Muslim, he neither drank nor smoked. He wore a prosthetic just below his knee; he had lost his leg when he'd tripped two Russian Claymore mines on his wedding day in Chechnya. Aqil was mistrustful, but soon he was telling me of life on the front lines of several wars, and not just any wars but jihads, holy wars, in obscure places like Bosnia, Afghanistan, Kosovo, Tajikistan, Kashmir, and Chechnya. He didn't brag or attempt to impress; I had to pull the stories out of him. He was known as a killer of Russians. He described his style of war as "up close and personal."

Aqil is a beefy-linebacker all-American apple-cheeked Irish American mujhid and Aqil wanted to die; he wanted to be *shaheed,* or martyred, to ensure his place in heaven. Aqil needed a shortcut because he had sinned.

He'd shaved his strawberry blond hair, and his head had two days of red stubble. I watched the fish in the aquarium as he sat surrounded by his children's toys. He was uncomfortable talking so openly about his past, and more reticent talking about his future.

Aqil found Islam while incarcerated at a correctional camp for boys. He was "a bad boy, nothing serious." He was sent to the camp for stealing cars and for multiple offenses. One day he saw an open Koran and started to read. When he got out of the camp he went to the mosques in San Diego, and in time a man named Zaki told him that he should go to Bosnia. Without any military training he entered Europe's nastiest war. He looked at it as a calling to stop Serbs from killing Muslims.

He showed promise, so he was sent to Afghanistan for training in the camps that the United States would eventually bomb with cruise missiles. There he met a man who'd kidnapped a group of foreign tourists in Kashmir, Osama bin Laden's men, and others. The camp had to hide him whenever Pakistani army officers visited, because he was American.

He was supposed to go to Tajikistan but ended up fighting in Kashmir, where he was ostracized by his Arab commander for being too aggressive, too eager to die. In Chechnya he walked from front line to front line until he finally met up with a group of misfits who wreaked havoc and destruction on the enemy, sometimes attacking entire Russian firebases with only six people. He narrowly escaped all manner of explosives, bullets, and attacks while participating in ambushes on convoys or acting as bait for Russian gunships. But it was not his time.

At a roadside stall in Chechnya, he met Ayeesha, a beautiful local girl. He asked her to marry him and she agreed. On the morning of his wedding day an old woman told him that Russian Spetnatz were trying to sneak into the village. On his way into the village he set off a booby trap that riddled his legs with hundreds of steel ball bearings. Before he would let the Chechen fighters take him to the field hospital, he made good on his promise and married Ayeesha. They left for Jordan and Turkey for surgery on his shattered legs. While he recovered they had a daughter. Frustrated by his attempts to get her back into the States, Ayeesha and his daughter had to return to Chechnya. When he returned to Arizona Aqil told the doctors to cut off his right leg.

He returned home to Phoenix, where he worked as a security guard at a local mosque where he had another wife, a local Phoenix woman. As a Muslim, Aqil is allowed to have more than one wife. They experienced the prejudice and hatred toward Muslims in this country and it angered Aqil every day. He wanted to move his family back to Chechnya before the war broke out.

He took me upstairs to an unused room. There was a pile of random papers. He rummaged through them to find something—photos of his child and a photo of his Chechen wife in front of a mosque wearing a full-length black covering. His wife's face was scratched out of the photo. Aqil wanted to know if I could take him inside Chechnya and bring his wife out.

He had tried to enter before but failed. His patrons were not Islamic fundamentalists. Aqil had a darker history than I first suspected. He first learned of me when his CIA handler gave him a copy of my book, *The World's Most Dangerous Place*.

Aqil hated terrorists. He offered to get Osama bin Laden and became an asset of the CIA. They passed him back to the FBI. Back in the United States, frustrated, penniless, and worried about his Chechen wife, he was told to infiltrate local Muslim groups. Despite his frustration he tried to do what he was told. Finally he told them that the local people did not support *jihad* or terrorism, and that he needed to be on the front lines, in the camps, to do what he could.

They agreed to send him to Kosovo to join the Kosovo Liberation Army, KLA. That is when his handler gave him *Dangerous Places*. Now he believed that I could get him back into Grozny where he could fight, and that I could get his wife out. I mentioned that I was concerned about his involvement with the CIA and FBI, something sure to get us killed in Chechnya. "Don't worry," he said. "I told the CIA to go fuck themselves a few months ago after they accused me of being a terrorist." Since then he said he had survived two assassination attempts. He never traveled without a gun.

There was more. Ayeesha's parents threatened to kill him if he returned to Chechnya. They felt that he had abandoned their daughter. They didn't know the truth because Aqil never could explain the bureaucratic red tape that prevented her from traveling with him to the United States. Aqil was turning out to be a dangerous man.

It seemed fitting that Grozny was now the most dangerous place in the world, where napalm, rockets, missiles, and thousand-pound bombs were raining down. By the time we got there Grozny was very likely to be under siege, surrounded by the largest military force the Russians had fielded since Afghanistan.

I would bring another person on this journey, a twenty-six-year old woman who had worked as journalist before and who craved the cutting edge of reporting from a war zone. Since Chechnya is an Islamic country,

I also needed a female who could leave with the girl and her mother and guide them out of the war zone. Like Aqil, she expected me to bring her safely in and out.

I explained the dangers. If we were caught we would be imprisoned, maybe even tried and executed by the Russians as spies. There was no guarantee of safety with the rebels. We would be entering a place where bandits and rogue militia hunted down foreigners for money, and where aid workers, journalists, missionaries, and even a top Russian general had simply disappeared. While I planned our entry, Moscow TV played videos of the torture and execution of hapless captives. The latest news said there were more than 160 hostages inside Chechnya—1,200 over the last year, according to the Russians. Six Red Cross aid workers were shot in the head while they slept. Russian planes were bombing villages and hospitals; artillery and rocket barrages were leveling civilians' homes. There were no medical facilities and little food. There were no safe places left inside Chechnya.

Despite my graphic portrayal of the world behind enemy lines and hidden from the news, she would not say no.

Why go? I had some soul searching to do. I have a wife, twin teenage daughters, a house, a ranch, three horses, a life, a job, a career. I called to see if anyone would help pay my expenses. A war in Europe, genocide, even the promise of bang bang, but no newspaper or television news showed interested. Every magazine turned me down. Even the Discovery Channel, a network that was paying me to do a show about "The World's Most Dangerous Places," said, "No, too dangerous." I was on my own. Life and times were good in America; no one cared about a war in Europe. A deadly stupid war whose root causes were little different from those of World War I or II.

I'd known from the start that few would care or notice, fewer would believe, and none would sympathize even if I died. I got the same responses when I went to other dirty little wars in Algeria, Sudan, Afghanistan, Uganda, or east Turkey. But this was a big dirty war. A Napoleonic-sized war. A replay of Stalingrad, a badly rehearsed production of the blitzkrieg, and a pathetically restaged big-budget sequel of the last war in Chechnya. I felt there was a message inside Chechnya.

But who cared about that message? What would people say about a man who entered a place everyone told him to avoid, bringing in a man who went to die? Well, what did he expect? What was he thinking? Just what did he think he was doing? All questions I asked myself.

This trip wouldn't be just about Aqil, his world, or my world. It would be about our world, how it changes, about what is right, what is wrong, why people don't care anymore, and why they should.

As I prepared for the trip a news report appeared. The Russians had sent a cruise missile into the center of a Grozny market, which killed more than two hundred people. The Russians said that it was an arms market. The Chechens said it hit a group of women shopping. Who was right and who was wrong? Someone needed to witness. I decided to go.

This was a tightly controlled war of both words and weapons, and any news seemed to come exclusively from the Russian side. The Russians took their cue from the American handling of the Gulf War and Serbia. This time they didn't want pictures of shattered soldiers who were hungry, begging, and dying. They didn't want stories of jubilant Chechen fighters. The Russians were keeping the journalists bottled up in Nazran, a small town well away from the fighting, granting quick PR tours to fill the airwaves with archaic images of happy Russian soldiers being sent off to defeat the Chechen bandits. I had a dark feeling that there were few if any journalists with the rebels in Chechnya because the Russians didn't want the rest of the world to know what was about to happen. The honest journalists datelined their reports from Ingushetia, while others literally stepped just inside the border so they could byline their stories from Chechnya. But the real war was inside Chechnya.

Chechnya is where Europe ends. A place where a severe mountainous ridge that separates Europe from Asia physically and geographically, but not ethnically or politically. Georgia lies to the south of the Caucasus Mountains. Once part of the Soviet Union, Georgia is Christian, with its own language and ancient culture. The Chechens who lie on the northern side are Muslims and Semitic in origin. They are an olive-skinned, intensely persecuted people separated in every possible manner from the Russians and the Georgians. The mountains of southern Chechnya have always been an impenetrable and confusing place. Invaders have claimed victory there, but there was never any real victory, whether it was in the beech forests, in the steep canyons, or in the dark eyes of the Chechens who hated every conqueror and vowed revenge.

Chechnya is a tiny place, only six thousand square miles, with a population that used to be 1.2 million. It was refused its self-declared freedom ever since Georgia broke away from the Soviet Union in 1989. A map of the region looks like the results of bad Russian dentistry, and each small toothlike region has a different reason to hate Russia. Ossetia, South Ossetia, Kabardino-Balkaria, Dagestan, Karachay-Cherkessia, and Stavropol-Kray have been held in place by Russian military force. Inside each republic is a volatile mix of religious, cultural, ethnic, and criminal groups that make the Balkans seem homogeneous by comparison, and of all the Transcaucasian republics, Chechnya has been the most troublesome. The Chechens are sometimes called the blacks of Russia because of their swarthy skin and dark complexions. They practice Islam, a religion that has always caused paranoia in Orthodox Russia and even in the communist Soviet Union. They are called criminals because Chechens are a potent force in the criminal world in Moscow and St. Petersburg.

Chechens call themselves *Nuokhchuo,* or *Nuokhchi* in the plural the descendants of Noah. Their religion is *nakh.* Their country is not called Chechnya or Chechenistan but Ichkeriya.

Noah had three sons, Japheth, Shem, and Ham. From these three men came all the peoples of the world. Japheth spawned the Europeans, Ham was responsible for Asia and Africa, and from Shem came the people of the Middle East, or the Semites.

Some say that the Chechens come from the *Nephilim*— "those who cause others to fall down," from the Hebrew *na phal* (to fall). According to the Bible, God was unhappy with men, and in Genesis 6:1–4 the Nephilim are mentioned as the "men of fame" or the "mighty ones." They, too are the descendants of Noah's son Shem, and came to what is now Chechnya after the great flood.

Chechens were first mentioned in history during the seventh century A.D. The name Chechen was given to the mountainous "Notche" people along the northern edge of the Caucasus Mountains by the Russians after a failed attack on the village of Chechen-Aul in 1732.

Three-quarters of Chechens speak Russian, but 98 percent of Chechens speak Chechen, a truly unique and ancient toungue that has no sister languages outside the immediate region. Chechens are often described as Islamic fundamentalists, or Wahabbis by the Russians, but this isn't true. There is a core group of fundamentalists among the Chechen commanders, but the large bulk of Chechens are not strict Muslims. Many combine mysticism with Islam, which is to some devout Muslims a sin as great as being a disbeliever.

Chechens were first converted to Islam in the sixteenth century by Kumyk and Avar missionaries from Dagestan. Islam came first to the northern flatlands, and then the mountainous south. In modern-day Chechnya the influence of Islam mingles with older, little-known superstitions. Half of Chechens belong to a Sufi brotherhood, or tariq. The two Sufi tariqas that spread in the North Caucasus were the *Naqshbandiya* and the *Qadiriya*. With Islam came the first sense of organized resistance in 1556 against Christian Cossacks and the first stabs of fear from the expanding Russians. The Russians were repulsed twice in 1594 and 1605, leaving the Chechens alone for 120 years.

Sheikh Mansur Ushurma led the resistance against the Russian invaders at the end of the eighteenth century, and Imam Shamyl, a educated man and a daring fighter, became the main leader of resistance in the nineteenth century. Both were Naqshbandiya leaders. After Shamil's surrender in 1859, the Naqshbandiya became less popular and the Qadiriya tariqa grew in importance. Islam was brought to Ingushetia, by missionaries of the Qadiriya tariq. Naqshbandiya is particularly strong in Dagestan and eastern Chechnya in the north Caucasus, while the Qadiriya has most of its adherents in the west of Chechnya and Ingushetia.

Among nearly all Chechens is the unbreakable web of *adat*, or custom. There are about 125 Chechen *teips*, or clans in nine tribes or *tukums*. Each of the nine *tukums* are representd as stars on the Chechen flag. *Teips* are groups that are bound by land and blood; Chechens can marry or move into a *teip*, but once bound they must give their loyalty to the *teip*. Like Afghanistan, this is a land of blood feuds, long memories, and strong loyalties. Hospitality and sanctuary are given even to enemies, and outsiders are mistrusted. Violence and passionate loyalty are common. Nothing is taken lightly in Chechnya.

Modern *teips* are not unlike the city-states of ancient Greece in that the commander of a clan can choose to align or to fight other groups. Business and control determine the wealth of the clan. These clans may have their differences and blood feuds in what passes for peacetime, but they are ordinarily united under the nine *tukums* against outside invasion. This is why the Chechens have always achieved an unwritten sense of purpose and national identity whenever Russia has attacked. This combination of blood and religious ties is what makes Chechnya so volatile during peace and so resilient during war.

The Russian empire wanted to expand southward into the Caucasus in the late eighteenth century under Catherine the Great under the "Greek Project." An army of three hundred thousand Russians could not fully subdue the Chechens. They came across a type of warfare they had never experienced before. Large massed groups of European-trained cavalry found themselves against small groups of raiders unafraid to strike behind the enemy lines and disappear. The Russians did not know if the enemy was in front of them, behind them, or around them. They reacted by building a chain of forts with impressive-sounding names and terrorizing the population by cutting down the forests, flattening villages, taking hostages, and executing thousands of Chechens.

Catherine's attempt to expand the empire and to create a strong border to the south had a major effect on the Chechens. In 1783 the king of what is now Georgia appealed to the Russians for help, and his kingdom became a protectorate of Russia. The Russians built a military road through the mountains of Chechnya and Georgia, and built forts like Vladikavkaz ("Ruler of the Caucasus"). This arbitrary expansion of Russian rule angered an Imam named Sheikh Mansur. In 1784 he proclaimed a "Ghazawat," or jihad, against Russia. He'd studied Islam in Dagestan, and when he returned to Chechyna he started to enforce strict Islamic code, replacing ancient customs and superstitions with Islamic law, called sharia, and interpretation of the Koran. He also united the Chechens to fight against the Russian invaders. Fighters from Dagestan joined the Chechens to create an army of 12,000 men. They initially defeated the Russians on their own territory but were defeated when they tried to enter Russian territory. The Russians pulled back from Georgia to the north of the Terek River. In

1786 the Russian abandoned their fort in Vladikavkaz. Sheikh Mansur was finally captured in June of 1791 and died in prison three years later. The Russians had united the Chechens, created a hero, and hardened the Chechens as an Islamic group. Three years after Sheikh Mansur died, a child named Ali was born in Dagestan near Ashilta. His parents changed his name to Shamil when he became ill. The young man grew up listening to stories about how Mansur defeated the Russians.

The Russians made moves in 1816 to pacify the Chechens. Under the command of General Yermolov, a hero of the war against Napoleon, the Russians built a series of forts and methodically sealed off and destroyed Chechen resistance. Yermolov's choice of names for the forts spoke volumes—"Grozny," or "Fearsome" was the largest of his forts. Between 1817 and 1827 he cut down forests, burned villages, eliminated livestock, and committed genocide against the men, women, and children of Chechnya. After a series of disasters, including the murder of one his Generals and the loss of an important post, the Tsar recalled Yermolov for cruelty. By then the Russians had lost an estimated 100,000 men and almost wiped out the Chechen race.

The Chechen Imam Shamyl became a hero during that war, and would serve as a role model for a new hero named Shamil in the most recent war against Russia.

Historically the Chechens have never totally submitted to outside rule. Despite their defiance, however, they have lived under foreign power since the thirteenth century. The Chechens were conquered by Mongols (1242–1295), Persians (1295–1380), Timurids (1380–1405), the Ak Koyonlu Horde of the White Sheep (1405–1502), Persians again (1502–1516), Ottomans (1516–1620), Persians again (1620–1817), Russia (1817–1834), the Dagestani Murid Imams (1834–1850s), Russia (1850s–1918), were integrated into the Soviet Union (1918–1991), declared themselves a republic (1991–1994), were invaded by the Russians (1994–1996), and enjoyed a brief state of semiautonomy (1996–1999) before being invaded again by the Russian military.

Russia is the largest country in the world, and rational outsiders would assume the loss of another breakaway republic like Chechnya would make little impact on its troubled state of affairs. But Chechnya is strategically important as the southern border of Russia. As a bridge between East and West, the Chechens have been forced to fight the Russians in 1817, 1850, 1920, 1991, and again in 1999. Each time an uneasy sense of peace came until a charismatic leader emerged to unite the Chechen *teips*. In some cases the Russians deliberately planted the seeds of rebellion by heavy-handed treatment or direct interference. In this modern age there seems to be little economic or constructive purpose for the world's largest country to fight and lose a war with a tiny border region. But the roots of the conflicts between Chechen and Russian lie in fear, not politics.

The Russians feared Chechens so much that in 1944 the entire population of eight hundred thousand was deported to Siberia and Kazakhstan. Stalin was worried that the Chechens and the neighboring Ingush would support the Germans if the Wehrmacht reached the Caucasus. After the exodus, Stalin ordered Soviet cartographers to erase Chechnya from Russian maps. When Krushchev finally allowed the survivors to return in 1956–1957, an estimated 450,000 had died. Chechens found their homes occupied by Russian colonists and people from the neighboring region of Ossetia. This traumatic event shapes every Chechen's opinion of the Russians. Most Chechens over thirty-five were born in exile, and the Chechen diaspora in Russia, the Middle East, and Turkey still have a fierce desire not only to return but also to create a homeland. It is a story similar to that of the people of Israel, Armenia, and Kurdistan, but few view the Chechen cause in the same light.

In 1989 the Russians counted 957,000 Chechens throughout the entire Soviet Union. Of these 734,500 were in Chechnya, or what was then called the Chechen-Ingush Autonomous Republic. There were about eight thousand in the neighboring Dagestan republic, in and around Khasavyurt. Smaller groups lived in various republics and in many larger towns of the European part of the Soviet Union. Less than 1 percent of Chechens dwelt in Grozny, the target of the Russian's fury. At the beginning of the first war Grozny had a population of about 1,150,000. At the beginning of the second war there were only 450,000 Chechens and Russians left inside the city. As I made plans to enter, there were between twenty and forty thousand infirm, destitute, and elderly unfortunates. Most of them were ethnic Russians.

Another aspect of the conflict was trade and oil. There is a modicum of high-grade, easily refined oil in Chechnya, but nothing that would justify the billions spent on sending a 150,000-man army to destroy Chechnya, twice. Chechnya is also a transshipment point for oil from Russia and points east. Oil can travel via pipeline and railcar through the turbulent countries of Iran, Iraq, and Syria, or it can be routed north through the Russian Transcaucasus. The loss of a northern route would put the control of this oil inside a hostile nation or through American-influenced Georgia. Chechnya is also the natural geographic boundary for Russia, a country that is itself paranoid about foreign invaders. The sharp spine of the Caucasus Mountains creates a natural barrier between radical Islam and Russia—except of course for the Muslim Chechens and Dagestan. It makes sense that when ex-Soviets look at a map in Moscow, they think of the mountains as the natural border of Russia, but their goals extend much farther, into Georgia and strategic alliances with Iran, Iraq, and the CIS states. The Great Game did not end in Afghanistan. It is still being played in the fractured little states and enclaves sprinkled along Russia's mountainous borders.

Russian-controlled pipelines run from oil rich Baku in Azerbaijan through Dagestan at Makhachkala via Grozny, where there was a large refinery, and then northwest to Novorossiisk on the Black Sea. A different pipeline goes through Baku to Azerbaijan, Georgia, South Ossetia, and Supsa, another Black Sea port south of Novorossiisk. Another pipeline is planned to leave Baku, pass through Azerbaijan, miss Ossetia, Abkhazia, and Adjara, pass through Georgia, and then cut down through Turkey to come out at Ceyhan. Ceyhan is a port tucked in the top northeast corner of the Mediterranean, and avoids shipping oil through the strategically important and Russian-controlled straits of Bosporus.

If the pipeline in Grozny was destroyed or in enemy hands, then oil and the revenue it generated would pass through nations friendly to the United States and bypass the Russian-controlled areas completely. A independent Chechen republic could control or cut off oil from Baku. This is why, when Chechnya declared independence after the August 1991 coup attempt in Moscow, Russia simply said "No." Chechnya officially considered itself independent on November 1st, 1991.

When the coup against Mikhail Gorbachev failed, Dzhokhar Dudayev, a former Soviet air force general, was appointed to the presidency of

TRANSCAUCASIAN PIPELINE REGION

RUSSIAN STATES

KARACHAY-CHERKESSIA   STAVROPOL-KRAY

KABARDINO-BALKARIA   NORTH OSSETIA   DAGESTAN

CHECHNYA

INGUSHETIA

Moscow

Rjazan

RUSSIA

KEY

— EXISTING PIPELINE

--- PROPOSED PIPELINE

Novorossiisk   Tuapse   Budennovsk

BLACK SEA

Bosphorus Strait

Adjara   Vladikavkaz

GEORGIA

Supsa   Tiblisi

CASPIAN SEA

Baku

ARMENIA   AZERBAIJAN

TURKEY

Ceyhan   SYRIA   IRAN

IRAQ

Checheno-Ingushetia. In the fall of 1991 he won an election on a nationalist platform with the support of around twelve hundred members of the National Guard, and declared Chechnya to be an autonomous republic. Ingushetia remained within the Russian Federation. He had ex-Soviet weaponry, aircraft, and the Baku/Tikhoretsk oil refinery, a large facility with a processing capacity of twelve million tons per year.

Ruslan Labazanov and a group of other prison escapees comprised the nucleus of Dudayev's presidential guard. Labazanov and Dudayev had a split, however, and Labazanov soon formed an armed group of around five hun-

dred men, basing them in the Chechen city of Argun. The Russians immediately began a covert operation to supply and direct Chechen forces against
each other, a policy that was being conducted in all breakaway states.

Another defector from Dudayev was Bislan Gantemirov, the mayor of
Grozny. When he left Dudayev's circle he commanded an estimated eight
hundred troops. The fighting started on June 11, 1994, when the combined
forces of Ruslan Labazanov and Bislan Gantemirov entered Grozny and
tried to grab control by attacking the National Guard compound. The
failed attempt resulted in one hundred dead. Gantemirov retreated to his
base of support in Urus-Martan, while Labazanov went back to Argun.

By the summer of 1994 Dudayev had three thousand men, around
twenty working tanks, 150 military vehicles, and ten artillery pieces. Their
major arms were small arms. In October 1994 this anti-Russian force began
receiving air support from unmarked Russian-supplied gunships and fighters. In September Dudayev ousted Ruslan Labazanov from Argun and
imposed martial law. In October Dudayev attacked Bislan Gantemirov in
Urus-Martan.

The Russian government decided to take matters into their own hands.
In November, the Federal Counterintelligence Service (FSK) hired fifteen
hundred Russian soldiers to attack Dudayev in Grozny. They made it to the
center of the city but were destroyed, and with them went any hope of
removing Dudayev from power. Echoing the beginnings of the war in
Afghanistan, the Russians urged a puppet regime under Umar Avturkhanov
to formally demand direct intervention in the Chechen civil war.

On November 30, 1994, President Boris Yeltsin signed a secret directive
to "disarm illegal armed formations in Chechnya and re-establish the con-
stitutional order." Eleven days later Forty thousand Russian army and Interior Ministry troops entered Chechnya from Dagestan, Ingushetia, and
Stavropol with five tanks. The Russian forces were a quickly assembled
hodgepodge of units whose members had had no training for winter or
urban warfare. In addition, the commanders were not thrilled about being
ordered to attack their own countrymen. Many officers respected the
blockades that were erected by angry Chechens. Russian bombers began
the old business of killing their own people, however, and the first exodus
of Grozny began.

On January 1, 1995, the Russian forces assaulted the center of the city. Two days later Freedom Square fell quiet as Russian forces withdrew. More than two thousand Russian soldiers had been killed, and despite Russian news reports that Grozny had fallen, the Chechen flag still flew above the presidential palace. By February the Russians had regrouped and sur-rounded the city. The Chechen fighters abandoned Grozny in the begin-ning of March, and the cities of Gudermes, Shali, and Argun fell by the end of the month. The Russians then moved into the mountains to surround the villages and systematically clear them of Chechen "bandits." By June the Russians were satisfied that they had chased the Chechens from their strongholds of Shatoi and Vedeno.

During this whole process more than thirty five thousand people were killed in Chechnya. Most of them were older ethnic Russians who did not have the money or the ability to flee. OMON and MVD troops, the inter-nal security troops supposedly charged with protecting the people, were accused of atrocities and even of firing on federal troops when they tried to retreat from battle. There was the usual hue and cry about indiscrimi-nate bombing, destruction of infrastructure, looting, and the execution of civilians, but it didn't make the news. The Russian explanation was that this was an internal matter, and for the rest of the world, this explanation seemed sufficient.

Then, on June 14, more than one hundred Chechen fighters led by Shamil Basayev were caught in the southern Russian town of Budennovsk, about 120 kilometers northwest of Chechnya. In a reprise of his namesake's daring raids, Shamil was on his way to Moscow to take the war to the Rus-sians—a tactic that is a traditional part of warfare in the Caucasus but was to be played out on a much grander scale.

Suddenly the war had been placed in a new historical and religious per-spective. There are a handful of legends in the Chechen's wars against Rus-sia. One of the greatest is of the original Shamil, or Imam Shamyl, a Chechen who rose up in the 1850s during the first Russian invasion of Chechnya. Shamyl kept the Russians at bay until he surrendered to live as an honored guest among them. Shamil Basayev was born in 1967 in Vedeno, and has become a living legend among Chechens. He took his name from Imam Shamyl, and was a religious fundamentalist who had fought for his beliefs in Russia, Abkhazia, Dagestan, and Chechnya. He was considered daring, hotheaded, and unstoppable. His ultimate goal was an Islamic imamate that would stretch from the shores of the Black Sea to the Caspian. In an odd twist of fate, Basayev was also the man who protected Boris Yeltsin—along with his future enemies Generals Grachev and Lebed—with only two hand grenades—during the August 1991 coup in Moscow. The Chechens say his presence on a battlefield turns a small firefight into a firestorm.

So it wasn't surprising that after Basayev and his men had bribed their way across Russian checkpoints and run out of money in Budennovsk, a city with a population of about one hundred thousand, things heated up dramatically. They were stopped by local traffic police and escorted to the police station in the center of the city. Once at the police station the Chechens took control, killing forty police officers and soldiers. When they realized they couldn't hold the police station, they chose a stronger base from which to make their stand. The Chechens moved to the hospital, gathering fifteen hundred hostages along the way. They initially released 250 hostages, but on day four, Russian special forces attacked the hospital, which resulted in the deaths of about 150 Russian civilians. The effort didn't dislodge the Chechens. They demanded safe passage home, and to make their point they shot eight hostages as Yeltsin negotiated with Basayev live on Russian television.

On June 23, Prime Minister Chernomyrdin of Russia promised to grant a cease-fire, begin negotiations, and guarantee safe passage for the rebels. There was supposed to be a peace agreement, and Chechnya was to be independent. The seventy three remaining Chechen fighters retreated. Among the commanders on that raid were Turpalov Ali Atigirov, Abu Musayev, and others whom I would come to meet.

The summer of 1995 was a time of sporadic fighting but overall détente as Russians stayed in their defensive positions and Chechen self-defense groups patrolled the villages. The Chechen fighters had promised to hand over their weapons, and by the end of August 1995 approximately a thousand had been given to the Russians. The Russians then gave these weapons to the self-defense units, which consisted of demobilized Chechen fighters—the same people who had just handed them over. Eighty percent of

Chechnya's men were unemployed, and there were an estimated ninty thousand guns in the region. The men who were armed tended to work for groups that had a working relationship with the Russian secret service and military. The Russians had set the stage for the region to become a haven for the mafia and kidnapping gangs.

The world was not really interested in what was going on inside another tiny breakaway republic in Russia, but stories coming out of Chechnya at that time were unusual in their curious causes and effects. The disappearance of Fred Cuny, an American relief expert from Texas, was the first story to stir interest. In 1971 Cuny had started a company called INTERTECT Relief and Reconstruction Corporation. His specialty was to create and maintain the basic systems that people needed so that they would stay in their own village, preventing the problems associated with refugee camps. His company had been active in seventy different countries when he was sent to Chechnya on behalf of the Soros foundation. He disappeared in April 1995 around the village of Stari Achkhoi in the foothills of western Chechnya. Although many searched for Cuny, his family admitted that he was dead by August 18, 1995. Author Scott Anderson pointed the finger at Abu Musayev, one of the ringleaders of the daring raid to Budennovsk, as the man who ordered Cuny's execution.

In December 1996 masked gunmen invaded the Red Cross compound in the village of Novye Atagia, twenty kilometers south of Grozny. The killers went room to room and shot four Red Cross nurses and two volunteers in the head with silenced weapons as they slept. The seventh victim, a Swiss who ran the project, was wounded.

The operation appeared to be a carefully planned and executed hit. The attack was successful in scaring foreigners out of Chechnya; international aid agencies soon began to leave. The task of finding the perpetrators fell to Abu Musayev, who had now been appointed as the Chechen government's national security chief. Strangely, no killers were found. Abu Musayev had been called a secret agent for Moscow, a cold-blooded killer, and the mastermind behind a number of terrorist operations. Fred Cuny's killer was determined to be Risvan Elbiev, who shot Cuny, his translator, and his driver. Elbiev was later killed and is now just another elusive ghost in the war in Chechnya. Soros never setup any aid programs and few outsiders saw any reason to risk entering Chechnya.

January 1996 saw another daring raid by Chechen guerrillas. Ultraseparatist Salman Raduyev lad a daring raid on Kizlyar in Dagestan. It was a replay of the assault on Budennovsk, and Raduyev took two thousand hostages from the local hospital. Russian troops surrounded Raduyev's position and shelled both the rebels and the hostages for several days. When the Russian troops attacked, Raduyev led the rebels and about one hundred hostages on a near-miraculous escape to the nearby Chechen town of Pervomaiskaya. But the Russians caught up to them there and destroyed the rebels. Despite heavy casualties, Raduyev escaped to fight another day.

On January 18 Chechen commandos under the command of Muhammed Tokcan, a Chechen living in Turkey, hijacked a ferry with 150 tourists on the Black Sea to call attention to the atrocities that were occurring in Chechnya. They released hostages when they claimed that their goals were met. The situation in Chechnya was threatening to spill outside its tiny borders.

On March 31, 1996, Russia's President Boris Yeltsin surprised his country by announcing that military operations in Chechnya would cease immediately and that peace talks would begin. A tentative peace plan was created in May. Unimpressed by Russian promises, the Chechens continued fighting. President Dzhoklar Dudayev was killed the next month when the Russians launched an air-to-ground missile that homed in on Dudayev's satellite-phone signal as he talked from his stronghold south of Grozny. It was the Russians' first major victory. The peace talks were left to Aslan Maskhadov, the Chechen prime minister and a former Soviet army officer. The Russians made gains in the flat northern areas due to superior military power but were unable to control the southern mountains or large urban areas. The peace talks progressed then faltered through the Russian presidential elections of June and July. The war faded from view. In July the Russians controlled Grozny, or thought they did. Yeltsin was reelected. On August 7, three days before Yeltsin's inauguration, the rebels retook Grozny. The Russians sent in wave after wave of troops only to find themselves lost and under attack from all sides. They had sent ill-prepared, badly supplied, poorly led, and confused young conscripts into a vicious guerrilla war on the enemy's home turf. Images of stunned, starving troops littering the ground were broadcast via a newly liberated media live to Russian homes. Soon there was no doubt that the military might of Russia was being eaten alive in the charnel house of Chechnya.

Russia's General Alekzandr Lebed was sent to negotiate a deal and on August 31, 1996, Maskhadov and Lebed signed the Khasavyurt agreements. As a result of the successful negotiations, Maskhadov was democratically elected president of Chechnya in January 1997, with Shamil Basayev, the legendary Chechen commander, second in command as prime minister. The war had killed 4,300 Russian solders and 100,000 civilians; 240,000 had been displaced. The scars ran deeper, though. A study of Russian troops who fought in Grozny found that 72 percent had some type of psychological disorder from the combat.

The impoverished fledgling government of a destroyed republic could not stop the internal forces from plunging the country into anarchy. Chechen groups that had focused on killing Russian invaders now found themselves at peace with no economy or hope.

Kidnappings and murders in Chechnya increased as conditions in both countries deteriorated. The Russians estimated that 1,094 people were kidnapped in Chechnya between January 1997 and August 1999. Five hundred known victims were being held inside Chechnya when I would enter. Chechens were worth between $5,000 and $145,000, according to a Russian hostage broker. The Russian Interior Ministry's General Gennady Shpigun was kidnapped from his plane in Grozny on March 5, 1999. The kidnappers wanted fifteen million for his release. On December 28 village elders in Achkhoi-Martan, a large town about twenty miles southwest of Grozny, said that Shpigun had been moved to the mountains and was being held for a five-million-dollar ransom.

Yeltsin's time was limited. He deputized Vladimir Putin as the man who would rebuild Russia. But Russia was falling apart. Some say that when a country is sliding into oblivion, the fastest way to rebuild confidence and national pride is to start a war. Many Chechens believed that the second war in Chechnya was inevitable. Like two boxers hanging on the ropes exhausted, they stood back and glared at each other. There were tentative talks about the Chechens working with the Russians to rebuild the country. This money quickly vanished into the pockets of Bislan Gantemirov, who was later jailed for the embezzlement. The security apparatus under Abu Musayev and Turpelov Ali Atigirov met with their Russian counterparts but ended up either ignored or arrested before being released. Soon the Chechens realized that there was a dark cloud on the horizon. This was not to be Yeltsin's war but a colder, darker type of war led by Vladimir Putin. Russia needed a war. Russians were starting to doubt their new democratic leadership. A war takes the focus off the mundane topics of poverty, hunger, and corruption, and rallies people behind the nation. The Russian Generals demanded vengence for the humiliating defeat. Putin, a former spy and careful planner, would ride from obscurity to popularity on the success of this war.

This war would be different. This war would show that Russia was smart, tough, and successful. It would act as a wave that would land Putin, a tiny, dour, tough-talking man who kept his ambitions close to his vest, into the presidency.

In August 1999 Shamil Basayev and his Jordanian born right-hand man Ibn-ul-Khattab took a few hundred troops and crossed over into Dagestan. Basayev had been provoked to launch this personal crusade to defend Muslim villages because they were coming under attack by Russian soldiers. Both Basayev and Khattab had both religious and *teip* allegiances with the villages. Khattab's wife was Dagestani. Many of the volunteers were mujahideen trained in Afghanistan and took great pride in fighting Russians inside Russia—just as Imam Shamyl had done 165 years earlier when he tried to set up independent rule in Dagestan. The historical message was not lost on the Russian government. They fought the small band of rebels back into Chechnya. But that wouldn't end things.

On March 19, 1999 a bomb exploded in a crowded market, killing more than fifty people in Vladikavkaz in southern Russia. On September 4 a car bomb exploded outside a military housing block in Buynaksk, Dagestan, killing sixty-four people, mostly the wives and children of Russian military officers. On September 9 a bomb inside a Moscow apartment block killed ninety-four and injured more than two hundred. On September 13 a fertilizer bomb placed in the storage area of an eight-story Moscow flat killed 118

Russians. Ten days later police discovered a timer, detonators, and three sacks of sugar mixed with explosives in the storage area of an apartment in Ryazan, 125 miles southeast of Moscow. The FSB said it was only a security test.

The series of apartment bombings in Moscow was blamed on Chechen terrorists. Oddly, the apartments were leveled quickly by Russians and no proof was ever entered to back up the Russian claims. There were rumors that FSB agents, the new version of the KGB, were caught loading explosives to blow up a fourth apartment, and that maybe the Russians were desperately trying to invent a reason for war.

Russia, a nearly bankrupt country, had begun amassing an initial invasion force of one hundred thousand men and an entire battle plan within days. The market price of crude oil had jumped, generating an unforeseen windfall; suddenly Russia had cash in its accounts. They declared war on Chechnya and began spending between forty to fifty million dollars a day.

On the surface the latest invasion of Chechnya was optimistically named "Operation Whirlwind," an antique war of might against right. A massive World War II style army rolled into Chechnya. The Russians met little resistance on the flat northern part of Chechnya and even less in the public opinion forum. The Russians were the cavalry coming to the rescue, although it was not clear whom they were rescuing, since the attacks were on their soil. The personality of the quiet, dour Putin contrasted with the loud, bellicose blustering of Yeltsin.

The Russian FSB circulated a letter that carefully laid out how this war was to be presented to the media. The Chechens were to be described as terrorists and bandits. The recent bombings and kidnappings were laid directly at their feet as a pretext to cast aside the peace treaty and promises. The media was not to wander freely, focus on front-line conditions, see troop movements, or offer any argument to Russian claims of victory. Journalists would have to sign papers, go through censors, have official escorts. The Russians began to capture and interrogate any journalists found in the wrong places. Eighteen journalists had been killed in the first war, most caught in the indiscriminate crossfire and bombings. But now the Russians had determined that Chechnya was to be a very dangerous place for journalists or for any outsider who dared enter.

The warning I received from the BBC and from others was not

intended to frighten me. It was a simple statement of fact. My obsession with the regional history was an attempt to understand and predict what was to face me. But all I had learned was that this war was unpredictable, there were no bystanders, and the violence was going to be staggering. Inside Chechnya, Russians and parties unknown were killing or kidnapping journalists, aid workers, missionaries, and politicians.

Peter Kennedy, Darren Hickey, Rudolf Petschi, and Stanley Shaw were in Chechnya working for Granger Telecom to install a regional satellite telephone system that would have provided phone service for three hundred thousand people. The men were accused of being spies, and on October 3, 1998, twenty armed men kidnapped them from their fortified and guarded compound. There was a gun battle between the two dozen guards and the camouflaged attackers. Russian troops launched a rescue attempt on December 7. The next morning, four severed heads were found in a sack by the side of a road near the village of Assinovskaya, 25 miles west of Grozny. Ruslan Akhmadov, one of eight Akhmadov brothers who worked the kidnap trade, had kidnapped them and handed them over to Chechen warlord Arb Bareyev from Alkan Kala. No one was safe. Everyone knew that Chechnya was going to be the most dangerous place in the world.

I called Aqil about to ask about the danger. He confirmed that he'd nearly been kidnapped the last time he was in Chechnya. Another thing he forgot to tell me. He was invited into a home for tea and was asked to leave his gun outside. His guests assumed that he was defenseless and brandished weapons to take him hostage. Aqil slowly opened his jacket to reveal grenades taped to his chest. He smiled as he went to pull the pin from one of the grenades and asked them if they were ready to die. He would go to heaven, they would go to hell. As for the grenade trick . . . he advised me to do the same once we got inside.

Just before the trip, Aqil drove up the California coast from San Diego, where he'd gone to have his mechanical leg tuned. He wanted a safe place to meet, a public place. He'd also promised to take his kids to the beach. I suggested a pier about a hundred yards from my office. He arrived at twilight as a cold fog rolled in off the ocean. His wife Samaya came with him and she occupied her time with their young daughter and son. She was dressed in a black hijab, which covered her head. The little girl was a bundle of energy chasing seagulls on the concrete tables. The boy had the grubby face of an urchin and followed his sister's lead. Aqil ordered a meal, but when it arrived he let it get cold. I asked why he wouldn't eat.

"Too many years on the front lines." His eyeballs did a sideways dance whenever the pain hit. "It drives people nuts when they see me sitting here waiting for it to get cold."

It was the first time I'd heard him say anything that sounded like a war story.

The fog glowed pink from the sunset above us, surreal and dreamlike.

"What will happen with your wife and children if you die?"

There didn't seem to be a satisfactory answer.

"They'll live with my wife's family."

We went to the office so that he could copy some pictures for me—his strawberry blond daughter in Chechnya standing on someone's hand, the picture of Ayeesha in front of a large mosque in a black head-to-toe chador with the face scratched out. His family waited in a gold Chrysler in the parking lot. He needed to get back to Arizona tonight.

I asked him if he was excited about the trip.

"Naw. I don't get excited. It's just another time. I keep thinking this is the time I will be *shahuda*. But I don't know, man."

Aqil got in the car and drove away. The red taillights glowed dim in the fog and disappeared.

We locked in our plane tickets on the fourth of November. That day, Aqil got a phone call. It was his daughter. She sounded like she was close. The four-year-old babbled to her father, and Aqil asked her to put her mother on the phone. Please. The phone went dead. Then the phone rang again, but there was just the sound of people laughing in the background. His daughter was alive, but he didn't know where.

To enter war you cannot journey in a straight line. This is for practical and sometimes psychological reasons. The war in Chechnya was no different. The first stop on our trip would be London. Through Aqil I arranged a meeting with someone who could help us on our journey. Someone whom we would meet to determine our suitability to go behind enemy lines. These decisions are made only by looking people in the eye and asking tough questions. I was instructed to phone my nameless contact from a public pay phone. He asked us to meet him in a bookstore in Victoria Station. Once there, I waited patiently, and of course he was not in the bookstore but outside watching me. He was a tall young man who had the appearance of a Pakistani. He introduced himself as Ali from Bangladesh. All I knew is that he'd set up a computer system for Khattab, Shamil Basayev's commander, in Khattab's compound in Azerbaijan. The man I was meeting was to either grant me the key to the first door or politely disappear, leaving me stuck in London without his blessing or forward contacts.

Ali was polite but not chatty. In a unspoken way I felt he had a strong sense of instant prejudice. We got a corner table in a Pizza Hut to have some dinner. I almost expected a lecture on how American culture was spreading its tentacles around the world, but he recommended the veggie pizza instead.

Ali wouldn't allow me to record him or take notes. He said that the only reason he was talking to me was that he had read my book, *The World's Most Dangerous Places,* and that I actually said some nice things about Islam and Muslims. He had a slight twitch in one eye, and his mood seemed to change from contempt to suspicion to trust as he spoke to us. He and three others ran a Web site called www.azzam.com. It was dedicated to mujahideen and the concepts of jihad and martyrdom. A photo of a dead fighter usually appeared on the front page, and there were photos inside that showed videotaped attacks on Russians. Their efforts were concentrated on Bosnia and Dagestan, two places where Ali seemed to have first-hand experience though he would not admit it. He was cagey about revealing his background, because, as he casually mentioned, people like him are often called terrorists.

They also had an English-language site named qoqaz.net. *Qoqaz* is Arabic for "Caucasian." He said he collected information from fighters in the field so that he could translate and post their reports on his Web site. It was a one-sided effort, not a news service, but he was careful to provide photographs, dates, and names to avoid having his site dismissed as propaganda. When I asked about backers, he laughed; "they work on the site in their spare time and pay for it out of their own pocket," he said. Much of the information came from Arab-language sources in the Gulf and directly from fighters inside Chechnya. It was obvious that Ali had connections with the people who supported the recruitment and transportation of Muslims to fight in these wars. But he was providing quite possibly the only reliable counterpoint to the Russian propaganda machine. I wanted to know more about his take on jihad and the people who volunteered to fight in these wars.

Jihad (struggle) is a basic tenant of Islam (or submission). There are two kinds of jihad: offensive and defensive. It is the highest duty of a Muslim. Anyone who loses his life while while engaged in jihad is guaranteed a place in heaven. At described the conditions of the *shaheed*, or martyred, he had seen. "Perfume comes from their bodies, their mouths are smiling, they bleed musk. Even after eight days their bodies do not smell." He had smelled a *shaheed* who had been eight days dead, and it was a nice smell.

Ali wanted to talk about real jihad, not the jihads that were claimed by Saddam Hussein and other leaders to bolster their defense. Jihad could only be fought for the sake of Allah, not a nation or a person. "That is why you will see fighters from every country standing shoulder to shoulder on the front line of a real jihad."

He listed the true jihads as Chechnya, Kashmir, Kosovo, Bosnia, Sudan, Algeria, and some others he couldn't remember. He had a lot of respect for Osama bin Laden because he ate and fought with the troops. He said that the Chechens would never have blown up the apartment buildings in Russia. Only Russians would do that. Mujahideen only fight against the enemy. They do not kill women and children.

He got emails from people who wanted to fight. People from Syria, Canada, Indonesia. He advised them to go to Pakistan, where they would meet someone. He figured there were two kinds of Muslims: apologetic Muslims and real Muslims. The first were Westernized. The volunteers were real Muslims, fighting not for the Chechens, but for Allah. One man's terrorist is another man's freedom fighter.

What was jihad like?

"You need a word-of-mouth introduction to become a fighter. You should be sent in by someone they trust. There are fifteen different nationalities fighting in Chechnya. Brazilians, Japanese, Germans, Swedish, the rich and the poor, all in active competition to get killed.

"There were three thousand foreign muj in Bosnia. Many came and went between 1992 and 1995. About two hundred had been killed. Many mujahideen cried when their friends died, not for their friends but for themselves. 'Why didn't Allah choose me?'"

Ali told me stories of other fighters. His initial distrust was dissolving. "Among the most notable was a mujahid who had cleaned toilets, washed dishes, and died fighting. His identity as a thirty-year-old Bahrainian prince was only revealed when they looked at his passport before burial." He seemed proud that the rich and royal fought next to the poor and embattled.

It was obvious that Ali had been to Bosnia and possibly Chechnya. He knew too many specifics to have learned them secondhand. His Web site posted photographs and news from the front lines before the news services learned about events. He was angry, and rightfully so. Despite providing accurate counts of Russian dead, specific actions, and photographs and video, the Western media ignored his tiny window into jihad.

He used to think that it was fifty-fifty when it came to lies versus truth in the Western media. Now he thought it was 95 percent lies. Although he was less reticent to talk, he still kept his reserve. Out of the blue he asked me, "Why are you not a Muslim?"

I didn't have an answer since I had never really thought about the question. By the end of the evening, Ali agreed to forward information to relevant parties who might assist our entry into Chechnya. Our next stop would be Turkey, to make a pact with the devil.

I needed a cameraman to film what we were about to see and do. My choice was Sedat Aral, the younger brother of my former coauthor, Coskun Aral. Sedat was a Kurd from Turkey who was living as an exile in London. He was inside Chechnya during the last war. We discussed the conditions and my task. There was a problem, though: After he'd gotten out of Chechnya during the last war, he swore he would never go there again.

"Wait until you get to Chechnya," he warned. "The Chechens are psychopaths. They love killing Russians. They made a movie of Russians being injected with a drug and then slowly having their throats cut. Other than that they are nice people." He said he would go with me as far as Georgia, but he didn't want to go to Chechnya. We agreed that he would document our trip as far as Georgia and then he could return if he wanted. His wife made him promise to bring a flak jacket and a helmet.

+ + +

Our next stop was Istanbul. Sarah, Sedat, Aqil, and I were now a tiny band of four misfits heading into an unknown future. we were here because Turkey is a center for the Chechen diaspora where many wounded Chechen fighters are sent for medical care. We needed to buy food, supplies—anything we might need for the trip. More important, we needed to find a man named Beshious, or "Five Hundred." He was in the epicenter of death but not from any war.

I was told by an Islamic charity that Five Hundred could be found in Düzce. There had been a terrible natural disaster, Turkey was in mourning. I rented a car and drove to Düzce, a farming area 120 kilometers east of Istanbul. The gray, grubby town had suffered a 7.1 earthquake less than a week before, and I'd been told that my contact was somewhere in the rubble of the disaster zone. All I had was the nickname by which he conducted his business. He was a Chechen hitman, a famous *mafyia* head who could arrange my entry into Chechnya. If he believed in my cause, he would introduce me to "The Fox," a man who brought money into Chechnya. The Fox had negotiated the release of Russian hostages when the Black Sea ferry was hijacked in 1996. There was little doubt of a direct connection between Chechens in Turkey and Chechnya.

Even if we met The Fox, there would be no guarantee that he would arrange our safe passage into Chechnya. These were Chechens, after all, people famed for treachery, surprise, and perfidy. I could expect a scam, a rebuff, or genuine assistance.

The sight of Düzce wiped any silly or idle thoughts out of my brain. The reality of disaster on this scale required complete focus. I drove past row after row of large, cheaply made apartment blocks that had simply folded in on top of each other, some leaving less than two inches between collapsed stories. Other buildings leaned as though they were tired, or were just piles of rubble. Some were untouched. It was close to the look, feel, and smell of a heavily bombed war zone. The sweet, rancid smell of death emanated from the week-old cadavers that had been compressed and buried under tons of concrete.

A few yellow bulldozers pushed paths between mountains of personal possessions and collapsed buildings. Some people had punched holes in the concrete floors of their flattened apartment buildings and brought up their possessions like landlocked scuba divers. There were several haphazard villages of tents and plastic sheeting. It was muddy, raining, and cold. A passerby guided me to a grubby intersection where he said my contact could be found. We were welcomed into a tiny four-foot-high enclosure with a mud floor. The four of us got out of the cold gray rain and sat on simple mattresses. Choking cigarette smoke hung low in the air.

Our welcome was genuine. There was the usual exchange of niceties. I offered a pack of cookies to my hosts. They asked if they were American, and when I told them that I bought them at truck stop on the way, they handed them back. Five Hundred, or Beshious in Turkish, took his high school ID number as his nickname. He was stocky and swarthy, and about as close to the neckless, bowling-ball-headed caricature of a gangster as you could get. He lets his second in command, Kamal, a former professional boxer, do the talking. Kamal contrasted with the stern, dark, round-featured Beshious. He was a happy, square-headed, square-shouldered, muscular buzz-cut Chechen, and he wanted to spar a few rounds. It was his way of saying he liked us.

My Chechen hosts never questioned my desire to go to Chechnya. It was, after all, what should be done. Who would not want to go to Chechnya to fight or to come back with the truth? It sounded so simple and true in the blue smoke of laughing gangsters. They seemed to envy me.

The Fox entered. He was well dressed and had the appearance of a banker or businessman. I was startled at his stated purpose. He wasn't here to give aid to the thousands of homeless and hungry earthquake victims; he was here to collect money to support the fighters in Chechnya. He admitted that the earthquake had made a serious dent in the effort, but the people still gave money. It was a measure of the commitment, durability, and charity among Chechens I would witness time and time again. I wanted to know more about the war but he signaled to our small group. First we must witness what had happened here.

Kamal the boxer was my new best friend. A group of others argued who would carry my tripod and camera gear. In the blue light of dusk, Kamal explained that the earthquake hit on November 12, at dinnertime. The locals told us that 850 may have been killed, and there might be 1,500 people still in the rubble. There were thirty-five thousand buildings in the town, twenty-five thousand of them were damaged. After the quake the officials told the people that they could move back in. The government started to collect the tents to force people back into their damaged homes, sometimes cutting the tent ropes while people were inside. Then the next quake struck.

I'd been in earthquakes but I'd never seen the aftermath of one of this magnitude. I walked along the muddy streets with a gaggle of Chechens who continually vied with one another to carry my gear. The people in the wooden homes had fared well, but the flats were killers. They had brick walls and concrete floors supported by thin cement columns with rebar. When the quake hit, the columns twisted and snapped, dropping the entire floor on to the one below it, again and again, until the six-story buildings were transformed into perfectly flat piles of concrete only twenty feet high. The scandal here was that many of the building inspectors had allowed shoddy construction in exchange for payoffs. Luckier people lived in older or better-built apartments. Commercial buildings didn't seem to be as badly affected. Now there was no plumbing and no electricity, save for a few generators. The toilets overflowed with human waste. The mud was everywhere. The rain drizzled. The snow would be coming soon. It was the definition of misery.

White tents were pitched in playgrounds and empty lots. Since there had been no preparation, the tents were surrounded by mud six inches deep. Blocks of wood and cement were used as walkways. In a mess tent five-foot-diameter pots cooked beans and chicken for dinner. As part of an unusual PR program, a FedEx truck pulled up and delivered hot meals from the city. There was a tent set up for the media. There was something bizarre about the epitome of Western efficiency delivering hot meals to this godforsaken place.

Kamal was told his flat was okay by government inspectors; he could move back in. When the second quake hit at 7 P.M., his house was flattened. He pointed out how many dead people were buried in the rubble. Twelve there, seventy-four here, unknown there. The smell was enough to make me believe him. There were only two pieces of heavy equipment moving through the streets. The job ahead was incomprehensible.

After the tour we sat in a large white tent. They offered us cheese and tea in front of a thirty five-inch television. They had adopted the curious Turkish habit of treating a television like a guest; it was the center of attention and elicited much comment and conversation. When the news showed coverage of the war in Chechnya they stopped talking and watched intently. The only coverage coming out was from the Russian side. Propaganda, they said.

A Turkish army officer came in to ask politely for tents. He explained that they would be for his relatives. The tent was quiet, and lit by the light of a bare bulb. It was a scene from *The Godfather*. Outside, people were fighting over packets of clean underwear being thrown from a back of a truck. I started to wonder about how the Turkish controlled the Chechens—and whether it wasn't the other way around.

We agreed with our hosts that a meeting would be set up with Chechen officials back in Istanbul. Somehow it made perfect sense that we would be sitting here surrounded by the sights and smell of death to arrange a trip to a killing zone.

There was a humanitarian group in the Fatih district of Istanbul. There was no sign, no listing. You needed to know someone to find it. Our contact in Düzce had introduced us to the right people, and had arranged for Chechen officials to meet us there. Based on our words and deeds in Düzce, The Fox agreed to make an appeal on our behalf.

It appeared that in addition to the blessing of the *mafyia,* the mujahideen, the Chechen money people, we also needed to meet with the Chechen government before we could enter Chechnya safely. I use the term safely in a relative way. No one had actually said the trip would be safe. Local journalists had been telling me it was completely possible to fly to Georgia, Dagestan, Ossetia, or Russia, make arrangements with a local smuggler, and get in. The French photographer Bruce Fleutiaux had just done this and was promptly handed over to kidnappers just inside the border of Chechnya. The Interior Ministry's General Gennady Shpigun visited Chechnya without incident, was driven to his plane, and as he waved goodbye to his military escort discovered that he was being kidnapped. There were no guarantees here.

The humanitarian organization had provided aid in Bosnia, Somalia,

Kosovo, and Chechnya. In the overheated bottom-floor apartment I sat patiently amid a pile of calendars and Korans that had been bundled up for shipment into Chechnya. What fundamentalists would do with more Korans I didn't know, and decided not to ask. There were two maps of the region and a 1920s-era book on the Caucasus in Turkish. I enjoyed the yellow-striped wallpaper. It was like visiting your grandmother.

The business of these people was to get food and medical supplies into Chechnya. The source of their funding was indeterminate, but a lush annual report that I flipped through while I waited showed photographs of their work to help Muslims in Bosnia, Kosovo, and other recent hot spots. Looking at the photos I had a sense of benign serenity until a photograph just inside the front page of the report chilled me. It was Mohammed Zaki, described as a volunteer from San Diego and the first American *shaheed*. According to the book, he was killed in a Russian air raid. I remembered Aqil's description of how Zaki died after being hit by a jet-fired rocket. It had something to do with Zaki blasting away at the Russian jet from the back of a truck with a Dashika anti-aircraft gun.

I pointed at the picture and asked the people at the center who Zaki was. "Someone who sent medical aid."

We were directed by our host to a place up the street where volunteers sought entry into Chechnya, a place where we could meet Basayev's people. We waited for a Chechen representative to show up. The talk of the day was the conference held by the Organization for Security and Co-operation in Europe, known by the acronym OSCE. Bill Clinton's parade of dark Suburbans had blasted by with lights flashing the night before. The Chechens wanted to gain audience with world leaders to present their evidence of Russian war crimes, but they'd received little sympathy here. They wallowed in the political machinations that had decreed that even an informal meeting would be tantamount to showing sympathy to terrorists.

They presented their case in a florid style with heavy-handed verbiage, and had even made a CD-ROM and a brochure that graphically detailed the atrocities being committed by the Russians. They even insisted that that they'd captured a Russian spy who could prove that the Russians had blown up the three apartment buildings in Moscow. The Russians scoffed and said that the spy the Chechens were talking about was dead. The only news that was hard to ignore was the treatment of the 150,000 refugees streaming out of Chechnya. The delegates looked grim and nodded their heads and agreed that it was a humanitarian catastrophe. Then, nothing.

The Chechen delegation finally showed up to meet us. They were not happy. They were led by tall-hatted men in leather jackets and double-breasted suits who surrounded an even taller-hatted man in a leather jacket and a double-breasted suit. The body guards looked burly and seemed to be uncomfortable in their cheap clothes. We went into a small office off the main room. The atmosphere was formal, stiff, and uncomfortable, not at all like our meeting with the *mafyia*.

The Fox appealed on our behalf before I could make my request to enter Chechnya. He spoke in Chechen, and nobody bothered to translate what was being said. The the tall-hatted, blue-eyed Chechen in the dark double-breasted suit listened without emotion and commenced what seemed like a formal speech. Our host translated.

"There is a war inside Chechnya. There is bombing twenty-four hours a day. The Russians attack everything and everyone. There is no quarter in this war. There is no guarantee that can be provided for your safety. If you accept this we will help you enter Chechnya."

I nodded our agreement.

"You will be assigned a Chechen guide, a student, who wants to go back to Chechnya for business or to see his family. You will pay his tickets and expenses, but you will pay no more than that. You will fly to Tbilisi in Georgia and be met at the airport. Someone will pick you up there and take you to a safe hotel. The next day we will stage a meeting at the Sheraton so that the locals can see that you are with us. There will be less problems this way."

I asked why we would hold this sham meeting.

"So that the other Chechens and the spies will know that you are with us. This will prevent anything unfortunate from happening to you."

I nodded as though his answer made sense. Just to be cautious I asked about going in or coming out on the Russian side. He smiled flatly at my stupidity.

"The Russians do not allow journalists in from the north. If they try they are kidnapped. The Russian government says they offer protection but you will not get close to Chechens. There is no kidnapping inside Chechen-held Chechnya. But the Russians will kidnap you and say that it was Chechens."

"Do Chechens kidnap people?" I asked.

"Yes, there has always been kidnapping in the Caucasus. But the Russians started the kidnapping of journalists when the *mafyia* thug Berevosky paid two million for the two British journalists. Since then, no one is safe from the Russians."

I was wasting his time with my concern about kidnapping, so he proceeded like a bored stewardess showing the safety features of an airplane.

"After the meeting you will be driven to the border of Chechnya. You will walk for one hour and then we arrange a meeting with senior commanders on the other side. There is a war inside Chechnya. We cannot guarantee your safety. You will need to get warm clothes, second shoes, and travel light." He had obviously done this routine before.

"Are any other journalists inside Chechnya?" I asked.

"You mean not kidnapped? Some, not many."

He wanted to know how long we expected to stay inside Chechnya. It was a tough decision; every day inside Chechnya drastically reduced the odds for survival. I said fifteen days but I really had no idea. He looked at me.

"Maybe ten?"

He stared.

"Maybe less?"

He smiled. "You will experience life under siege."

"How long should we expect?" I asked.

"Total travel time from Tbilisi to Grozny is one day."

I had assumed that it would take a week to ten days to get from Tbilisi to Grozny. Then came the windup.

"You will be given protection. We will give you twelve bodyguards. Seven will cross with you. They cannot save you from bombardment. But if you are attacked I will give the guarantee that you will not die until the last one of men has died. The Russians have killed over one hundred thousand people in Chechnya. There is a lot of blood in the soil."

With that he and his retinue stood, shook hands, and walked out.

✦　✦　✦

Aqil's wife Samaya called me at the hotel in Istanbul. She wanted Aqil to know that she would be staying with friends. Aqil's two-year-old son was taking it hard. He hadn't stopped crying since his father left. He kept looking at a picture of his father, asking him to "come here."

I offered to take Aqil out to a nice restaurant before we left for Chechnya. His choice for a final civilized meal was McDonald's. Aqil said he would eat there three times a day if he could. He had been looking for painkillers but hadn't found any. He had just enough old pills to get him to Chechnya.

I mentioned Samaya's call to him. I told him that his wife sounded pretty shaken up over the phone.

"Yeah, I'm pretty rough on my wife. There's a lot of stains on the carpet. When I come home I'm hungry and I want to eat. My wife, she's not too good a cook. I get mad and throw the shit on the walls. Usually after I calm down she'll make me a hot dog or macaroni and cheese. Yeah, I am pretty rough on her.

"I met my wife when I was seventeen in the youth camp. She was a horsey girl. Loved to ride. She and I hit it off. She even helped me escape once. We've been together ever since. She converted."

I didn't tell Aqil that I'd promised his wife that I would look out for him, and for her to call my office if she needed anything. A thought nagged me. How can you take care of someone who wants to die?

Despite the need to travel light, Aqil was a walking hardware store. He'd brought a laptop, a solar charger, a GPS, and God knows what else in his new yellow North Face pack. He also had a spare leg but he couldn't find an Allen wrench to pop the top off. I offered to carry it but I didn't quite know what I would say to people seeing a perfectly healthy person carrying a prosthetic leg. He even brought his Phoenix police force badge. I asked him how effective it would be in Chechnya if the Russians captured him.

"There's only one way to go and that's by emptying a full mag on someone," he said.

Outside in the cold he told me that he had the precombat jitters. He always got them when he realized that hot lead soon would be flying at him. I remember thinking that I may have made a mistake.

+ + +

We left Turkey on November 24, 1999. The flights from Istanbul to Tbilisi, Georgia, were a couple of hundred dollars round trip. In a typical show of Western caution we chose Turkish Airlines over Aeroflot.

At the airport the check-in line was full of stocky, round-headed people with cheap, bulging, weathered baggage, like refugees on the last plane out. The surroundings and events were slowly sinking into Sarah. She was going to a place where people kill people, where she could be killed. She felt sick. She breathed deep but it didn't seem to work. She said she'd get over it.

I looked for our guide Ruslan, and found him chatting with a Russian-speaking woman who evidently was trying to look inconspicuous in her lime green fake fur coat. Ruslan was dressed as though we were going to a night-club: black turtleneck, a natty black leather jacket, trendy boots, and a neo-prene cell phone holder but no cell phone. It was a uniform we would come to know well, because he never changed his outfit in all the time he acted as our guide. He was twenty-one with trendy hair and a goofy attitude. He told us that he was an engineering student and that he was studying banking and enjoyed playing guitar and video games. His father had worked with internal security. In the last war he carried RPGs (rocket-propelled grenades) for the soldiers and was wounded by shrapnel. His father found out about his adventures and shipped him to school in Turkey. He had urgent business with President Maskhadov in the form of a mountain of papers contained in a an overstuffed green backpack. It would appear that we were wired on this one.

The lime green fake fur coat lady worked at the airport in Tbilisi and said that she would take care of everything once we landed. She told us that the weather was fine inside Georgia. Although December was right around the corner, she assured us that there was no chance that rain or snow would block the mountain pass we would have to take.

Ruslan told us to disregard half a dozen young men in their early twenties. All of them wore identical gray turtlenecks, black pants, and shoes. What set them apart was that some were freshly recuperated from wounds, and they exactly fit the profile of Chechen fighters. With their lean builds, two days' beard growth, deep scars, and habit of standing very close together in identical cheap clothing, they looked like a hockey team.

There was more good news. Ruslan was bringing in a go-anywhere Iridium satellite phone. The rumor was that it was for Shamil Basayev. Maybe our

precious cargo would ensure a smooth ride. But our first inkling that intentions and realities had parted ways came up during our brief banter. Ruslan
had tried to enter Georgia three times and was turned back at the airport
each time. He hoped he could get in this time. Considering that Chechens
were being turned back and arrested in Georgia, we didn't seem very low key.
I pointed out that his Russian passport, to which he had affixed a Kurt Cobain
sticker, had *Ichkeriya* plainly marked on the cover. He was also wearing a small
pin on his lapel that had the Chechen flag on it. Why? Because he liked it. He
was confident. We had the satellite phone, the woman in green, the hockey
players, and his packet for the president. How could we not get in?

Aqil thought Ruslan was an idiot and that we should ditch him before
he got us arrested or killed. He promised me that once he got across the
border he would get an armed group to come and get me. I couldn't decide
which was the least attractive option.

On the 737 we were seated directly across from the Chechens we had
been warned to ignore. Before we took off Aqil started to talk about the
war. In Russian. The Chechens crowded around and listened to his stories.
He showed them his mechanical leg. As Aqil talked with the other fighters
they laughed nervously and traded their *noms de guerre*. Aqil was Abu
Mujahid; in the States he called himself Abu Saif. The Chechens liked him
for his bulk and seriousness. They looked at his graphite and stainless-steel
mechanical leg in awe. He was finally among his own kind.

Aqil told them a story he had told me before, about the last time he was
in Chechnya.

"I was the sharpest fighter out there. I had two braids coming out of
my face, grenades across my chest, sharp uniform. Man I looked good. I
scared the Russians. The only time a warrior is allowed to strut is out on
the front line. Here's this guy with this big beard and sharp equipment. I
looked good.

"At Zandak, me and Abu Terab, a Hindu from Texas, we were in the
village on the border of Dagestan in a valley behind a twenty-meter hill.
The plains beyond were Dagestan. We were on the main road into
Chechnya through Zandak, and northwest of there was my first tactical
position. Our job was to hold the road. Zandak was the main R and R
village for the fighters.

"There were tank teeth across the border. One day two guys came running up from the road to the top of our hill saying the Russians were coming. It was like fourteen hundred years ago. Just two guys against all these Russians. I told my friend to cover me as I went down among the rectangular blocks to see what the Russians were doing.

"The Russians had their line two miles inside the border. We put on our vests. The other guys said he had to make some satellite-phone calls.

First we looked and we didn't see anything. They had the BMPs in the hauled-down position. We got to the top of the hill and started to walk down. I told Abu to stay at the top and cover me.

"I walked down the hill to the concrete bocks into a small depression. There were two Chechens whose car had broken down near the Russians. One was scared, the other one was excited. One guy radioed and said get back up at the top of hill.

"We waited about ten minutes and a car full of Chechens came down the road. They drove toward the Russians. The guy keeps calling to make sure he's not down there. He finally is asked to bring a radio down to the Chechen commander. More Chechen fighters show up until there are fifty Chechens and a hundred Russians. Some of the Russians stayed in their foxholes, some just sat on the BMPs.

"The Chechen commander gave the Russians half an hour to pull back or we would attack them. Nobody moved, so it was like a showdown in a Hollywood movie. We had a forty-millimeter cannon and pointed it at the back of their truck. Maybe soon it would be Pray-and-Spray time. It was too exciting to miss. It was *maghreb* prayer time. We had two Russians in our unit who wanted to give the *azzam*, but the commander gave me the privilege of making the call to prayer.

"It was five minutes before sundown. In war half of the fighters pray and the other half stand guard. The fighters were yelling '*Allah u Akbhar!*' over and over again, and it echoed back and forth through the valley as the sun went down. Then everybody started loading and chambering. The guy next to me positioned himself with his RPG and painted the BMP. The Russians freaked. There was a flare, the signal for the Russians to move. They threw cases of ammunition into their trucks and took off. Some of our guys threw little rocks at the Russians to disgrace them. That was the best day of my life."

Someone else on the plane told a story that made everyone laugh. On one of the earlier flights, a Chechen fighter tried to open the rear emergency door to go to the toilet. The flight crew stopped him and explained what he was doing just before he figured out how to open the door.

We were carrying heavy camera equipment and sitting with a group of lean, mean Chechen fighters with satellite phones, scars, and identical Converse-logo jackets, talking about the war in Chechnya. Not very covert considering Georgia that had just announced it was suspending all visas for journalists and sworn to turn back any young Chechens entering the country.

One of the men, Sayifhudeen, was a thin, handsome, angular-faced man who was charged with guiding two Turkish television crews that would be coming with us. He was cool and distant, and was in the business of bringing people in and out of Chechnya. He said that his little brother had driven Aqil's Chechen wife and daughter to Iskadar, an area on the Asian side of the Bosporus. She was with a group of 130 Chechens who lived in Istanbul. Her name was Ayeesha Sulemano and her daughter was Nusayba.

Aqil didn't seem shocked at the news. My primary reason for entering Chechnya disappeared as the plane took off. So what now? It seemed pointless to enter Grozny with only an American mujahid, a young woman, and a nervous cameraman and no good reason to go except that no one else would. But so many people had brought me this far that turning back didn't even seem like an option.

As the long flight wore on Aqil rocked back and forth and complained about his leg. "My leg, my leg, my leg . . . it hurts me man," he said. "I've been on it all day and it's pounding." I wondered how he was going to survive when his painkillers ran out.

Ruslan had something to tell me. One of the Chechens had heard about Aqil. He told Ruslan to take him inside Chechnya, tell the first commander he met that Agil was a spy, and then shoot him.

It was cold and raining when we landed in Tbilisi. The stewardess told a young Kangol-hatted man behind me to just hang on until everyone got off the plane. "It'll be much easier that way," she said. As we got off the plane a white airport van pulled up. My Chechen hockey team and the lady in the lime green coat were whisked away, safe behind the closed bus window curtains. The rest of us went through normal channels. The thin, dark, very Chechen-looking Ruslan joined a different line and tried to fit in among the neckless fireplug Georgians.

Customs took a long time but was simple. There was a serious-looking official standing behind the two female passport agents and another walking through the lines staring intently at faces. Something was up.

The agents didn't ask us any questions and I was surprised that we got through without much scrutiny. Even Ruslan was waved in. Was the fix in, or did they have other things on their mind? Ruslan could barely contain his excitement. Now we had to meet our contact, the man who would ensure that we were taken to a safe place. Just in case the Georgians changed their minds, we moved our bags outside the door and hung around outside. Suddenly, a man was escorted past us and into the parking lot. He was trying to wriggle out of a double hammerlock and was led by two burly Georgians. It was the same Kangol-hatted man who had been politely told to wait in the plane until everyone disembarked. Everyone stood back and made way. The man was hit and roughly shoved into a waiting car. Welcome to Georgia.

Finally our contact arrived. He demanded the satellite phone. Ruslan eagerly showed it to him, and before Ruslan could ask what our next move would be, our contact grabbed the phone and started to leave. Ruslan started yelling that he was our only ticket to Chechnya. The man turned around, shrugged, said something rude, and disappeared into the parking lot.

We were in the land of cheap leather jackets, five o'clock shadows, and sideways glances. At least we had Ruslan for our guide. To this point he had been unfailingly unreliable in his predictions.

Our lime green lady showed up and tried to arrange a car for us. She found us a limousine whose driver offered to take our group to the four-hundred-dollar-a-night Sheraton. It was a price so far beyond everyone's abilities that we thought he was joking. He wasn't. We insisted that there must be something cheaper, and drove the streets of Tbilisi at 4 A.M. looking for a hotel. We saw a lot of Tbilisi that morning because technically, there were no hotels. The big, multistory tourist hotels were packed full of refugees. There were small homes that rented rooms, but nothing that could put up both the hockey team and our crew. It was an interesting round-and-round tour of castles, cobblestone streets, and fading, rundown estates. There were bright glittery casinos next to art deco mansions. Not quite the Asia I had expected.

By crossing the snowy mountains north we would be back in Europe. Georgia was the door into Chechnya simply because the Georgians hated Russia more than the Chechens; Georgia was the first republic to leave the Soviet Union, and its citizens had been paying for it ever since. Russia started proxy wars and even occupied Abkhazia on the western shoreline. Georgia turned a blind eye and an outstretched hand to the Chechens who crossed the border. Russia had demanded that Georgia close its border, and even bombed the Georgian border posts to make its point.

The best lodging we could find was a new homestay that charged us an inflated sum to sleep for a few hours. The next morning we discovered that we were supposed to go the Turkish hotel and wait. Everyone who went to and from Chechnya waited at the Turkish hotel. They sat in the dining room in a cloud of blue smoke, endlessly drinking Turkish coffees. And waited. It appeared that this would be no one-day transit as promised; even the secret meeting our Chechen contact wanted to arrange to prevent our being kidnapped never happened. I wondered if the limping hockey players were our bodyguards, but even they would disappear in the first few days.

The morning we arrived at the Turkish hotel one group left to cross the border. We would see if they made it across. If they did, we would follow. Contrary to the lime green lady's predictions, it had been snowing heavily, and there was a rumor that the Russians might try to seal the border with paratroopers and gunships. A couple of two-man Turkish television crews showed up at the hotel like a convention of linebackers, wearing Camel adventure gear and chain smoking. Sedat huddled in the corner with them as they made their plan. They didn't want to go in unless I did. I don't know why they thought I had any magic talisman other than the sulking argumentative Aqil. The Turkish people were quite interested in Chechnya because Turkey is also a Muslim country that borders Russia.

The Turks were from Show-TV and Star-TV, and each had a guide. Sedat didn't want to go in with them. He didn't even want to hang out with them. He said that the Turkish crews had a bad reputation with the

Chechens. "They just go inside and take pictures and leave," he said. Pretty tough talk for someone who didn't want to go in at all. When CNN Turkey offered him five thousand dollars for an interview with Basayev, suddenly he wanted to go.

Sedat said he had been to this region three times before. The last time he'd met with Basayev, who did not like journalists and had little patience. He advised me to keep the questions short when I interviewed Chechens. "Don't anger them. They are odd people." Sedat was making me nervous.

A young Turkish photographer who had just escaped from Chechnya appeared one day. He had been left behind by his colleagues. He didn't show up at an appointed rendezvous and they panicked. He had walked forty kilometers by himself to the border through the ice and deep snow. He said that there had been a snowstorm just the day before and there were few, if any, civilians inside Grozny. He'd been there for twelve days, but spent all his time in bunkers. The Russians bombed all day, not so much in the city, but around the rebel positions on the periphery. He'd wanted to be the only journalist in Grozny. When he arrived there were fifteen people from Japanese TV. The Chechens had just video-taped 220 Russian paratroopers who'd been shot out of the sky and killed. The Chechens sold it to the Japanese for forty thousand dollars. It showed two wounded Russians with head bandages staggering around and the bodies of the rest littering a snow-covered field. The Russian news agencies insisted that nothing had happened and refuted the tape as Chechen propaganda.

The Turk said that the Chechens wouldn't take journalists to the front so that their positions wouldn't be revealed. Journalists had to go to the accreditation center first, but when he checked in, he didn't see any other names on the list. One bodyguard accompanied each foreigner on the streets. The Chechens had tried to kidnap one of the Turkish crew members on the Georgian side. One of the kidnappers pulled the pin out of his grenade but accidentally dropped it and blew himself up, which allowed the crew member to escape.

It was a very bad trip, he complained. Every day there was some problem; they had no organization here or in Grozny. It took eight hours to get out. The Russian gunships and jets fired on any convoy. Most of the time he shoveled snow to dislodge the car. Finally he abandoned the car and walked here.

As he spoke to us the photographer realized that he had forgotten to take pictures on the way out. He'd thought he was going to die.

Five days after we arrived, thick, geometric snow flakes began to fall on the streets of Tbilisi. The Chechens didn't want us on the streets but it was too festive and beautiful outside to resist. They wanted us to stay put until all the arrangements were made. They intimated that the odds of getting kidnapped in Tbilisi were higher than inside Chechnya. Russian agitators here had put a bounty on journalists. Judging from the number of stocky chain-smoking thugs who hung out around the casinos, there was also no shortage of gangsters. The Turkish hotel was considered safe, but only the drivers who lounged in the lobby were said to be reliable. They were controlled by someone who was not to be messed with.

I enjoyed Tbilisi when I could escape for an occasional walk. It is technically in Asia, but at first glance it has the look of Paris in the 1920s. There were a lot of old European-style buildings interspersed with balconied wooden homes. The Georgians were handsome and dark, the women attractive. There was a sense of being somewhere undiscovered; it reminded me of Hemingway's *A Moveable Feast*. Georgia is a Christian country, and America has a strong presence. Coca-Cola signs with that odd Georgian typography lit up the empty streets. The one American I bumped into at a cafe turned out to be ex-military and ex-CIA and seemed to be involved in some local intrigue.

I found that the retro gaiety was illusory when I looked inside the baroque buildings. The interiors were dark and cold. Honda generators were chained to the storefronts. Electricity was a luxury here, and heat was a creative matter of positioning portable heaters. I visited an Internet café where the customers checked their email by candlelight while their computers ran off a battery backup device.

Back at the prisonlike Turkish hotel I had the first big decision to make.

A mysterious helicopter flew from Tbilisi to the border. The price was four thousand dollars divided among three groups: the two Turkish TV crews and ourselves. We discussed whether it should be split by person or by group. The Turks said that they wanted to split it by person. I said no, we should split it by group. I insisted that if we waited the *mafyia* would clear the roads, to take us in. But there was still the danger of avalanche, and the rivers would be too high. The Turks were irritated because I wouldn't automatically agree to take the helicopter.

At night the Chechen fighters at the hotel played with the new Sony Handycam video cameras they'd bought to document the war. The Turks smoked cigarettes continuously. The waiter emptied ashtray after ashtray, brought tea, and made jokes. We could see the snow through the small, grimy windows. I opened them to clear the air and smell the fresh winter day. The Turks would close them whenever I left and the miasma of blue cigarette smoke returned to the restaurant. Aqil would stumble in at midday in his usual dark funk. He didn't sleep or come out his room much. He was soaked with pain in his own personal hell, halfway between reality and dreams. Waiting to die, coasting on a morphine high, strangely resigned to the waiting. He would order a chicken dinner, let it get cold, eat a few bites, and disappear. The Turkish journos descended on his uneaten chicken and finished it.

One day, Ruslan asked us to write down our names and left. The problem now seemed to be getting permission from the government to do something illegal. We were crossing into a country that didn't exist, but we needed the right paperwork. In a Catch-22, we had to ask permission to cross the border although there was no law or policy that specifically forbade it. We even had press credentials from the government of Chechnya. It rained, then it snowed, and every day Ruslan promised us success and asked us to wait. And every day we waited and every day we were disappointed. I soon learned that whatever was promised foretold the opposite. If we were told to stand by, it was a false alarm. If we were to be ready, we could plan on another day before seeing Ruslan. If we were to be *packed* and ready, it meant another three days of waiting.

The time crawled by slowly. I went to a new restaurant for dinner with Sedat and Sarah. It was a pale imitation of American culture that was becoming popular in Georgia.

Sedat and I played a silly tic-tac-toe game afterward over Georgian brandy and cigarettes. I invited Sarah to play, but she got mad and said that she was being set up to lose. She wasn't, but it didn't matter. She wanted to convince herself that she was made to lose before she started. Sedat and I looked at each other.

Sarah withdrew into her own world and started to draw shapes on the wooden table with spilled sugar. She was fascinated by the gentle curves and elegant shapes made by the round base of the saltshaker. When we tried to add to her shape she pulled away. She wanted this to be hers and no one else's. The boredom was getting to us. We had been in Tbilisi for five days and four nights, sleeping on hard mattresses, eating bad food, and inhaling thousands of other people's cigarettes. It wasn't long by normal standards, but it was more intense for Sarah because of her desire to succeed as a journalist. She viewed the trip as a final gamble, a do-or-die event that would determine her future.

The restaurant of the hotel was like a lounge at an airport. People waited, listlessly ticked off the minutes, made idle chatter. Countless numbers of unshaven men watched us as they pulled deeply and quietly on their imported cigarettes. The smoke built up to a thick cloud and mingled with the smell of fried food. Besides the two two-man Turkish film crews, a small cast of new characters appeared.

I spent time getting to know the Chechens who were waiting. At night a bored violin-and-piano combo sang "Das Vadana" Wayne Newton style, as well as Russian folk songs. When nobody listened, the band sat glumly in the corner and stared at us. Russian folk songs didn't go over big here. On one occasion, the Chechens told the band to shut up. The Chechens were listening intently to a tiny shortwave radio. There was news from Grozny; the heaviest bombardment to date. The Russians had made advances. The Chechens yelled at the newscaster's voice and called him a liar, but they agreed that they had to go in before there was only rubble.

One day a tall dark man in a suit entered, accompanied by four stocky men who looked uncomfortable in civilian clothes. He had dark, thin, triangular features, a dark mustache, a thin nose, and black hair. Very intense. The kind of person that makes you nervous just by sitting in the same room. He always seemed to be sitting alone, back to the wall, smoking low-tar cigarettes. Waiting, like us. Ruslan told us that he was an ambassador, and had been an important commander in the last war.

He watched us but didn't come over. When I passed by I said hello. In a brief, formal conversation he gave me his room number and offered to answer any questions we had. He introduced himself as the Chechen ambassador to Finland. "Call me Osman," he said and smiled for the first time in two days. I sat down across from him.

"I drink," he said, as though excusing himself for having a vodka. "I try to tell my bosses that you have to drink at these diplomatic functions or else they'll think you are a fundamentalist."

I liked talking to Osman. He sat stiffly and politely and had black eyes. Osman said that Chechnya had oil only four or five thousand feet below the surface, and that there were 300,000 to 350,000 people left there. We talked about the peace treaty that had ended the last war in Chechnya.

"Lebed is like a fish you know?" He made snaking motions with his hands to describe the Russian general who negotiated peace over the objections of the Russian military and politicians. "The Chechen people were naive. 'I will stop this war,' Lebed said. We believed him.

"We have one American guy in war on our side," he said out of the blue. "Our Secret Weapon."

"Do you know his name?" I asked.

"Yes of course."

"Do you know where he's from?"

"Yes of course."

"West or East?"

"Doesn't matter," he said.

The next day Osman was sipping a vodka in the restaurant. He was sitting with small, young man who could only be an American. He saw me and called me over.

"Our Secret Weapon!" He winked and smiled.

Their Secret Weapon was a nervous man named Joel, and he looked like he had just gotten off from cheerleading practice. Curly headed, over animated, and over-bearing, he had come here for his religion. The surprise was that he was an Episcopalian. He had converted to the upper-class religion not known for crusading. Joel said he'd knocked around in Bosnia and was looking for action in Chechnya. He was from North Carolina, a graduate of the Citadel, and was vague about his military background. He also had a degree in history. He'd studied the Ottoman Empire and the Balkans. Surrounded by the serious-looking Chechens, the thirty-one-year-old was about as far removed from a secret weapon as I could imagine. He had another credential to fight in Chechya. His final college paper was on Ptolemaic Egypt, a subject he loved to bore Sarah with at great length and in minute detail. His former occupation was that of set builder for a movie studio in North Carolina. Furthermore, honest discussions with Aqil revealed that he apparently had no money and was without a clue. He latched on to unsuspecting Aqil as though he were an older brother, and they disappeared together for long periods. When Aqil slept, as he often did, Joel would latch on to Sarah and regale her with a pause-free endless discourse on Jesus Christ Our Savior, Ottoman history, or Egyptian deities.

Osman and Joel met on the Internet. Before the first war in Chechnya Osman was a businessman. Then he was a sniper. Then he was in charge of security for Dudayev. He funded fifty men with guns, RPGs, and ammunition. He had two Land Cruisers, one for personal use and one for fighting. Although he started his military career in the Chechen army as a sniper, he was promoted rapidly by Dudayev. He'd been in Grozny during "the fall." Like a great rock concert, a famous speech, or a turning point in history, every Chechen spoke of the defense of Grozny with reverence and affection. It was their biblical revenge, David versus Goliath.

"We had no one to help us," he said. "We turned to Allah and we now say that only Allah will help us."

Osman was in charge of the prisoners, and then he became Dudayev's personal bodyguard. He showed me a photograph of himself with Dudayev. They looked like twins with their pencil-thin mustaches and thin, dark miens. He paused and rubbed his thumb over the photo before he put the picture back in his wallet. He showed me his passport, labeled ICHKERIYA. Despite the auspicious passport number of 00003, it was meaningless because it wasn't recognized by anyone.

One day they would have their own currency, he explained. It would be called the Nakhar, and its value would be pegged to the British pound. It would have the Caucasian wolf as its symbol, the borz.

Like most Chechen government supporters of President Maskhadov I met, he didn't have a high opinion of Shamil Basayev. "He is not educated man but the media like sensation," he said as he mimicked a journalist writing down everything Basayev said. "When Basayev asked the Chechen government to invade Dagestan, we said, 'Go do what you like, Shamil.'"

The news was broadcast over the radio in the restaurant. The Chechen congressional member heard the news of Chechen gains and laughed.

When he was a sniper during the war in 1995, Osman would slowly make his way within three hundred yards of a Russian outpost and watch for hours as the soldiers goofed off. When someone appeared who made the soldiers snap to attention, that was the man he would shoot. "Poof," he said, smiling, as he mimicked a head exploding with hands and wide eyes. After his kill, the Russians would wildly rocket the village behind him. He would wait two hours and drop another Russian. He would drink strong tea to stay awake but he couldn't smoke.

"You don't feel cold or hunger in war, you know," he said.

We were coming to know Tbilisi as a gangster city not unlike many other cities in other former Soviet regions. There was either too much money in the form of very expensive casinos and restaurants, or there was abject poverty. A peek into one casino revealed a newish, undecorated place with guilty-looking inhabitants. As I entered, the gangsters moved away from me deftly and quietly. They stared at me with a slow, weird suspicion, as if I was pulling a gun and everything was in slow motion. Then I was escorted out after the slightest nod from a man inside the casino. Outside the casino the big thrumming generator sounded exactly like an approaching Hind gunship.

That night we went to a restaurant on Pereskyia Street, which had a collection of theme eateries whose doormen were dressed in costumes appropriate to the fare. We chose a Mexican in a sombrero over an aging Georgian cavalry officer. At the restaurant we bumped into Ruslan and the other guide. They seemed surprised to see us.

As usual, Ruslan had more important information that we were used to ignoring. The situation was developing rapidly. Special conditions existed in the Shatili region, where we were to cross. The Russians were pressuring the Georgians not to clear the snow off the road we would take, and were sending troops to close the Georgian border. The civilians had been evacuated.

The most alarming news was that the French and English governments had demanded that all journalists leave Grozny as soon as possible. The Chechen ambassadors said that there was speculation that the Russians were planning to use gas on the Chechen capital. Most civilians had left, but there was an ominous feeling in the air that with all journalists and foreigners out of the region, the Russians would begin the killing in earnest.

Aqil was in a dark funk. He stared down at the floor with a slight tilt to his head. The morphine the Chechens found to replace his prescription painkiller was not working. We talked about leaving the smoke and the grease of the Turkish hotel and finding a new place. "Man can I come with you?" he asked quietly. "If I stay there any longer I'm going to hurt someone."

As we waited we learned that the weather was not our friend. The roads were closing. In Tbilisi, big wet flakes of snow made the city festive, but in the mountains there were avalanches. Osman told me that our choices were down to one: the mysterious and expensive helicopter, which required coordinating cars on the other side to get us into the besieged city. Depending on whom we spoke to, the helicopter landed just inside the Chechen border, a long way from the border, got shot at, or didn't exist at all.

We learned slowly through the rumor mill that it was a Georgian military helicopter that made a slight detour for a few dollars. It required a special arrangement with an unnamed pilot who could ferry in people and supplies just short of the Chechen border. The cost was three thousand dollars. It wasn't an unfair price, but expensive at $350 per person. The helicopter would only leave at dark, land in the forbidden area of Shatili, and make it back to Tbilisi by dawn.

I suspected that we would be paying a different price than the Chechens who would accompany us, Osman being one of them. There was also a group of doctors and medicine waiting to go over. Instead of jumping at the chance, I told them that if they could get the price down we would go, but for now we would wait. Everything was getting clear and fuzzy at the same time.

Some of the Turkish hotel players tried to mess with Sarah's mind. Sedat continually scared her with dire warnings. Joel thought he had found a companion before he headed to his death in a blaze of evangelistic glory, and his big saying of the day to her was, "I hope you die quickly." Sarah was quiet and she felt sick. She thought she had a bug. She wouldn't believe that the fear was getting to her.

Osman sensed that Joel was talking too much and started to keep him away from the journalists. Then Aqil and Osman got into a shouting match, during which Aqil suggested to the Chechen ambassador that Chechens were stupid, incompetent, and lazy. I separated Osman and Aqil and tried to make light of the situation, citing Aquil's lack of painkillers. Between Aqil and Joel, Osman surely had to think that all Americans were crazy.

Aqil slept in his room for the rest of the day, tired of the continual exhortations to have patience. He didn't think he could make it through the winter with the little bit of money he had left. He'd made a decision, and wanted to know about the next flight to Istanbul. He would go back to find Ayeesha and his daughter, and take them back to America. He said that it was a job he should have finished before.

Aqil was angry. He thought that I was just being jerked around. He was mad at the Chechens. Everything up to this point had been a disaster. We would never get in. He got mad at the sniper-turned-diplomat again and I had to hold him back and calm him down. Aqil's rage was turning against the Chechens. He told me to tear up anything he'd ever told me, forget it. It never happened.

For now it appeared that Aqil's jihad was over.

The people who'd left before in the helicopter returned. The Médecins Sans Frontières doctors and humanitarian supplies had been turned away. Osman, who had told us so vigorously that passing by road was impossible, magically disappeared the next morning. It seemed that he'd left by road, and that he'd just wanted us to pay for his helicopter flight.

We were awoken the next morning at 5:20 A.M. We were supposed to be downstairs ready to go. The cars were waiting. Bad Russian disco music played on the radio as we sat and drank tepid Turkish coffee. When we checked out, the hotel bill was twelve hundred dollars. We had also eaten three hundred dollars' worth of food. Aqil was charged for drinking the mini bar. He'd taken everything out and put it in the closet because he couldn't stand to look at the alcohol.

We were taken to a compound somewhere in Tbilisi by taxi. It was cold, very cold. Standing around outside seemed purposeless. There were three Lada Nivas, small Russian-made four-wheel-drive vehicles. There were also military transport vehicles in the compound. Hard to explain. Maybe they were on loan. Ruslan was happy. He had more news. The Chechens had retaken Gudermes and they'd also shot down a Russian helicopter. The footage of the two hundred dead Russian paratroopers and two prisoners was on the news. On our end, Aqil was gone, our main camera had broken, and Sarah was sick. The helicopter that we were promised had disappeared. The mountain pass that was described as impassable was suddenly passable. But it had snowed heavily since our arrival, there was no one to clear the road, and the Russians were bombing the pass and the road inside Georgia. Things were looking up.

The men who were to drive us looked like out-of-work stevedores. They all had three-day growths, slight stoops, broken noses, and cheap wool hats that sat too high on their heads. Translated, their names must have been Sluggo, Lefty, and Rocky. I assumed they had a little down time between contract killings. As always, we waited. In Georgia, men always congregate in clusters, stamp their feet, and complain about waiting.

There were the two two-man Turkish TV crews, a Polish crew, a member of the Chechen parliament, and our little crew. There was even a man who was given the oblique description of "military official" to ensure that we'd get through the checkpoints. Together we formed a small convoy. I knew that we would be traveling in a convoy because Ruslan had warned me that we must never travel in a convoy or else the Russians would bomb us.

Despite Ruslan's urgent warnings to be ready to leave instantly, the gangsters hung around, stamped their feet, and discussed the latest news. They were provisioned by a Chechen who was in "the transportation business," as Ruslan described it—the Technical Joint Venture Company, to be more precise. The cost per person to the Chechen border was $150. This was the standard rate for people traveling over the mountain pass to Shatili.

We had official-looking press accreditation from the Chechen government, a government that theoretically didn't exist. We also had double-entry ninety-day Georgian visas. Nobody wanted to see a Russian visa.

We were waiting for the big boss. I could tell he was coming before he arrived. The gray Series 7 BMW, missing both bumpers, was the trademark of the Chechen *mafyia*. Way-too-loud Russian disco music poured out of the luxury car when they opened the door.

He was there to make sure everything was in order, and that he would get paid. The three Ladas he provided for our covert trip through the patrolled mountains were bright red, brilliant orange, and, mercifully, one sparkling white one. Finally, after another hour in a coffee shop, we were off.

Ruslan promised that the trip from Tbilisi would take about five hours. When we turned off the main road we were stopped by a bored cop for a quick check of our paperwork, and then we were off. Then the road climbed up into the snow and mountains. They hadn't cleared the roads because the Russians would bomb the snowplow operators. Instead, the tiny Ladas acted like snowplows as they bulled two grooves into the snow with a flat center all the way up the mountain. Fresh water springing from the ground created dramatic frozen waterfalls with perfectly smooth sheets of ice across the road. There was also evidence of avalanches in the form of stress cracks and blocked road sections.

The bold blue sky above the panorama of snow-covered mountains made the trip seem festive as we occupied ourselves by watching our driver cheat death.

Our driver, if described charitably and without use of his real name, was slack-jawed, dim witted, and unconcerned with the Newtonian effects of ice and gravity. He negotiated the thin frozen corniche road like a despondent suicide victim, driving as far out on the lip of the crumbling road as possible, often hooking an outside wheel over the precipice. Why, I asked? That's the best part of the road, he said. It's hard to argue logic like that. It took a while, but we convinced him that there was more mountain underneath the inner side of the road and therefore that was the best part of the road.

Toward the border we formed a convoy with five cars and two Gaz vans loaded with indeterminate bundles. The first border check went fine. The Georgian soldiers spoke perfect American English here. The U.S. embassy told me later that the United States was advising Georgia on subjects like high technology as it applied to border control. We watched their training in action as they pulled out a weathered hotel guest book and laboriously hand printed each person's name and address. They were quite concerned about our paperwork. In fact, one of the main reasons for our delay was the need for an official press pass from the Chechen government, which had absolutely nothing to do with leaving Georgia. Everyone in our small group took great pains to act as though we chose this lonely road into a war as part of our vacation plans.

We were journalists, the fighters were—well, maybe they were hockey players. We handed out cigarettes, joked with the guards, and wondered why this charade was so complicated. Joel was the one person who didn't seem to have any documentation or reason to be there. Luckily, he was the only person in the group who was small enough to fit in the trunk of a Lada, and we would eventually hide him there for the last checkpoint.

At one checkpoint delay, a Georgian soldier jumped in our car and a special Chechen fixer took over the wheel to drive to the commander's house up on a hill overlooking the checkpoint. The three of us were stuffed in the tiny backseat of the Lada like oversized carnival prizes. We had been told not to talk—to just nod our heads. But what if we didn't understand the questions they were asking? Yes, we are criminals. Yes, we want to go to jail for illegally entering Russia. Yes, we want to be kidnapped.

The Georgian bodyguard turned around and asked, "Where are you going?" in perfect English. Nodding was futile at this point. We stumbled, trying to avoid answering the obvious. Our driver hit him stiffly on the shoulder, as if to say *you stupid,* and then the driver said, "Grozny *pow! pow!*" He took his hands off the wheel to make shooting motions with his hands. So much for our cover. There was much discussion inside the commander's house, and our animated Chechen fixer swore up a storm describing his Georgian friends. But after another laborious session filling out forms and writing down mothers' maiden names and home addresses we were sent through the checkpoint.

The first clue that something bad was happening inside Chechnya came when we met a family of people walking toward us in the deep snow. They were climbing across the eight thousand-foot mountain pass in the deep snow with no luggage or food and wearing only city clothes. Their twin ten-year-old boys did a few takbirs, or "Allahu Akbars," for the Turkish cameras. Then there was another family whose car had run out of fuel. We stopped at the summit to take pictures, mistakenly thinking we had finished the hard part.

At another Georgian checkpoint we heard the steady drone of a large plane. The Chechens yelled and waved frantically for everyone to get back inside the cars. The silver plane circled slowly, possibly to take our pictures or to call in a jet strike. The shortwave broadcasts said that the Russians had begun bombing inside Georgia.

We waited for hours in the car. The windows iced over. My feet went numb. Since the jet strikes didn't occur, we were apparently avoiding the high-resolution cameras of the circling four-engine Antonov. But what moron wouldn't know what our convoy was up to? And why wouldn't they bomb the cars? Shouldn't we be sitting on the nearby hill or under a tree? These are all questions our guide Ruslan pondered but to which he had no answer. I was getting increasingly concerned with Ruslan's newfound ability to take long answers in Chechen and turn them into a few English phrases. Soon he'd found the ultimate shorthand for his translation duties, an answer that he used with increasing frequency: "I don't know."

It turned out that we were waiting because the Polish journalists from the Turkish hotel had thought they would be clever if they applied for permission to travel to Shatili, but not beyond. Once at the border town of Shatili, they thought they would just bribe their way into Chechnya. It didn't work, and now they would have to take the daylong trip back to Tbilisi at night and pay whatever their Chechen driver demanded. Somehow they made it worth the guards' while to let them pass, but the Georgians outsmarted them. During the entire wait it didn't dawn on our guide to jump the line and let the Poles sort themselves out.

But we were all delayed; there was nothing to do but watch the Georgian border guards stamp their feet and hunch up their shoulders in the frigid valley. The sun slid slowly up the wall of the valley and kissed the summits with an orange glow. Then it was blue, then it was dark and cold.

When we were allowed to pass, we had another small problem. Our car was broken. There was no specific reason why cars didn't work there; they just broke. We were towed with a thin cable like a red Christmas sleigh as we wound through the start of the Argun River gorge. It was bad enough to have our slack-jawed driver under his own power, but now we glided silently in the dark through the sparkling snow along a curving and winding river. Every two hundred yards the cable would snap and a furious argument would ensue between our confused driver and the tougher, less patient man who was towing us. The driver in front was going too slow, we were too heavy, we shouldn't use our brakes. They were like a bad comedy team with their too-small hats, Adidas track suits, and dangling cigarettes waggling in the dull yellow glare of the headlights.

It was not a comforting ride staring thousands of feet down the white slopes glowing in the yellow headlights. But it was doable. Barely. When the road tilted upward again we got stuck and we'd have to clear the snow from beneath the wheels.

Shatili was the last town before entering Chechnya, or rather the last dot on the map before the jagged border. It was the site of a medieval slate fortress in the Argun River valley, a rough-and-tumble structure piled on the side of steep pass that dated back to the eigth century. Like most mountain redoubts it was used to control passage along the pass. Although its function was strictly scenic now, it was a reminder that the region had always been a wild frontier.

Shatili was a classic mountainous border town. There was no law, no delineated border, but there were very real rules and penalties. The curved pole carved out of a small pine and weighted with car parts was not the real border. It was where the Georgian guards stood around and argued about how much they should charge the Chechen refugees to enter and whether or not they should hassle the fighters and drivers headed into Chechnya. The border was officially closed, so it took a little longer than normal to cross.

The four hundred or so people who lived along the border were called Khevsurs—men of the passes. The official story was that they earned their living by hunting, but the truth was that they rented their mountain ponies and knowledge of the passes to smugglers. The Georgian border guards worked with the Chechens who showed up in tiny Ladas and vans in order to expedite unknown materials into Chechnya. Although they were Christians and spoke Georgian, the Khevsurs were more closely linked to the Chechens to the north.

There were supposed to be twenty-two families here. The Russian bombing took care of that and now there were hundreds of deperate Chechen refugees here. At this altitude everything was frozen. The waterfalls were solid cascades and the river flowed under a sheet of silvery gray ice.

The main trade in Shatili consisted of taxi drivers preying on refugees who were eager to get to Tbilisi. The cost was two hundred dollars per Lada and six hundred dollars for the bigger Gaz jeep. There had been 1,650 refugees through here in the last three months, but most couldn't afford that kind of money.

We had made it through four checkpoints; it was late at night. The snow crunched under my feet and the stars burned like spotlights. When we arrived at the last checkpoint we were delayed again. It was something to do with the Poles again. The Polish reporter was wearing thin leather street shoes, a suit, and a green business overcoat. His only concession to traveling into a war zone in December was an Ellesse ski headband. I imagined him chained to a rusty radiator in a Grozny basement, and the evil thoughts warmed me up. Finally he was sent back by the stubborn Georgians.

I could see houses in the dark. Single yellow squares of light came from the windows. One of the Chechens asked if we wanted to meet the refugees.

I tripped over the barbed-wire fence and banged my head on the frozen laundry on the way to the door. The heat and humidity from inside fogged up my glasses and camera. A row of children appeared, lit by a single kerosene lantern in a portrait of despair. Slowly, more women and children came out of the darkness of the back room. The yellow light of the lamp softened their faces and added bright sparkles to their eyes. They were happy to see us but they don't know where to begin. They had come here to escape the bombing in Chechnya. Their men were not allowed to cross and could only go back and forth to bring food. Now they were being bombed here and they were scared. Some of the women cried and sobbed hysterically.

They were trapped here. They'd to had pay one hundred dollars per person to be allowed to cross the border. Now they had no money for a taxi or even food. A family let them use this four-room house but there were more than twenty-four people here. As the women talked they became more animated. They told stories about family members who had died trying to escape Chechnya: children, brothers, sisters, husbands. Even when they were told it was safe to pass, they were bombed and strafed. They didn't care who ran Chechnya. Russians, Chechens, Americans. They just wanted to live on their land in peace. I filmed their terrible stories and took pictures.

They started to cry. The only happy one was a tiny baby who giggled and smiled through the wailing and yelling of the women. Tears glittered in the golden light as they rolled down their women's faces. "Are we terrorists? Are we bandits? What shall we do? Why is this happening?"

All this and I hadn't entered Chechnya yet.

PART TWO

O Allah! Who sent down The Book . . . Who makes the clouds drift . . .
Who defeats the armies . . . Defeat Russia! O All Mighty! O All Powerful!
O Allah! Indeed we ask that You Scatter their firing, and Shake the earth
beneath their feet, and Strike fear in their hearts. O Allah!

Cripple their limbs and Blind their sight, and send upon them an epi-
demic and calamities. O Allah! Separate their gatherings and Scatter their
unity, and make their condition severe amongst themselves, and make their
plots go against them, and show us in them the amazements of your Power,
and make them a lesson for those who do not learn lessons. O Allah! Hurry
their destruction, and make their wealth as booty for the Moslems.

O Allah! Aid our Mujahadin brothers in Chechnya. O Allah! Unify their
rows, and gather them on the word of truth. O Allah! Aim their firing and
strengthen their determination, and make their feet firm, and descend upon
them tranquillity, and satisfy their hearts and guide them to that which is all
good. O Allah! Make for them from Yourself an authority, and aid them
with the army from Yourself, for to You belong the armies of the heavens
and the earth, O Lord of the Worlds. May Salaah and Salaam be upon the
Messenger of Allah and upon all his followers and companions.

—From www.qoqaz.com, a Chechen mujahideen Web site

Finally we were allowed across the border into Chenya. The roughly hewn
sapling that served as a barrier at the border crossing was lifted. We drove
across the snow-packed road for a few hundred yards and stopped at a
three-sided shale structure, the last exit from Georgia. A gaggle of refugees
huddled around a tiny wood fire. Georgian soldiers mooched cigarettes and

CHECHNYA REGION

RUSSIA

CHECHNYA

INGUSHETIA

Kizlyar

CASPIAN SEA

Grozny   Gudermes

Chechen-aul   Argun   Khasav'yurt

Nazran   Achkhoi-Martan

Urus-Martan   Shali

Duba-yurt   Stari   Vedeno   Makhachkala

Sovestskoye

Shatoi

ARGUN
RIVER
VALLEY

Shatili   DAGESTAN

CAUCASUS MOUNTAINS

GEORGIA

25 mi

25 km

Tbilisi

money. The night was piercingly cold and the waiting chilled us. I handed out cigarettes with my numb hands. An English-speaking border guard smiled and laughed after he lit his cigarette. "Welcome to Hell," he said. There was a gaggle of people I didn't recognize in the darkened canyon. I could hear someone familiar babble in Russian and Chechen. It was Aqil.

Aqil had not returned to find his wife and then give up jihad. The night he left to go to the airport to return to Istanbul, his Chechen driver had told him that there was a seat available in one of the cars going to the border. He took it and had been waiting here for a day.

From this point we had to walk to get to Chechnya. We paid our driver. He complained about the lack of customers and said that he was never coming back. But he would wait and see who appeared at the border for a ride home. The refugees usually showed in the early morning to travel the hellish narrow gorge road into Georgia. Estimates about how much of the road ahead was destroyed varied from two kilometers to forty. The gorge was steep here; razor-sharp stones cut a jagged dragon spine on both sides. The Argun River carved its way from the gorge toward Grozny. The road to Grozny followed the river as it turned from a churning powerhouse to a slow, muddy waterway.

The word was that the Desant, or Russian paratroopers, were coming. They would be dropped onto the peaks and then fight their way down to the road tucked along the river. Rumors are rife in warfare, and fear acts as a superconductor. All I knew for sure was that the Russian reconnaissance planes had been flying nonstop, taking photos, mapping the rebel strongholds, monitoring activity. We were at their mercy in the mountains.

At this time of night the path was frozen glasslike and treacherous, but we were warned to stay on it. The Russians had been dropping aerial mines that were impossible to see in the darkness. They were also using the new Ka-50 Hokum-A helicopters equipped with night vision. The Chechens' defense was a pair of thirty-millimeter cannons salvaged from a Russian troop carrier. Their strategy was to lure the helicopters into the narrow gorge and let them have it. The gorge was safe from helicopters now because it was too treacherous to fly through at night, but there were thousands of air-dropped mines left from their daytime forays.

Despite my paranoia, the walk was enjoyable. There was no moon; above the dark V-shaped silhouette of the gorge, I could see the stars. The ragtag column of fighters and civilians chattered and sprayed their flashlights around the canyon, creating the atmosphere of an Easter egg hunt. I sweated from the exertion in the still, frozen air. We'd been told that we would be bombed while crossing the gorge but there was no sound of aircraft yet.

We came across a collection of green vans and trucks hidden under some trees. The commander was in a brand new Land Cruiser, playing with his winch as he tried to pull a van from the bottom of the hill. The winch broke with a snap. He didn't seem too perturbed. He could always get a new one—truck of course. Chechnya was a haven for stolen and smuggled goods. Commanders here talked on their five-dollar-a-minute Iridium satellite phones as though they were cell phones; there was no other phone system in Chechnya.

The green vans weren't carrying anything evil, just green wool balaclavas for the soldiers. There was even paperwork to be filled out on the hood of a jeep as the Chechens in the Land Cruiser took delivery of three or four boxes. The Chechen fighters were all in uniform and spotlessly clean. We showed them our passports and then waited around. The smell of pine trees, the roar of the river, and the stars would make this a great site for a hike. But the darkness was being kind.

The first official sign that we were in Chechnya was a confused outpost called the Customs House. It was a small rock structure tight against the base of a cliff that was camouflaged by twenty-foot pine trees. The steepness of the gorge didn't allow for any large structures. Inside was a small stove and two dozen fighters crammed together to hide from the cold outside. Inside, the temperature was at least one hundred degrees. I walked forward to move out of the way and fell into a four-foot pit. Oops. I climbed back out and crammed myself inside. The fighters were lounging around and yelled out greetings: "Robert, come in!" For some reason they all knew my purpose here. News traveled fast. I was inside Chechnya.

After a few minutes I went from hypothermic to sweating under my heavy winter clothes. Tired and now drenched, I decided to go outside and look for a flat spot that didn't have rocks or ice. I commandeered one of the cardboard boxes that had been delivered as my bed for the night. But night was when men and matériel moved, so we waited while Ruslan sorted through the chaos.

Aqil still had that pissed-off attitude, moderated slightly by fatigue. The cold was causing him great pain. The nerve bundles at the end of leg and his weight of 220 pounds conspired to make his stump red. The Chechens had found him some morphine but it didn't have much effect. The only good thing was that it knocked the edge off his anger.

We milled around and had decided to spend the night in the cardboard boxes that the uniforms came in when half a plan was hatched. Ruslan told us to leave our luggage in the jeep and not to worry, so I made sure I held on to everything. Aqil made the mistake of tossing his pack into the jeep.

An hour later we were told that cars had been arranged. There were more people than cars, and the scene soon became a replay of the last few minutes of the *Titanic* as diplomats, civilians, and fighters jostled for space. No one wanted to be there when the sun came up and the bombing began. The twenty-foot craters and collapsed road meant that they dropped very big bombs here.

Ruslan ran around yelling in English, "I need four small men." There is no such thing in Chechnya. Worse, he was supposed to be finding us a car. We pushed our way into an available car. Three gunmen pulled and tugged at our baggage, trying to pull it out the door, so I grabbed it back and pulled it in through the other door. For a few seconds it looked like we'd have to leave everything behind if we were going to escape this place. An urgent, angry argument in Chechen started up outside, then we were told to get in.

After a short wait I heard an insane giggling as a furry face popped into the driver's side. Then another furry face, framed in the passenger's side door. They poked their Kalashnikovs into the car. I pushed the barrels out of my face. They pushed them back in again. I looked closer at the little furry one's face. He was trying to hand me his "Automat." I took the heavy, double-clipped weapon wrapped with rubber tourniquet tubing around the stock and put it on top of my pack, which was already pinning me into the backseat. He smiled and yelled *"Allahu Akbar!"*

Nice to meet you too.

The taller furry face on the other side of the car echoed back: *"Allahu Akbar!"* They giggled in sync, jumped in the car, and fired it up. We were on our way into the war zone.

Our front seat was quiet as we drove off. The taller one was praying. I hadn't even noticed a smaller fighter sitting in the middle of the front seat. All I could see was the top of his hat. The driver identified himself as Yusaf, and Yusaf was excited. After the prayer was over they all yelled their takbirs—*"Allahu Akbar! Allahu Akbar! Allahu Akbar!"* Yusaf's taller, mirror-image passenger was Isphael. They looked at each other and giggled. Then they erupted: *"Allahu Akbar! Allahu Akbar! Allahu Akbar!"*

Shit, I thought. I'm going to be killed in between stereo fundamentalists.

Yusaf repeated the phrase with even more enthusiasm and banged the steering wheel for emphasis. *"All-Ah-u-ak-bar!"* Isphael yelled back and giggled and yelled louder, *"Allahu Akbar!"* Like a crazed tennis match, they repeated the phrase over and over. We skirted swimming-pool–sized missile craters, edged along collapsed cliffs, and climbed over crudely made bridges as the icy road wound along the gorge. The only time it quieted down was when Isphael said another prayer. Then the giggling would start again. It wasn't reassuring that that the highest calling of a mujahid is to die. It reminded me of Aqil. When I looked past the luggage that was pinning me to my seat, I realized that we had lost Aqil again.

It was four hours before sunup, and it was supposed to take five hours to get to our destination, so we were an hour late to avoid the beginning of the bombing. The car was nice and warm but my hip and side were jammed against the cold steel and window. My main occupation was to gingerly balance the gun, which was set on my pack with the barrel pointed toward the window, in case the trigger snagged as we bashed and slid down the road. When we hit a large pothole, Yusaf yelled out a healthy *"Allahu Akbar!"* as though it would prevent any serious damage to his car.

Yusaf was a Georgian volunteer from Batumi in Abkhazia. Like the others, he was obviously here for a good time, not necessarily for a long time. He enjoyed swerving around the bomb craters as he whipped the Lada down the icy road. Every time we hit a bump, the front seat erupted with Ping Pong choruses of *"Allahu Akbar!"* finished off by hysterical giggling. I was starting to like these crazy mujahideen.

There was also a little bobbing black hat in the middle. At first I thought it was a child, but it was another fighter named Megam, who seemed satisfied to be the quiet mysterious one, *Allahu Akbar'*ed into both ears.

They told me the road was not safe. Nothing serious; some question as to whether the Chechens still controlled the road to Grozny. If we bumped into Russians I was sure they would let us know.

After a while the road calmed down as it followed a wide river on the right and a sandstone cliff on the left. Confident that the AK wouldn't go on full auto at a swerve in the road, I nodded off to sleep. I was awakened by the sound of gunfire next to my ear. Shit! I thought. Russians!

I couldn't get out of the car. Wedged in by my pack and the Kalashnikov with the double-taped banana clips and rubber tourniquet wrapped around the stock, I resigned myself to being a front-row spectator at a firefight. I peered out the frosted windows to see the enemy.

I heard that crazy giggle and *"Allahu Akbar!"* again. Then silence. Then gunfire. A white rabbit zigzagged madly in the headlights in a crazed attempt to escape. Then more gunfire. The bullets sent up sparks and flits of ice all around the rabbit but it was unscathed, somehow determined not to be shown up by Isphael's bad shooting. After watching the fun and fire-works, Yusaf bolted out of the car and tried to catch the rabbit by hand. But that didn't seem to phase Isphael, who kept firing wildly around the feet and head of the scrambling rabbit and the laughing and skidding Yusaf. It was a crazed circus of gunfire, sparks, ricochets, furry laughing terrorists, and a tiny white terrified rabbit flitting in and out of the headlight beams. Finally the rabbit escaped. I took it as an omen that we would come through this even if we were subjected to direct fire, since the Chechens were considered to be good marksmen.

Panting and laughing, they explained that there wasn't much fresh food where we were going.

We passed groups of fighters walking toward Grozny who were carrying small packs and RPGs, RPKs, and AK-47s. They were in good spirits and waved as they received Isphael's obligatory but highly enthusiastic *"Allahu Akbar!"* They had the same serious, burly look as Aqil. Yusaf rolled down his window and yelled, *"Allahu Akbar!"* over and over. Even after we'd passed the fighters and he'd rolled the window, he exchanged his favorite phrase with Isphael and a few *"Alla humdillahs"* afterward for good measure.

When we'd run out of bomb craters, potholes, and passing fighters, it was now time to teach me how to yell "A-loh-who Ak-bar," with a heavy roll on the "r." They made me repeat it until I got it right and screamed with laughter when I didn't. Finally, I too could start a Ping-Pong match of *"Allahu Akbar!"* if a bomb hit or we swerved past a crater.

They called me "Amerika," and subjected me to long questions posed in the incomprehensible language of Chechen. After Sarah pulled out her Chechen-English dictionary, the education of "Amerika" began.

The words *I love,* or more correctly in Chechen-English, *I luff,* were coupled with every possible object by the two fighters. "I luff Amerika!" "I luff Bill Cleenton!" "I luff Dzhokhar Dudayev!" Yusaf luffed his *makina,* or car. He luffed jihad. The possibilities of the word were endless, so we played twenty questions to explore politics.

"You . . . luff . . . Dzhokhar Dudayev?" Yusaf asked.

Easy one. I gave a thumbs-up and a hearty "Dudayev Number One!" Two grins split their bearded faces.

The next one was over the plate.

"You . . . luff . . . Maskhadov?"

"Okay, Maskhadov Number One!" Big thumbs up. *"Allahu Akbar."*

Good answer.

"You . . . luff . . . Basayev?"

Oh shit. I remembered something about a split between Basayev and Maskhadov. Are these Basayev's men, I wondered? Oh, I'm on thin ice now.

My answer was tentative, without the eager thumbs-up.

"Basayev . . . Okay? . . . No . . . *No* . . . very bad!"

They scowled.

I knew I should have boned up on the latest politics. Yusaf and Isamael were loyal to President Maskhadov. The only thing that Basayev and Maskhadov agreed on one thing: They both wanted the Russians out of Chechnya. Oh well. Down to a local basement I'd go for six months, and after a few million in ransom I'd be forgiven. I would learn later that Maskhadov controlled most of the formal external contacts into Chechnya through Georgia and accordingly had dibs on the few journalists who came this way. Basayev and Khattab controlled the entrance through Dagestan and Azerbaijan, and a group of commanders controlled the entrance from the north. At that point, if you hated Russians you were okay. In peacetime all bets were off.

My new Chechen friends told me that they were *terroristyi.* Or so the Russians said. They pointed to their passports and smiled. They couldn't go anywhere with their Russian passports because the Russian customs service had classified them as terrorists in their computers.

Yusaf made a suggestion. "Maybe I will come to America and fight jihad."

Around 4 A.M. we made it to Shatoi, the first major city on the way to Grozny, which was still forty kilometers away. Despite the confident estimate that the bombing would start at 5:30 A.M., the city of Grozny was being pummeled. I heard the sound for the first time when I got out of the car. It is difficult to describe heavy bombardment. Bombs have both a low register and a violent physical concussion that arouses animal fear inside rational people. It is too powerful, too big, too subsonic to comprehend or measure. The impacts blended into a constant soundtrack. Even from our vantage—far enough away to be fearless—it was the equivalent of a distant rock concert. The weapon of choice was the Grad missile, mounted on trucks in batteries and fired twenty at a time. *Grad* means "hail" in Russian. They were designed to destroy artillery positions, but here they were being used to destroy sanity, houses, and lives. They had an odd double *wa-whump* thud, like the most ominous double beat on a kettledrum. Then there was a massive tower of dull orange flame that rolled into the sky. It was hard to estimate the size of the explosion, but the tower of fire must have been at least half a kilometer high. Then the sound arrived like a movie out of sync: a diaphragm-thumping, brain-squeezing subsonic thunder. Another pillar of flames rolled into the heavens. What could it be? Yusaf giggled and pointed. "SCUDs . . . Grozny."

It was the first time I'd heard the continuous explosions that would become a soundtrack for the trip. Grad barrages were fired about forty to sixty seconds apart, jet bombing runs came every fifteen minutes, and SCUDs landed two to three times a day. There was no sound of return fire, no sense of battle, only demolition. Yusaf explained with sign language and bad English that the fighters were in the bunkers but that the people still lived there. He shook his head.

The first day of December 1999 started with a beautiful morning. The sun melted the ice in the courtyard of our safe house in Alhuervo. The drone of the Russian surveillance planes sounded almost lazy. I snapped to wide awake under a soft comforter. I had forgotten where I was. The room was frigid. I could hear the sound of children playing outside and the sound of bombing, like the crash of waves outside my home on the coast of California, or like houseguests watching a war movie in the next room. We were in a small two-bedroom house inside a compound. The windows were frosted, so I rubbed one to see outside. It was a rural scene occasionally interrupted by the rattling of the thin glass window every time a bomb hit. The hockey players were here as well, with Aqil's yellow pack but no Aqil.

We rolled up the thick mattresses and covers and tried to rouse ourselves after just a few hours of sleep. Some women came in with trays and a vinyl mat for flatbread, butter, and jam. We had a tiny cast-iron woodstove with a pot of Turkish tea to be thinned with water. We were guests, but we couldn't leave the eight-foot steel walls of the compound. I peeked at the women as they went through the green steel gates to gather water. It didn't look like a war. I felt like we were being punished, but they just didn't want us to be kidnapped. I made an excuse to go outside and visit the outhouse.

On the way I watched children build snowmen and toboggan down hills in their backyard. It could have been any rural community in America or England if not for the telltale ba-boom, BA-BOOM, BA-BOOM, of Grad barrages. I watched the spotter plane above. It would make a slow circle. Within minutes two jet fighters would drop bombs in the center of the circle. The good news was that spotter planes meant no SCUDs or cruise missiles. The bad news was that the spotter planes were looking for any concentration of people, like marketplaces or a water pump to bomb.

The Chechen fighters didn't move in the daytime like the civilians, who walked or drove very quickly. We had to sit and be patient. We were supposed to meet with senior people to understand the situation. The village was far enough from Grozny but in the middle of the bombing. The villagers said that it had never been rocketed or bombed because no one was allowed to use electronic devices here. It was a "safe village," used to give visitors and new fighters a chance to find their contacts and sleep after the trip in. So far the Chechens had been very efficient despite any visible signs of organization or planning.

That morning the hockey players put their orders in for weapons. The fighters and volunteers bought their own gear. Ruslan was happy he was getting a Makarov pistol despite the fact that he wasn't a fighter. The standard weapon was the newer, smaller-caliber Kalashnikov AK-74 or Automat. Although most of the weapons and ammunition were courtesy of the Russian army, who sold or lost them in great amounts, they were not cheap. The older AK-47s went for $150, but their larger and scarcer 7.62-millimeter bullets were five for a dollar. The AK-74, which fired smaller 5.45-millimeter bullets, sold for five hundred dollars but the bullets were plentiful and dirt cheap. Our guide settled on an AK-74. The prices were high because the Chechens hadn't really come in contact with the Russians yet. Once they did, the weapons and ammunition prices would plummet. A Makarov 7.65-millimeter pistol was $250; $300 in new condition. Hand grenades were five dollars each. You could get high explosives or chemical grenades. An RPG 7 cost three thousand dollars, and fifty dollars for each rocket; pretty expensive but ultimately the best weapon when the Russians rolled in. The fighters bought their own weapons here. Volunteers without money went to the front lines and waited for casualties to render up their guns.

Chechens didn't lend weapons because of blood feuds. If you borrowed a weapon and killed someone, the owner of that weapon was responsible. Another odd custom was the dime-novel concept that there was a bullet somewhere with your name on it. A popular souvenir was a bullet with the owner's name engraved on it. That way you knew where it was at all times.

The snow was melting. Like a zoo animal, I could only peer outside at the white world around me. Everything I saw was beautiful, quiet, real. A woman milked a cow, the lady next door banged a carpet, and her beautiful teenage daughters ran away giggling when they saw my camera. Women fetched water, children had snowball fights, cows wandered slowly down the road.

Despite the tranquil scene, I could see, hear, and feel the falling bombs around us. Time moved slowly inside the brick house. The Turks chain-smoked and talked endlessly. They didn't really want to be there. They slept when they weren't talking, drinking tea, or smoking. The metal pan under the tiny round stove filled with cigarette butts. More food, then tea, then cigarettes. I hung around outside in the snow and the mud. The bombing didn't really have an exact pattern yet. The silver four-engine reconnaissance plane appeared and droned in a circle. I timed its appearance with the sounds of bombs. Within sixty seconds, I'd hear great explosions. There were usually two attempts to destroy the target. The background was full of the *carump, carump, carump* of rocket salvos. Jet attacks were at their highest in the midafternoon. They came in low over the hills behind us, and two minutes later the five-hundred-pound bombs would hit their target. You could judge the distance only by the feel of the impact on your cheeks and diaphragm. The people on the street didn't even look up when the windows rattled and the doors clattered. Watching from behind a steel fence I could feel the boom reverberate through the metal. Around 4 P.M. there were two SCUD attacks about ten minutes apart. The SCUDs made an apocalyptic sound, and the tower of flames usually burned for a minute and a half. I had a strange, irrational desire to be under the bombing rather than beside it.

At dusk the bombing continued. Like rain in the English winter, it was noted but not discussed by locals in much detail. We waited patiently for the blue kettle to boil on the tiny round stove. We didn't even notice the house shaking anymore. Some fighters came off the front line to be our bodyguards. They prayed in the room next to ours and cleaned their weapons. Big, hulking fighters with black wool hats and bulky green-and-brown camouflage utility vests. One had a broken nose and asked us not to take his picture. He was a businessman and had to do business with the Russians after the war.

At sundown the fighters got ready. We prepared to go to an undisclosed location at midnight. The news from the shortwave was not good. The Russians were pressing in. Getting to Grozny would be a little iffier, and there was a possiblity that Argun would fall.

The six fighters and our hosts sprawled all over each other with affection. They were close, leaning their heads on each other's laps so that they almost looked like lovers. But they were bonded by something deeper.

It was hard to figure out how this war would end. The Chechens had met the Russians and beat them the last time, but their country was destroyed and quickly fell into anarchy. This time they were full of confidence, but they complained that the Russians wouldn't fight them. Instead, they formed large, sweeping pincer movements to surround cities. They probed inside the cities and bottled up the civilians. The Chechens would put up a token resistance and then abandon the city en masse. They didn't want their women and children killed in the house-to-house fighting the Russians specialized in.

The Russians were using a different tactic. Instead of a haphazard blitzkrieg they were slowly strangling the life out of the country. Once the people were trapped, the Russians smashed them with a hammer. Just like General Yermolov over a century ago. Chechen refugees were being pushed northward, about 150,000 at last count. They were charged money to pass the border, their houses were looted by soldiers, and they were shot at, bombed, or rocketed as they lugged whatever they could carry. The Russians enjoyed this climate of fear and profited by it. To them, these people were bandits and terrorists who could be given no quarter. The border with Dagestan had been closed to refugees. Georgia was too difficult to travel to; Ossetia directed them right into concentration camps. When they arrived they were sent away or ignored in large tent cities. Many Chechens wanted to go back but the Russians charged them money to return.

That's why many preferred to stay in their homes under the bombs. It felt cowardly not to be there directly under the hammer. There was no relief even at night. As we got in the cars to go to our secret meeting, the explosions got closer. I listened as the bombs overlapped and faded into the background. I nodded off even though I knew I shouldn't. We were told that we were going to meet an unknown person in an unknown place.

Strangely, the streets were full of cars and people at that late hour. I learned that people did not sleep here, they just had catnaps. Most of the houses were full of refugees, and they took turns sleeping in the beds. There were no lights and the city seemed ghostly. Small candles illuminated rush hour in the town of Shali as people conducted business, escaped, or looked for lost relatives. We drove around and around on our way to the "secret" location. We saw the same buildings and landmarks go by once, then twice, then every five minutes. I wanted to tell our driver to just park and save gas.

Finally we were ushered through some formidable steel gates to a simple house decorated with carpets on the walls and military goods covered with gray army blankets. Ruslan was nervous and tried to prop up a large Chechen flag and a portrait of former president Dudayev that had a garish frame and a plastic cover. A bare bulb hung from the ceiling to light the room.

President Aslan Maskhadov entered. He was a short man in his fifties and had a patient gaze and inanimate manner. He had acted as defense minister under Dzhokhar Dudayev and had served in the Russian military before that. He refused to serve in an army that was trying to destroy his homeland, and he knew exactly how to bait the bear.

When Dudayev was killed by a Russian missile, Prime Minister Zelimkhan Yanderbiev took power. The Chechens elected the minister of defense, Aslan Maskhadov, to the presidency in January 1997. After the raids of Basayev and Raduyev, the Russians felt they could negotiate with Maskhadov. Basayev warned that he was wasting his time. Even though Maskhadov was elected fair and square and was favored by Moscow, he was dumped nonetheless in favor of a blatantly fake puppet army led by Bislan Gantemirov, a man who had been imprisoned by the Russians for stealing aid money sent to rebuild Chechnya.

It was time for an interview. I asked Maskhadov what the current situation in the war was.

They were fighting the Russians, had taken back some cities, and would defend Grozny. Like most Chechens he was calm and confident even though there was now an army of 150,000 invaders inside his republic.

What was his opinion of Shamil Basayev?

He was a Chechen citizen and free to do what he liked.

Very diplomatic; it was an answer designed to smooth over the power struggle between the fundamentalists and the mainstream. Basayev had two thousand men and was considered a terrorist and a fundamentalist by the outside world. His right-hand man, Khattab, was a young Jordanian born commander of foreign volunteers. The Georgians disliked Basayev because he supported the Russians in the Georgian province of Abkhazia, and the Russians wanted him for his adventuring in Dagestan. To the political elite, Basayev was an uneducated man, a politically volatile substance, and a hell of a fighter: someone who had the potential to save Chechnya or destroy it. Basayev controlled the pace of the fighting, while Maskhadov was often credited with directing the strategy. The truth was that all Chechens were united in the war against Russia. After the war, all bets were off.

"Why are you fighting this war when the women and children are the ones who die?" I asked.

"I must solve this problem now. The Russians attack us every fifty years and I can't allow this to happen again." He didn't have a choice. The Chechens didn't have a choice.

During the interview, Maskhadov deflected my questions about kidnapping, criminality, and fundamentalism as Russian propaganda. When asked about Arabic or other foreign volunteers, he said that most of the volunteers were from Russia and former Soviet republics. He was not about to feed us ammunition. He sat stiffly and played president until the end of the interview when his aides begged off.

Outside, I bumped into a tall, giant-faced man with a wide lambskin hat and blue steel-capped teeth. He was a shoo-in for the James Bond villain and brandished a three-foot long *sulificar*, a very large, double-bladed sword like the one used by Mohammad's cousin Ali. Imam Shamyl had also had his own executioner, complete with large ax, to carry out sharia punishment on the spot.

It was a nice touch, but Maskhadov had about as much fire as a Rotary leader, and about as much authority. He made speeches and did interviews, but independent commanders like Basayev did the real fighting. Maskhadov, however, was the reason we had been brought there. The Chechens had a government and an army. Unlike most desperate wars there were no children pressed into service, the fighters were well groomed and neat, and they jumped into the fray at a moment's notice. There was no debate as to who was in charge or whether the independence of Chechnya was valid or not. Whoever won this war would determine all that.

Although the total number of men under arms in Chechnya was estimated to be thirty thousand, the fighters told me that there were only five thousand at any one time. In truth, no one knew the actual figure. There were militias, private bands, and volunteers whose numbers were never recorded. I never saw more than twenty armed men in any given place, and that was in the nexus of the Russian advance. Most of the troops were groups of twelve to twenty, dug in and awaiting the Russian attack on Grozny. The mood was cheerful, almost giddy. They would fight the Russians on their own turf. But there was something disturbing about this war. In the first war the Russians did not destroy the cities. In this war they were methodically pulverizing every last vestige of Chechnya. They also killed the villagers or pushed them out of their homes, destroying or stealing anything of value. How could the Chechens win the war when there was no country left? The answer was simple.

We were to go to Grozny. There were stories that the Russians were using fuel-air bombs to clear the bunkers the Soviets had built in case of an American nuclear attack. The Russians were slowly surrounding Grozny in a large Pincer movement, afraid to enter the city. In the last war the Russians had used textbook assault tactics against fighters who had just served in the Russian army. They entered the concrete maze of Grozny without maps. The fighters had created a network of underground tunnels that would allow them to attack the front and back of an armored column as it moved through the city. The troops in the middle had been trapped, and with nowhere to go the Russians and their tanks were picked off one by one. Before reinforcements arrived, the Chechens disappeared down the tunnels and popped up hundreds of yards away.

The Russians could do nothing against snipers, labyrinths, booby traps, and hit-and-run attacks, so this time the military adopted very different tactics. Since the fighters didn't have major supply bases, the villagers were their source of food, intelligence, and support. This war was against the people of Chechnya rather than the entrenched fighters.

A typical attack on a village would commence by controlling the roads with checkpoints. Villagers were asked for bribes when entering and leaving, and the men were arrested. Those who would not or could not pay, or who didn't have proper documents, were sent to "filtration" camps, a euphemism here for concentration camps.

Then the Russians bombarded the outskirts of villages in an effort to cause panic. Aircraft dropped bombs on clusters of people gathering for water, funerals, meetings. The casualties put stress on the medical and support systems. In some cases commanders demanded payments from the village heads to prevent bombing or attacks. Often they were told to turn in a certain number of weapons and fighters or they would be attacked.

The week before an attack, the bombardment would be nonstop and completely indiscriminate. The goal was to force the entire population to flee. Other safe corridors were negotiated and paid for. Often these clearly marked convoys with preagreed paths and times were strafed and attacked.

The village was then finally attacked by regular Russian troops and armored vehicles. There were usually high casualties. Interior Ministry or OMON troops mopped up from house to house. The OMON used grenades to kill the inhabitants. Some were tortured and raped until they handed over their money, then shot. The tanks and trucks overflowed with household goods looted from the villages.

Any man between the ages of sixteen and sixty was sent to a filtration camp for questioning and detainment. Many were simply murdered and thrown in pits.

When the troops left they stayed in heavily fortified bases because they were afraid to enter the population. The Chechens then used mines, snipers, and booby traps to kill off the Russians. The pattern was repeated over and over throughout Chechnya. Soon it would be Grozny's turn.

After interviewing Maskhadov we were handed over to a driver to find us a bodyguard. The Russians were advancing rapidly; no one was quite sure where anyone was at any one time. We had to go to Shali to find someone who could help us. Our car broke down after we left our safe house. There isn't much to do when your bright red car breaks down in Chechnya except time the bombs and rockets.

Sedat, Sarah, and I we were told to stay inside to prevent kidnapping. Nobody could tell me who was responsible for the kidnappings, but everyone knew that a foreigner was at the top of any kidnapper's wish list. Being an American and, for all intents and purposes, a journalist, I was about as good as any kidnapper could hope for.

The Chechens explained that the phenomenon started after the Russians left in 1996. There had been a campaign of high-profile, big-money snatches. The victims were Russian journalists, foreigners, and wealthy people, many of whom were grabbed outside of Chechnya. Some Chechens opined that the kidnapping was a purely Russian affair that took place outside Chechnya because captives were often magically rescued inside Chechnya. I was told that I would be kidnapped because the Russians had put a bounty on any journalists caught here. In an odd way, it made the Chechens even more determined to make sure that I wasn't kidnapped.

As in any good business, there was a flourishing wholesale trade in captives. Snatchers "flipped" their victims to blackmailers for quick cash, and many were bought and sold before the brokers could find someone to foot the ransom. Victims were traded between Dagestanis, Chechens, Russians, and Ossetians. Locals went for between two thousand dollars and forty thousand dollars. Foreigners started at one million dollars and went up to five million dollars. Before, kidnapping was a very low-key affair in Chechnya. The Russians had turned it into a big business.

Those were the facts. They didn't help when you were stuck in a car with only a Swiss Army knife to protect you. The rocket barrages made the car shudder. The windows compressed with every shock wave, like a metal sheet being vibrated louder and louder. A light haze was on the fields and the roads were covered in slush. Grozny was identifiable at all times by the black pillars of smoke that boiled up and flattened at the inversion layers. The bombing sounds weren't distinct anymore, just a continuous booming. After sitting in the car for an hour, a Japanese sedan with tinted windows drove by slowly, then again. We decided to go to the nearest house for tea.

The next day we went to the main market in Shali. The Chechen flag flew tattered and defiant outside the main building. The weapons market was next the to the food stalls. There was a small room where the soldiers could drink tea, eat, and relax. The Russians didn't bomb the main market in Shali because they needed the buildings for an HQ to stage an assault on Grozny. Downtown Shali looked just like the main square at Universal Studios: There were cheap Greco-Roman public buildings, a cheesy town square, and the constant hubbub of people shopping, as if the war were just an ugly rumor.

There was much disagreement between village leaders and fighters. Many wanted the arms market outside of town because of the cruise missile the Russians had fired into Grozny a few weeks before. They thought it would save lives. The commanders didn't seem to care. They set up their bunkers and bomb shelters in the large basements of the buildings at the center of town. Soldiers lounged around the city square. They weren't worried about attracting the Russians. They were coming.

Our next stop would be Grozny.

Within a few minutes of entering the most dangerous place on earth I felt a sense of injustice. The city was not ringed by defenses; instead, the first people that I saw were selling chocolate bars and cigarettes at the side of the road. Others walked down the street with plastic shopping bags. Men stood on corners and watched the cars pass by. There were bright red brick houses between the faded wood and concrete structures—homes that had been rebuilt since the last war. There were playgrounds, and fences, and stores, most of which were deserted, but all undeniable evidence that normal people lived there. Those who were left behind either could not or would not leave. The Russians dropped leaflets from the sky. The message to their fellow countrymen: Leave or Die.

Grozny sat astride the pipeline that sent fuel from Makhachkala on the Caspian Sea to Novorossiysk on the Black Sea. There had been a great refinery, but now it was all gone. The oil tanks that had been destroyed in the first war were now perpetually burning pyres, still belching up black pillars of smoke into the cold winter sky.

The news reports told of flattened buildings, pillars of fire, a wasteland, but we were driving through neat suburbs, many with rebuilt red brick houses. There was no damage here. Occasionally there was a missing house or a cratered yard, but otherwise it looked like Mayberry RFD on a Sunday morning.

We soon found ourselves parked in front of the beautiful, newly built house that belonged to Turpalov Ali.

We took our boots off and unloaded our gear. Inside there were kittens by the stove and a pretty young woman who introduced herself as Turpalov's sister. His men were dressed in black, spotless and clean.

Turpalov Ali Atigirov was the minister of interior security. He was twenty-nine, had just fixed up this house, and didn't want to leave it. After I saw the bathroom and the beautiful windows, I didn't want to leave either. There was no water or heat and no basement or protection from bombs. Turpalov told us that we could use the bomb shelter next door if we wanted.

He hadn't seen any outsiders for a while, so it was nice to have company. He put on a fine meal, better than some of the meals we had had in Tbilisi. He had some flour and cookies stockpiled, along with noodles, canned beef, and jams.

As minister of interior security, he felt he had to be official, so he told us that Grozny sat on a big reservoir of oil and water; they were worried that the bombing would cause the oil to mix with the water and cause an ecological disaster. Somehow it seemed silly to talk about the environment with bombs going off in the background.

I asked about the war. Turpalov said that it was the result of a series of missteps made by the Russian military and government, not a carefully designed plot. "After all," he said, "what does anyone win with this war?" He added, surprisingly "This war is because of me."

As deputy prime minister, he has been the head of security for Maskhadov's government. In July 1999 he went to visit FSB head and future Russian president Vladimir Putin to sign a cooperation agreement between Chechnya and Russia. Instead, he was arrested as a terrorist for fighting against the Russians in the Dagestani border town of Kislyar in 1996 with Salman Raduyev. Before that he had been in Moscow five times and nobody said anything about his presence. Somehow he had become a war criminal, a terrorist. Turpalov Ali said his arrest was a simple provocation designed to start a war. Three days after he was arrested, Russian Mi-8 helicopters attacked the Chechen fighters. He was held for two weeks but eventually released by then–Russian prime minister Stepashin. "The Russian generals could not accept that such a small army could defeat them, so they came back. The three years in between were just a time out. In the meantime, the Russians had supported the criminals in Chechnya."

I wanted to talk about the kidnappings, something that had scared journalists away from covering the war from the rebels' side. His explanation was simple and convincing. Russians had always kidnapped people and sold them back to their families. They even sold him the dead bodies of Chechen soldiers. Turpalov himself had had to buy two relatives back from the Russians for ten thousand dollars.

He blamed the kidnapping on freelance special forces, or Russians who actually hired the kidnappers and victims.

A Russian NTV journalist was kidnapped. Many people had an interest in this kidnapping and everybody won. The Russian politicians' ratings went up. The kidnappers got a ransom of three million dollars. One of the TV executives got a kickback of five hundred thousand dollars. Even the Russian Internal Service and the journalist himself got paid.

Turpalov Ali was at Budennovsk and looked back at the operation with pride. It officially made him a terrorist. He saw the hijacking of the ferry with two hundred captives notice a terrorist attack but as a military operation that startled and shocked the Russians.

He commented on the bombing around us as Grad (hail) and Urgan (hurricane) missiles pounded the city.

"The Russians didn't bomb the rebels, who were underground. There were no front lines, so they bombed the city; the large buildings, the apartment buildings, the hospitals, the markets, the schools, anywhere there were people. They didn't waste their ammunition on the bunkers or the suburbs."

"These type of weapons are forbidden by the Geneva convention," he said. "These are weapons that can kill everything around." But the Russians dropped mines, napalm, and phosphorus every day. They also used SCUDs and Topol missiles, rockets and bombs. They fired about two to three SCUDs every day, up to a hundred on some days. They used the SCUDs against the crowded areas, usually on women at the market.

"They want to destroy the thing that makes soldiers. The strength that builds this country. Kill the women and there will be no more young Chechens. For three centuries we have fought. It is our way of life now."

They were the one-sided statements of a man who had spent his adult life fighting Russians. Somehow I couldn't imagine Boris Yelstin or Vladimir Putin sitting calmly with his house under bombardment discussing Chechen policy.

It was getting late in the day and he wanted to show us something: the October cruise missile that landed in the Grozny marketplace as I was planning my trip. On the way to downtown Grozny he said that we were very lucky because we were the first journalists to escape bombardment on the road from Shatili.

After leaving the suburbs, it was plain that little inside the city was unscathed. The large apartment blocks on the main streets had been attacked relentlessly, destroyed by concrete-piercing bombs that penetrated the top five floors and then exploded in the middle of the building or in the basement. Buildings sagged; there were empty lots like missing teeth where bombs had blown a building into matchsticks. Splatterlike shrapnel marks were evident on every building. Twisted cars and burned black marks lined the asphalt.

There are places we never want to be true. Hard, cold empty places where it is impossible to deny that human's have no mercy. When I got out of the Lada it was cold, overcast, and gray. There was no sign of life, just broken, shattered, confused, and abandoned remnants of a busy market. Something powerful and evil had happened there. There was no color or life anywhere nearby.

Victory Avenue was a scene that every human should see once in their life. The main street of Grozny was to have a McDonald's. The guitar store was over there, Ruslan pointed out, the computer store was over there. Now there was a street of mud with a massive crater. The military couldn't even figure out what had caused the destruction. One commander who appeared on the scene offered his explanation: "a big bomb." Rusted red sewer and gas pipes were thrust skyward like civic artwork. There was a bus there, its skeleton blown apart. Odd bits of human existence were laid out as if it were a memorial. A shoe here, a sewing machine there. A cheap suitcase with a name and address. The bus was packed with refugees when it was hit by a rocket.

It was like the end of the world. The dogs roamed insane and barked at the rockets. A three-legged dog hobbled around. Two others growled and menaced us. One of the fighters racked the lever on his Automat a few times to scare them off. In the last war they shot all the dogs. They'd used them to warn of approaching soldiers, but then the animals started feasting on the dead. The fighters told me that once the dogs tasted humans they had no fear. They went crazy. So they had to die.

A nicely made-up middle-aged Russian woman stood patiently at the side of the road, selling cigarettes. She was strangely neat and well dressed in the gray devastation around her. The street was blasted and muddy for as far as the eye could see, strewn with the silly things for which people work all their lives. I walked through the pathetic possessions of the bus passengers to reach her. She lived here, in the apartment across the street. She made six dollars today.

A few blocks away I saw an unexploded SCUD missile up close. The fighters had already taken the two thousand-pound warhead. The sprawling complex had been blown down to its naked iron supports. It was hard to figure out what they'd made here. A sign on the way out said BAKERY.

The cruise missile landed on a group of mostly women vendors at around 2 P.M., when the market was at its busiest. The stalls were twisted and scattered from the impact. A large hole marked the epicenter of the violence. I peered down as if there was an answer in the center, but there was only more death—a dead German shepherd rimed with frost at the bottom of the twenty-foot crater. A group of fighters magically appeared from nowhere. They walked with a slow, cautious gait, like gunfighters sniffing each other out. Their faces had an oddly serene aspect as they sized us up. The leader had a headband with Arabic letters. He stared at me and gave me time to take in the scene, his silent vigil punctuated by upward glances to the sky to look for spotter planes. An inquisitive officer wanted to know why I was there. As he got closer he saw my camera. He broke into a grin and said, "You should get a medal for courage."

Turpalov Ali wanted to borrow my satellite phone to make a call. Using a sat phone sends a distinct signal to the Russian radio scanners, and it wouldn't take long for them to target a battery of rockets on the signal. We walked away from the house and made the call in the bright snow. He talked to the Chechen representative in France. Was there any news of the kidnapped journalist Bruce Fleutiaux? He'd hired the *mafyia* to take him inside Chechnya. They simply handed him over to his kidnappers once he was inside. The commander said, "Don't worry, we'll find him." He reflected on what was going on around him. As we walked back in the cold night air he said, "This war cannot be won, but it can be stopped."

A few minutes later the rockets rained down.

I liked to sleep in Turpalov's house on the wooden floor with the rest of the Chechen mujahideen. I didn't want to stay in a basement. The basements were hot, damp, and foul, like a tomb. The house was clean and happy, a human place. It was my way of fighting the fear.

The fighters talked and laughed in the main room, which was heated. RPK machine guns, ammo belts, spare magazines, and AK-74 Automats were strewn around the house. It was always full of mujahideen. The bearded fighters wore bulky camo jackets, utility vests, and waterproof pants, and came and left at all hours.

When they entered the house the fighter's routine was automatic: They stood up, hugged, and put an arm on each other's shoulder as they warmly greeted each other like old friends. They were obliged to give an update on what was happening, to convince each other that they were winning, to remind each other of the Russians' lies. Here, the nighttime was the daytime, the working time, the time to kill Russians.

The next morning one of the fighters came in with an armload of fresh bread. "They just bombed the marketplace. There are many casualties. Come quick." The market was five hundred meters from us. The three victims were gone by the time I got there. A white car was on fire, and the topsy-turvy debris of an explosion littered the area. A tiny gray puppy staggered around the deserted market stalls. Someone told me: "This is not an arms market. It is the place where you buy bread." A few fighters and old men stood around with their hands in their leather jackets. This was nothing extraordinary. Having outsiders to witness it was.

A large splatter of blood thickened on the ice around the corner from the burning car. A wavy trail of blood drops led us toward an apartment. People pointed the way for us, but the blood trail made their directions superfluous. The people weren't hiding in bunkers, they were out on the street. They weren't cowering, they were angry.

It was dark and cold inside the stairway. Normally people lit candles for us, but the old people navigated perfectly in the dark. I used the railing to guide myself upwards.

The apartment was very dark, and the people urged us toward the light. A single window illuminated the bed. Tears ran down a young girl's face in silent pain. Her mother was angry and distraught. "We couldn't leave because they had no money," she explained. "Why are we being bombed? Are we terrorists? Is she a terrorist? She was just going out to get water. I knew this was going to happen." The girl just looked up silently.

We were crowded into the small apartment by more old people. For some reason they didn't care that there was no light in the stairwell or the apartment. I looked closely at one of the older women. She was staring upward. She was blind. None of them blinked or shaded their eyes when they entered the girl's room. They were all Russians. They were all old. They were all blind. This was an apartment for the infirm and blind.

The mother of the girl broke down and cried.

I was told that the other wounded had gone to a hospital. We discovered that it was not a hospital but a nursery in a dingy basement entered from outside. Down in the subterranean hallways I stumbled into a tiny operating room by accident. "Please go back, this is a sterile area" a doctor yelled at me. I backed up, not from the warning, but from the sight of a young man with his face blown off lying in front of me. We talked to the wounded but there was little to discuss. They were here because they could not leave. They hid during the day and went out only when necessary. I asked a doctor if I could take her picture. She didn't want to. One of the fighters urged her to pose. She did, but with a pained smile. Sobbing came from down the hall—it came from the family of the man that just died from his wounds. We learned that he was the head of the Grozny orchestra.

Back at the house well after dark, a large man with piercing eyes, a hooked nose, big beard, and a red-checkered kaffiyeh—the headdress of the Arabic fighters—showed up. The Chechens we were with remained standing longer than normal. There was a sense of unease and seriousness about this visitor. He had come to take us somewhere He wouldn't say where, he simply told us to come with him.

I was told only that someone wanted to see me tonight. The visitor took us out to a truck. Unlike the beatup Gaz jeeps or worn Ladas, the visitor had a new white Toyota pickup. There was camo netting in the bed and a brand-new radio aerial in the backseat. The mujahid with the red scarf sat in the back and I crammed myself between the powerful radio antennas and supplies in the backseat of the pickup. I'd seen these types of trucks used as military vehicles by "Arabs" in Afghanistan, the same place I saw red-checkered kaffiyehs. It was the trademark of the Arabic men who trained in Afghanistan to fight jihad. Their main benefactor was Usama bin Laden, who introduced the Toyota Hilux as a weapon of the war to the Taliban when he purchased fifteen hundred of them from Dubai and donated them to the cause. I asked about the red kaffiyeh by pointing and asking "Arab?" The mujahid answered in Russian, saying that these were common and not necessarily the mark of an Arab. I felt out of time and out of place. It seemed like Afghanistan or Yemen.

Our driver's name was Sultan. He carried in his utility vest a selection of very large, wicked-looking knives stuffed between curved AK magazines. He had a Chechen-style army beret and a big black beard. He slammed the door and started the engine. He drove slowly and precisely toward the center of Grozny with the lights off. There was just too much evidence as to who I was with. The only sounds were the dull explosions outside. As if to liven things up, Sultan popped a cassette in the tape deck. The haunting sound of the Koranic chanting came through the speakers. The strong, eerie voice rose and fell and interspersed with the deep guttural voices of the fighters communicating on the radio. They signed off with a grim *Allahu Akbar.*

I knew why I recognized the man with the three ornate knifes protruding from his utility vest, knives the fighters used to cut the throats of captured Russians and send the infidels to Islamic hell. Sultan was from Basayev's personal bodyguard. Basayev had a price of one million dollars on his head. Sultan's reaction: The Russians just wanted to insult him by offering only three million. I asked Sultan if he'd had a chance to use his knives on a Russian yet. "Not yet, but Inshallah soon," was his reply.

My worst fear was coming true. I had been simply picked up by the very people the Russians, the media, and everyone else warned me about, with their full beards, cold dead eyes, large knives, red kaffiyehs, white pickup trucks, high-tech radio gear, and cold seriousness. I knew exactly whom I was going to see: the terrorists the Russians were so desperately trying to kill.

It would have been impossible for me to retrace my route from Turpalov's house to the grim center of Grozny, but I tried hard. I recognized a few familiar landmarks by now, the flooded underpass, the tombstone rows of destroyed apartment blocks, and the canyon like buildings backlit by the dull glow of explosions. Both our escorts seemed very serious. I wondered if it was because we were navigating through the middle of a bombard-

ment or because they intended to do something to us. The only hopeful
sign was that nobody had forced us to do anything. Unlike the meeting
with Maskhadov, filled with a modicum of planning and circumstance, this
was very intense and dark.

Finally we ended up in the frightening landscape of sagging and demol-
ished buildings that was downtown Grozny. We left the car and were guided
down curved basement steps below the surface by men who wore large
furry hats and bristled with machine guns.

It was hot and acrid inside the basement behind the steel doors. It
smelled of dirty feet, greasy food, and sweat. The heat was stifling and the
sweat instantly started to seep into my clothes. We were surrounded back
and front by armed men. There wasn't much I could do even if I wanted.

Bunk beds were jammed together in small rooms off the main corridor.
Skinny bearded men stared at us from their tightly packed cots. In the largest
room just off the hallway a generator-powered TV played a Chuck Norris
movie with Chinese subtitles. The fighters were watching war movies during the war. They looked up from their cots and wooden benches, then went
back to watching: Chuck was explaining something to a bad guy.

Most of the fighters spent their time in bunkers. Grozny was full of
bomb shelters and basements like this, partly because of Cold War paranoia,
partly out of function. Some of them were built to withstand nuclear hits
and came complete with massive air-filtration systems and door locks. The
people as well as the fighters had learned to live like rats in basements that
now doubled as homes, kitchens, bedrooms, offices, cold storage for the
government offices, and civilian apartment blocks. They also connected to
each other via sewers, underground tunnels, and corridors. The Chechens
had used these labyrinths to magically disappear and then reappear around
advancing and besieged Russian columns in the last war. For now they
were safe, dark, and dank command centers for the fighters.

We were led into a tiny office lit by a single yellowed bulb. On one wall
was a large green Islamic flag. On the other was the Chechen flag with a
gold background instead of green.

A bearded man with a shaved head sat on a bed that doubled as a chair.
He wore the pants and belt of a fighter but judging by his paperwork it
looked like his work was confined to management. I guessed he was in late

forties by the streaks of gray in his beard. He looked terribly serious and
didn't look us straight in the eye when introducing himself.

"I am intelligence commander Abu Musayev, head of Special Department of the Intelligence Service. I have brought you here tonight to meet
someone."

I felt relieved as I pulled out my small video camera to tape, but something about his name sounded familiar. His display of formality was almost
funny, considering that he had brought the three of us here without a clue.
The meeting was even more bizarre given the tiny size of the room and the
officious manner in which he sat on his bed. The two men who had
brought us crowded into the room and tried to look as formal and inconspicuous as possible.

Shit, now I remembered why I knew the name Abu Musayev. He began:

"I have brought you here because I want to prove not that we are angels
but that the Russians are terrorists." Musayev had a curious habit of turning his head away from me at the end of each sentence, as though he was
not happy to be photographed.

"A group of Russians were caught crossing the border on October 4,
1999. One of those men is here. This man came here to blow up buildings
and create havoc inside Chechnya. He has confessed to this."

Musayev held up a yellowed piece of paper with Russian text on it.

"He handwrote his confession on one and three-quarter pages and
videotaped his confession on the twenty-ninth of November. I will present
Alexi Galkin to you, but you are not allowed to ask him any questions
because we have not yet finished processing him."

I told them that I needed to ask him some questions to verify that this
wasn't a hoax. Musayev was nervous and didn't quite know how to reply.

"Well, you must only ask him certain questions."

I told him that I needed to ask questions that would confirm who he
was and that he had done what he had done. We struck a deal. He sent Sultan and the fighter in the red-checkered kaffiyeh to bring the spy.

Alexi Galkin looked traumatized. He was gaunt, sweaty, tired, hollow
cheeked, and had greasy hair. His hands, which he held together tightly
during the interview, had been burned. The result of torture or just my

imagination? Nonetheless, Alexi looked pretty good for a dead man. When his confession was shown to the Russians at the OSCE conference in Istanbul, the Americans asked whether Alexi's confession was true. The Russians said that he was dead. The Chechens wanted us to prove that Upper Lieutenant Alexi Galkin was very much alive and singing like a bird.

I asked Musayev if Galkin would be killed. Musayev smiled for the first time since our arrival. "You cannot kill a dead man. He has been tried and judged in a sharia court and sentenced to death. But now that the Russians say that he has been killed, we must do everything we can to keep him alive." He smiled at this odd turn of fate for the Russian. Alexi didn't find this funny.

Musayev repeated his preamble in front of Galkin and put a collection of materials on the table in front of me.

"He was arrested with Ivanoff and Bahanov trying to cross into Chechnya from Russia."

Musayev showed me a thick code book printed on cheap paper and a laminated code card with words to use over public phone lines. There was a handwritten notebook with instructions and diagrams for building explosives, some pills "to prevent him from worrying too much," and his military photo ID. I photographed and recorded all of it.

Alexi sat on the edge of the bed like a bird transfixed by a snake. I explained that I was going to ask him questions and that he was free to answer or not answer. I would videotape anything he wished to say and send it to whoever he wanted. I had only a small palm-sized video camera, and the bulb in the room glowed and dimmed as the generator sped up or slowed down, Sedat held a small flashlight to light Galkin. He looked straight ahead into the bright flashlight as he answered my questions, as though it were an optometrist's exam. Despite staring into the bright light, his pupils remained dilated. When I asked him to move forward or backward to make the most of the bare lightbulb, he obliged. I asked my questions through a translator.

"Why are you here?"

"I came to plant mines and blow up refugee columns and put explosives in buildings."

"What do you know about the apartment bombings?"

"I was not directly responsible for the apartment bombings but I had direct knowledge of the planning and execution of the bombings. I was with Ivanoff, the head of the mission, and we were together in Dagestan. During the first apartment bombing."

I asked if he had proof that the FSB planted the bombs and killed their own citizens.

Alexi wanted me to know that he was with the men who carried out the bombings, but that he had nothing to do with planting the bombs. Both were members of the GRU/FSB. He was sent to Chechnya to continue the same kind of sabotage that would be blamed on the Chechens.

Alexi didn't have much to say outside his confession. I asked if he'd been tortured.

"No."

Was he afraid talking to me right now?

"No."

Then why was he nervous and sweating?

I have never been on TV before and I hope I am doing all right.

Oh.

He was taken away. Musayev seemed happy. That made me unhappy. Musayev had stood off to one side as I questioned Alexi, seemingly ready to shut him up or shut me down. Was he concerned that Alexi would blurt out something that would destroy the illusion?

Musayev told me that one explosive called Hexagen was used in the apartment explosions, and that he had information confirming that the Russians had blown up the apartment buildings in Dagestan and Russia. He had the proof, he said, to convince the outside world of their evil intent. I told him I really couldn't believe that the Russians were that evil.

"There is a division in the GRU responsible for the assassination of political enemies," he said. "Putin's direct orders conceived and carried out the bombing. This is Putin's war."

He held his thumb and forefinger up as though to measure something. "You know," he continued, "Putin is a small man. The problem with small men is that the distance between their heart and their asshole is too little."

If what Galkin and Musayev said was true, then the Russian government deliberately killed their own people to start the war in Chechnya, an unthinkable crime. What made this idea less astounding was that I was in a place where Russians were deliberately killing Russian citizens in their own apartments. Instead of loading the bombs on trucks they were dropping them from the sky, and they made no apologies or excuses for it. According to the Russians I was in the company of terrorists, but according to the terrorists the Russians were the terrorists. From this point of view it made perfect sense. I wasn't fearful, but I would have been had I known that everyone here except Sedat, Sarah, and I would be dead within a month.

His job done, our host relaxed and ordered tea and food: pumpkin and flatbread cooked in butter. He showed a Sony shortwave radio he said was given to him by a *Newsweek* photographer, Robert King, who had spent time in his bunker. He wanted me to like him, to show that he was a friend of journalists and outsiders. I asked him what he thought about the position America had taken in this war. Like the other Chechens I'd spoken to, he knew that America didn't care about Chechnya. It cared too much about business with Russia to bother about right and wrong. Normally I got a lecture from people, but it seemed he was past it.

I remembered where I'd seen the name Abu Musayev. He'd been one of the leaders on the daring raid on Budennovsk and was wanted as a terrorist. He was also the man who supposedly gave the orders to kill Fred Cuny and his three companions on April 14, 1995. Others said the orders came directly from then president Dudayev, although Risvan Elbiev and his men pulled the trigger. It was assumed that as head of Chechen counterintelligence, Musayev ordered him liquidated as a spy. Some said that Musayev worked too closely with his Moscow counterparts.

I asked him boldly: "Who killed Fred Cuny?"

He reacted with anger. "Fred Cuny was a good friend of mine and stayed in my house. The Russians hired a man named Adam Deniyev, who is in Moscow. If the Russians are trying to catch terrorists why haven't they arrested Deniyev?"

"Who killed the five Red Cross workers?" I asked.

The Red Cross workers, he explained, were killed by Russian instigators to scare humanitarian groups out of Chechnya. Arbi Bariyev was a name that came up. The deaths of the telecom workers were also instigated by Russia.

"Who is responsible for the kidnapping of journalists?" I asked.

"In the last war there was no kidnapping, so why is there now? The Russians began the process of frightening the foreigners out after the treaty was signed. When we signed we were told, 'Be ready. You have three years before we come again.'"

Musayev went on to blame the phenomenon on high-profile kidnappings, where everyone took a slice of the ransom. He pointed to the Russian policy of selling bodies back to relatives as an example of how low they could go.

He encouraged us to eat more. I told him that every Chechen we met seemed to be concerned about feeding us. He laughed and said it was part of traditional Chechen hospitality to strangers. He wanted to know what we thought of Chechen food. The woman who served us wore a leopard-skin blouse and camouflage pants, and we gave her effusive compliments.

I noticed a windup penguin on his mantel. It was a toy for one of his children. Where was his family?

"They are not here, they are outside." He hadn't seen his wife in four months.

"What will win the war this time?"

"We have no secrets. No big power. Just our belief. How can we lose?"

After our midnight dinner we had to leave for another visit. As usual, our itinerary was not of our own making; it was being orchestrated by someone. Before we left we had our pictures taken with Musayev. He cautioned us with a smile: "Be careful. You just had your picture taken with a terrorist."

The icy-cold air aboveground was refreshing after the close, dank heat of the bunker, but the rocketing was ferocious. We were still traveling through central Grozny but I could no longer get my bearings. We went down into another bunker, this one smaller. The armed men who guarded it greeted our bearded driver with respect. The ceiling was low, and the basement looked like it was freshly plastered with gray cement. It seemed to be the command basement of a large office building. The commander's room was another tiny cell lit by a bright, naked bulb. Again the bed served as a chair, and there was another bed at the end of the desk. Two maps on the wall showed the current Russian military positions with large, sweeping red arrows and the Chechen positions with tiny prickly green lines. I asked if I could take a picture. They laughed to say no. I didn't bother to tell them that from the size of the red arrows and the thin, widely spaced green lines, the situation could be sized up in a second.

This was the headquarters of Aslambek Ismaelov, the man charged with the defense of Grozny. The presence of Chechen fighters in the capital was not strategically neccesary, but Grozny was symbolic. It was where the Russians could be bled to death, if they attacked. So far they hadn't. There was a difference of opinion here. The hardened mujahideen wanted to drift out of the city, leaving it for the Russians to occupy. Then they wanted to sneak back in, strike violently, killing all the complacent Russian troops inside. The government wanted to hold the city to show that they could defend their ground.

In the last war the most potent symbol had been the parliament building nearby. It was pounded into rubble by the Russian air force to show that they had crushed the rebels. The Chechens defended the building until the Russians resorted to lying: They simply claimed victory and announced that the Russian flag was flying over the building, when in fact a Chechen flag still flew above it and the Chechens still controlled the streets. I wondered whether it was worth dying for a patch of ground that could be taken as easily with lies as with the blood of soldiers.

Aslambek Ismaelov was thirty-six years old, a square-jawed, gravel-voiced man who sat stiffly with his hands clasped together and his green forage cap pulled low over his eyes. The hard light of the yellow bulb slashed a black shadow over his eyes. He stared straight ahead at me, awaiting my first question.

"How is this war different than the last?"

"The previous war was about destroying Chechen forces. This war is about taking as much ground as possible."

He looked like a boxer and had a mustache, but unlike Basayev's group, he wore no beard. He used to be in charge of the civil works in Grozny. His answers were curt and painfully polite. The Russian strategy was as plain as the map behind me. In military terms the Chechens had already lost. The red lines covered most of the country to the north and surrounded the city we were in.

"When will the war end?"

He cracked his knuckles and gritted his teeth. "It will be a long hard fight."

"How many casualties so far?"

"In the last three to four days, none. Since the defense began, twenty dead. Since the start of the war, in October, about one hundred." He guessed there were about five hundred Russians dead and reminded me it was the civilians who were dying here, more than five thousand and climbing.

I sensed that he was pressed for time and needed to get to other things. I asked if he had anything to say to the West.

He shrugged impatiently. "I don't think America thinks much about this. It's more typical for them to think about themselves."

The interview was over. He had a war to fight.

Turpalov Ali's driver waited for us outside the bunker in his red Lada. Sulatn, the bearded man, and the white Hilux had vanished like ghosts.

Our driver got stuck under the flooded overpass on the way back. We often passed through two feet of icy water at least two or three times a night, but this time the engine stalled. It wasn't a bad place to stall, since the bridge provided some protection from the rockets and bombs. Unless, of course, the Russians decided to aim for it. The rockets were putting on a show. Normally we were a few hundred meters to a few kilometers from where the rockets landed. When they were distant, there was little difference between the hundreds of detonations. But underneath them, it was easy to measure the progress of each rocket as it landed closer or farther away. It was an immense sound, somehow disconnected from reality. Something that big and deadly couldn't be measured. Each rocket had a *wa-wham* sound. The concussions and the noise combined in the lowest audio sound it is possible to feel—wa-whump, wa-whump, wa-whump, wa-whump, wa-whump, wa-whump, WA-WHUMP, WA-WHUMP, WA-WHUMP, WA-WHUMP! I looked at my watch and timed off sixty seconds. I didn't count each impact, but rather each salvo of Grad missiles. Eighteen rocket barrages the first minute. Fifteen, twenty, eighteen. I made a note to ask my hosts how to differentiate the five-hundred-pounders, the thousand-pounders, and larger bombs. The SCUDs were easy to hear, or rather feel.

I never thought I would be sitting in the nexus of the apocalypse, calmly timing the hammers of hell. Fred Cuny had estimated that the highest level of firing recorded up until that time was in Sarajevo, with thirty five hundred heavy detonations per day. In the last war one of Cuny's colleagues had counted four thousand detonations per hour. The estimates of this war started at six thousand an hour.

There wasn't much fear. Somehow I absorbed the attitudes of my hosts. Inshallah. If Allah willed it, I would die. If he didn't, I would survive. In any case, I was doing exactly what I wanted to in the place I wanted to be. My hosts respected that, and it appeared for now, so did the gods. I thought of Aqil and Joel somewhere out there. Sarah did her job and Sedat was very quiet.

Occasionally a Lada or Gaz would swish through the deep water, slow down to look at us, and continue. Our red car was concealed from spotter planes, but the firestorm of rockets and explosive missiles made every second in the center of Grozny a one-sided Vegas crap game.

Suddenly I discovered that I wasn't being very observant. A man in a white trenchcoat was hanging by his neck thirty feet above me. A sign identified him as a traitor. Later I found out that he was taping microtransmitters to candy wrappers and dropping them outside rebel-occupied bunkers. Allegedly. This was Chechnya. It didn't matter who was right or wrong, or if it was simply a ghost.

There were guests and food back at Turpalov Ali's house. As usual, the fighters rose and greeted one another whenever a fellow fighter entered the room. They kissed and then shussed us back into our seats. This is one of our customs, they explained, it's okay for you to remain seated.

A blond-haired, blue-eyed, round-headed fighter sat beaming at the end of the table without saying a word. He didn't have the thin, dark look of a Chechen. When our host could stand it no longer he asked if there was anything unusual about this guest. "He is a Russian," they said. They all laughed.

He was a former Russian Spetnatz paratrooper who landed in the hills during the last war. He eventually converted to Islam, and the Chechens welcomed him as a fighter. He told his story with some hesitation because he didn't want his family to know that he was now a Muslim and living in Chechnya fighting Russians. His family and the military thought he was dead. He said that when he was a Christian he didn't believe in God, but now that he was a Muslim he knew what he was living for.

How could he shoot fellow Russians?

"I know that the soldiers that are coming here are serving for the bad people," he said. "I shoot them because they are bad."

What did he think about the Russians bombing him?

"I just don't want to die yet," he said, and laughed.

Sarah, Sedat, and I were looking for prisoners to photograph and interview. They had a Russian prisoner in one of the bunkers. The Chechens called him Valet, after the close friend of Muhammad the prophet. I assumed they meant a valet, or a personal servant.

Like a pet monkey or dorm house mascot, he was ordered to sit and talk to us. One of the Chechens had a quiet chat with him and pressed some bread into his hand. He was young, round headed, and blond. He looked a little bewildered and kept his hands together. Like most of the Russian con- scripts, he had the look of a confused farm boy. He was from Irkutz, a draftee from a mechanized division. He ran away from his unit because his officers beat him. He still wore his grubby, poorly made Russian uniform and sat in an uncomfortable position. His right boot cap was held together with black tape and his soiled undershirt was fading. There wasn't much we could ask this low-level Russian prisoner in front of his smirking captors except how to contact his family and tell them he was still alive. He was a conscript, a draftee, occasionally paid the twenty dollars a week he was owed, brutalized by his officers, forced to pay protection, then sent to fight enemies he knew nothing about. At least here in this bunker he was safe.

Once again as if by plan, who should be waiting for us at Turpalov Ali's house when we got back from our bunker visits but Aqil. He was with his commander and was dressed in full fighting regalia. He was even wearing one of the winter hoods brought over on the trucks from Georgia. He'd bought an AK-74 at the market but he'd needed more bullets. He wouldn't tell me how much he paid for it, so I told him what he'd paid. He'd found an old commander who had assigned him to what he called a "kamikaze battalion" of sixteen men holding off five thousand Russians in an industrial area near Khattab. I didn't think there were anything but suicide battalions inside Grozny by now. Although they could see the Russians they wouldn't attack.

His commander asked me formally to make jihad with them, and after seeing what the Russians were doing to the Chechens I was tempted to join. Turpalov explained that their strategy was to keep the Russians out of Grozny. From the look of the maps in the bunkers, they were already here.

The latest news was that the Russians had advanced within two and a half kilometers from where we were staying. They wanted to get us out of the city before it fell. Aqil asked if I wanted any video footage of the bunker where he and Joel the Ptolemaic proselytizer were. He said things seemed quiet, although the entire factory next to them had collapsed after the Russians dropped a two thousand-pound bomb on it. I gave him my video camera to shoot some pictures. He promised to come back tomorrow with the footage.

The war was all around us now. Nighttime was when the rockets and missiles fell. The bombardment was the heaviest it had ever been. I listened to the conversation in the main room and then to the explosions outside. They told me they would wake us if the city fell, but for now we were told not to worry. It's just the Russians calling us. They called the rockets "Russian telephone calls."

They were using Grad rockets. After a week in rebel-held Chechnya, I could identify the different munitions by sound. The five-pound bombs had a flat bubble burst, the thousand-pounders had a violent *wham,* the Grad rocket barrages had angry double *wa-whumps,* artillery shells sounded like screaming freight trains, the SCUDs shook the ground like subsonic thunder. I listened to the explosions move closer and farther away like a confused giant's footsteps, crushing the land with each thunderous step. Eventually I tired and fell asleep.

What woke me up the next morning was the silence. Turpalov Ali said that we had to leave the city immediately. He had been up all night. "You should have left last night," he said, "but your guide said he was tired."

I kicked the perpetually slumbering Ruslan out of his bed and told him to get ready.

The Russians had advanced straight though the Chechen lines to within kilometers of the house. Aqil had promised to come back that morning, but now I had to leave. Turpalov told me that the Russians overran his position during the night in a battle of twenty Chechens against five thousand Russians.

"Is he dead or alive?" I asked.

"Inshallah" was the only answer my host could give me.

I walked through the deserted streets of Grozny as we waited for the Lada to be readied. There were no sounds except for the barking of dogs. Steam rose from my breath just as it did from the urgent animals. Usually the dogs were useful; they barked at approaching Russians. Today they were off in the hazy distance, foraging nervously like apocalyptic commuters, as if they were embarrassed that they hadn't warned us. Up above the crows waited silently in the trees. Is this what it will look like at the end of the world, I wondered? Nervous dogs watched by patient crows?

As I walked back to our house I saw several destroyed homes. Here, aboveground in the sun, I felt immortal. For today at least. Others were not.

Lost in my silent reverie I was surprised by two well-dressed middle-aged Russian women. They headed out to do their morning shopping as though nothing was going on. They stopped and talked to me, not surprised in the least to see a foreigner just hanging around the deserted streets of Grozny. I followed them back to where Ruslan and the crew waited and chatted with them. It was the same story. They lived there, they had no money, so they stayed and waited. For what? They didn't know. Turpalov Ali came outside and pointed at them: Russians. This was not a war against just Chechens. The Russian women were comfortable around the Chechen commander. After all, he was their neighbor. For some reason I gave one of the women a kiss on the cheek. She blushed deeply. Just a small act of warm humanity in this bleak monotone hell.

Turpalov Ali laughed good-naturedly at the woman's embarrassment. He decided he wanted to dance. His men started clapping as he flailed his arms, kicked his feet out, slapped his heels, thrust his arms into the air. It was a happy, defiant, manly dance accompanied by the firing of AKs. Not too many bullets, though. They would be needed.

When he was done Turpolov Ali told me that he recommended that all his men dance every day. He was worried that his people hadn't been dancing as much as they should be.

The cars were rounded up and we headed out. It had taken too long to leave. The Russians were less than two kilometers away now. The Lada started off slowly. Turpalov's driver and our bodyguard talked on the radio a lot. They were looking for Russians, not in the distance but around the corners. They stopped at intersections as though there were invisible stop signs, looked both ways, and started up again slowly. We made it to the outskirts of town. It was time to run the gauntlet.

At times like this, no one knew where the enemy was. The Russians could be in front of us, beside us, behind us, or in the air. There was no place to hide. The best information was that the Russians were one kilometer away on each side of the road, and closing fast in a pincer movement from either side. There was nobody to stop them, and we couldn't hear any gunfire, shelling, or bombing.

We finally reached the beginning of the long straight road to Shali, which was now the last lifeline out of Grozny. We would be safe in Shali, or so we were promised. Other cars full of civilians passed us at high speeds. Nobody seemed to be firing at us, so our driver put his foot to the floor. Our car lurched forward, stalled, then died. We rolled to a silent stop. We had run out of gas just as we entered the unprotected, wide-open fields. Our only salvation was a thin, six-foot concrete wall around a factory that hid us from the advancing Russians. I got out of the car to peer through a blasted gap in the wall. I could hear and see nothing, but like trained hunters, the Chechens were able to point out multiple invisible, silent "Ruskis."

The Russians were out there somewhere. At the spot where we waited for someone to bring us gas, a woman started to set up her tiny kiosk for the day. I walked over to videotape her. She set the chocolate bars, cigarettes, and cookies on the table carefully and neatly. Steam from heating pipes poured out of the ground around us as if we were alone in a dream. I asked her if she knew that the Russians be there soon. She didn't answer.

I realized how stupid my question was. She was Russian. She lived in Russia. She was here. Of course the Russians were here.

There wasn't much to do except wait and watch. Cars full of people and possessions whizzed by at over 120 kilometers an hour. I was a spectator on the racetrack to freedom, for the lucky ones at least. The thick, lazy pillars of black smoke that rose in slow motion above the city provided a dramatic backdrop. Bombed oil tanks took weeks, sometimes months to burn off. When the black smoke rose far enough, the soot cooled and flattened and formed a long black smear. I occasionally heard explosions far away. There were no aircraft in the sky. It was a perfect day for a siege.

Fuel arrived from the house and the fighters laughed at our predicament. It was now nearing 10 A.M. If there was any advantage to getting out early it was gone now. The latest news on the shortwave was that the Russians said they had surrounded Grozny. Now we had to look for Russian "checkposts," as the Chechens called them, Russian troops assembled into clusters about one hundred meters apart. If we ran into one of the checkpoints we would have two choices: hide from them or fight our way through. With only two gunmen, we couldn't fight our way through. Or could we?

Our driver told us not to worry. Last time there were Russians everywhere. He pointed to the Russians to our right and smiled. "Cat and mouse." After gassing up we sped to the exit road. The Russians didn't fire at us, or even notice us. We reached a tortuous, rutted road littered with blown-up vehicles, and finally we saw other traffic. We were out. We stopped to confer. According to the radio, the Russians were everywhere, including the road we were on now. The man on the other end of the radio asked, "Didn't you come across them?"

Lucky or blind—I'll never know. Later, according to the Russian army, the road was sealed at 11 A.M. It was 10:30 when we escaped.

Fuel was sold at the side of the road on the way to Shali. First for four rubles per liter, and then two rubles. People walked on the side of the road, and the kiosks hummed with activity. It was the Friday market and everything looked normal, eight kilometers from the Russian lines. The village was full of people for Friday prayers and the weekly market, but I shouldn't have been fooled. Our bodyguards told me that the village had been bombed four days ago. A helicopter strafed the market and killed a woman, then there were cluster bombs.

Cluster bombs with parachutes descended slowly and quietly. At a predetermined altitude they exploded, sending out smaller bomblets with flechettes, or tiny darts, that sliced through soft flesh. Ten adults and two children died.

Turpalov Ali's men dropped us off at the main square in Shali. We were recognized and welcomed by the fighters. They knew about Grozny already and were glad to see that we had made it out safely. The whole square was rooting for us, and people still approached us to talk. One man wanted us to know that the Russians had used gas bombs in Voykova yesterday, and that his son had lost his eyes. A town leader wanted us to know what was going on. Another wanted us to interview the head of parliament. Another wanted to tell America something. Our protectors needed to get back to Grozny. I thanked them and gave them packs of cigarettes. They said it was nothing, their pleasure. Aqil was still there. Was he alive or dead?

We were sized up by a number of armed men who walked by. At first they wanted us off the street. Mostly they were concerned that we were just milling around with no weapons. A tall, sharp-featured man was pressed into service as our security detail and guide. He was introduced to us as the official government journalist. He had a short AK-47 and wore a tall gray wool hat, camouflage, and a utility vest stuffed with twenty-clip magazines. I asked him what kind of journalism he did. Khampash Terkabyev was twenty-seven and worked for the Presidential Press Office. When there was time he put together a TV show. He showed us his new Panasonic video camera, which he hadn't quite figured out yet. He'd been a few feet away from some good hand-to-hand fighting between Russians and Chechens but a rocket blew up his car and his old camera with it. In the last war he shot four hundred tapes with plenty of good fighting, and used them to put together a show with the snappy title of *My Motherland Is the Place Where the Holy War Is Now.* The show he put together twice a week for this war was called *The Way of the President.* When he smiled I could see he had two gold eyeteeth.

We decided to look for the great Chechen fighter Shamil Basayev. Ruslan wanted to find some relatives. We drove out of town but discovered that their neighborhood no longer existed. It was smashed as if by a bulldozer. For some reason a man told me we that we were the first to film this, as if there was a contest, or that anyone would care. I didn't tell him we were the only outsiders here. We started to drive down the street but the locals warned us off because there were Russian tanks at the end of the road.

We tried another way past the homemade refineries that supplied the fuel. Any available steel container was buried into the ground and heated to boil off the distillate. This became the fuel that was sold at the side of the road. In normal times the Chechens tapped into the pipeline from Baku and processed the fuel.

The people standing around the homemade refinery waved us off. Once again we were told that it would be wise to turn back. Four hundred Russian tanks were advancing down the road. I didn't ask how he knew there were exactly four hundred.

It became obvious from our wanderings that we were being hemmed in slowly by the advancing Russians. We looked for the front lines, but there didn't seem to be any. By that afternoon a large column of black smoke boiled up from a dull orange flame. The Russians had attacked and blown up the refinery we'd just visited.

We got to see the rhythm of life under the hammer. There were no jobs or industry, but the Chechens were busy meeting and carrying on the small niceties of village life. Men sold lime green gas in five gallon jars perched on benches. Tractors dragged entire trees down the main street to be cut up for firewood. People came and went from red brick houses with green gates. Men in black coats and fur hats sat in circles chatting. Some smiled when they saw us. Most had beards or weekend stubble. The women and children pulled wheeled carts with battered silver milk jugs to collect water. Everyone was clean, friendly, and a little shy when they saw us.

No one seemed to notice the explosions. Occasionally they looked up to the sky to locate the jets. They would say "Argun," or "Grozny." Soon people would be saying "Shali."

Khampash couldn't find Basayev or even Khattab so he looked for a place for us to have tea. Our little group of three drew a big crowd every time we got out of the car, he wanted us out of sight for a while. We were invited into some complete strangers' home, and they laid out a feast as though we were invited for Sunday tea. Hospitality is not unique in the world but it took on a special significance for Chechens. When they were rounded up in boxcars and sent to bleak Kazakhstan they had only each other to survive, and that is why no Chechen will refuse a stranger food or shelter. Our hosts immediately brewed tea and brought out large glass jars of jam, along with fresh butter, and bread. They sat and watched us eat, making us try this and try that. We weren't hungry but once again it was humbling.

Their house looked packed away. The carpets were rolled up and they had put plastic across the windows. With Ruslan as translator I asked the woman of the house if she was afraid of the Russians. She was. Would she stay? They had nowhere to go. The man joked, "Maybe we will find out where the Russians came from and we will live there."

An older man came into the house, short of breath. He pushed aside the plastic that separated the heated kitchen from the cold outside, sat down next to me, and asked for a few minutes to rest while he caught his breath. He'd learned that we were journalists and pointed to my camera. He asked if he could say something to the American people. I pointed the camera at him and he began.

He wanted to know why, if we believed in freedom and justice, did we let the Russians kill women and children? If America was strong, it had to help the weak. The Chechens were a small group of people, and they didn't have any help from the outside world. He took his hat off as a sign of respect. "We just want to live in peace without the fear of death. Please help us before we are killed."

He thanked me politely for my time. I didn't know what to say.

Our lunch was interrupted by a tank barrage. The Russians were supposed to be about four kilometers away and moving toward Shali. But they were already here. Khampash said that we had to go. I didn't know what to say or do. Our hosts knew that their house would be looted, their possessions ransacked. I wanted to give them money, something they could use. Khampash smiled and said no. As we got ready to go the man of the house asked us to wait a minute. He went to the back of the house and came back with gifts. He gave each of us a clean handkerchief and thanked us for coming. I unbuckled my flashlight and offered my batteries to him. He was embarrassed but he accepted. We had to go.

◆ ◆ ◆

That night we were supposed to stay at Maskhadov's safe house and meet with Basayev and Khattab, but nothing happened. We slept at midnight but the rockets arched closer and closer, and the ground shook underneath us. The dogs barked furiously at two in the morning; I thought I could hear the sound of motorized columns on the road. But in the morning, nothing. Outside it was eerie. Only the children, women, and old men were out on the streets. The big chore of the day was getting water.

Kittens sat in stripes of sunlight on the brown linoleum floor of the hospital in Shali. The people there stood and waited; there were no chairs, but they didn't slump or lean. They had the dull, exhausted look of people who had used their last reserves and were now just existing. They waited because their relatives had been wounded and needed food. The hospital was full but not as crowded as I'd thought it would be. The building was bombed regularly, so the patients who could be moved were taken home as soon as they were able.

The stench was overpowering. The hospital was full not of fighters but of middle-aged women, most with horrific, oozing shrapnel wounds. It is a fact of war that it is often more effective to wound than to kill. The wounded burden the living and sap the morale to resist. Many of the seriously wounded would spend the rest of their lives requiring care, would be unable to work, and would bear deep physical and emotional scars. The most common wound was from razor-sharp, jagged shrapnel blades. Then there were the injuries from concussion, shock, and collapsed buildings. There were no bullet wounds yet. The real fighting hadn't started.

A doctor took us around and gently lifted each patient's sheet or covering to show the gory details. The smell of putrefaction and body odor escaped with each revelation. The women didn't mind being uncovered; in fact, they wanted us to see how they'd been disfigured. Each of their stories had a familiar theme. Some were at their stalls in the market when they were bombed in October. At least they were alive.

Dogman Alarkhanova was a middle-aged woman. The bones in her legs were held together with construction rebar. She was in her stall when she saw a sparkling flash. The two men in front of her were vaporized. That's all she remembered until she woke up here. I asked the doctor why the Russians bombed the hospitals. "That is where the people are," he said.

We were still looking for Russian prisoners. Someone told us there were sixteen in a village south of Shali. We jumped in the Lada and went to a compound with a large building. It took a while for a fighter to come out to talk to us.

"Where are the prisoners?" I asked.

"We don't keep them. They are too hard to feed. They take too many men to watch them, ten for every hundred. They are too much trouble."

"But what about the sixteen Spetnatz prisoners?"

"Not here."

"But they were just here."

"You are too late. They have all been shot."

We looked at each other. All shot. "Why?"

"We offered them to the Russians in exchange for safe passage for our civilians out of Argun, but they refused. If they don't want them then we surely don't."

Always hospitable, he invited us to tea.

I could see where they'd kept the prisoners from a room that overlooked the compound. They'd fashioned a crude six-inch grid made out of welded rebar to keep them in the back part of a garage.

"Can we still see them?" I asked.

"No, they are dead."

We asked again.

He give us that look. Sedat's warning not to ask Chechens too many questions came to mind. By way of reply, the fighter said, "Yesterday they killed forty civilians trying to leave Goyskoye." The fighter seemed perplexed to find logic in what he was saying. He couldn't believe that the Russians wouldn't let their own people leave the war zone, let alone take back their elite troops.

Argun still needed to be evacuated, so the fighters decided to attack the Russian checkpoint.

"We managed to kill the Russians who set up a checkpoint on the road, but the Russians retook it."

"So why don't you reopen it again?"

"It takes time to kill all the Russians."

On the way out of the compound, Colonel Umar Murtazaev approached to talk to us about the recent fall of Argun. He was husky in his uniform and looked deadly serious.

"I was in Argun. We were fighting to the end but we ran out of ammunition. We were around one hundred Chechens. I thought we were going to die but somehow we didn't. We abandoned the city but the Russians didn't enter for three days. They were too scared."

A lot of fighters told us that the Russians were afraid to enter the urban areas, and that the Russians thought that there were thousands of fighters holding each area. I thought he was telling us this because he wanted to impress upon us the fact that Chechens weren't cowards, and that they didn't abandon their people. They fought until there was nothing else to fight with, and then they left only when it was necessary to regroup and rearm. He said that the idea of having to fight this war again was bothering him.

What could the West do?

"If we could get help from the West, we could hold for ten years. The West says things but they don't do anything. With your help we could put the American flag in Moscow," he said, then added, "right next to the Chechen flag." He reflected on something, then drew in a big breath. "The Russians are a godless, stateless people. They have no nation and no law. They are a mix of peoples with no identity and no faith. We don't fight terrorists, we don't fight criminals, we defend Chechens. We will fight for democracy, for freedom, until it's over. The fighting has taken two months. Even though Argun is empty, they still bomb. There are still civilians inside Argun. It took forty thousand Russians to take Argun from a hundred Chechens. Eighteen Chechen fighters died inside Argun. Hundreds of Russians died [civilians], and their bodies are still there. The Russians threw the bodies in the wells and holes and burned them. In the spring they will find the rest of the Russian bodies."

"What should the world do?" I asked.

"Just do something."

✦   ✦   ✦

In the village of Shali, life seemed to go on as usual. They didn't want us to film the arms market because the Russians were selling weapons to the rebels, though you really couldn't tell it was an arms market by the loose cluster of approximately one hundred leather-jacketed men. Fighters wandered in and out of the leather-clad cluster. Occasionally they demonstrated the weapons with the sporadic fire of bullets into the air. Pigeons flapped from the tops of the buildings with every burst and faithfully returned, only to scatter again. The men had stacks of rubles, a useless currency for large sums. Most prices were quoted in U.S. dollars and then converted to rubles at a premium.

They sold plastic explosive for sixty dollars a kilo by slicing it like bread. A young boy said he would toss in a grenade worth six dollars if we bought a shotgun for sixty-five dollars. A man with a large scar across his face and a large white Chechen sheepskin fright wig hat pulled up with a massive 50-caliber machine gun poking out of the trunk of his car. He saw me taking pictures, waved me off, and then disappeared into the crowd.

There were plenty of other bargains in Chechnya. Snickers bars were five for a dollar, cheaper than in America. An almost new Series 7 BMW of indeterminate origin and ownership could be had for around three thousand dollars. Its front and back bumpers were missing. Not bad for an eighty-thousand-dollar BMW, but you had to enjoy it quickly. Once the Russians came the BMWs would be the first things to be confiscated.

We bumped into the security detail from Turpalov Ali's house just off the square. Our former driver bummed more cigarettes. The handsome young bodyguard who was always dressed in spotless black was there. I recalled how he once stopped to wipe the tiniest speck of mud from the side of his sole back in Grozny. Now he was spattered with mud and had messy hair. He looked tired, but happy to see fellow survivors. They had to walk to Shali when their Lada broke down. They told us that the Russians were using vacuum fuel-air bombs in Grozny. The bombs pumped out a massive amount of aerosolized fuel and then detonated in a massive blast. The vacuum that resulted from the ignition collapsed bunkers, detonated land mines, and pulled people's lungs out of their mouths.

We couldn't go back to the safe house in the hills because the Russians were too close, so we cruised around in Khampash's car looking for Basayev and Khattab. Their people were in town, as evidenced by a mud-splattered Land Cruiser. The only clean spots were the wiper areas and a small hole cleaned off the side window to see out. Perfect camouflage. We checked at Khattab's house but he'd gone back to Grozny to defend Khankala airbase. Basayev had also gone in. There was a muddy road into Grozny over one of the wooded hills that the Russians had been magically or financially induced not to watch.

The talk at the soldiers' center was focused on the continual Russian advance. The rumor was that the Russians would try to take Shali tonight, and I was learning to trust rumors. They'd closed the Bakuristov highway and were bombing the villages in the mountains. I drove around looking for Russian prisoners. Our guide suggested that we go to the front lines in Vendano, an hour and a half away by car and by foot. They were using Russian prisoners to dig trenches.

"And then what?" I asked.

"They are too much effort to keep around. When they are done they will be shot."

I decided to pass. A while later we stopped in the market to buy dinner. A fighter told Khampash that he'd heard a radio report that Vendano was now under heavy bombardment. Our timing would have been perfect; we probably would have showed up just in time for our annihilation.

A black Volga with tinted windows pulled up at the market. It was surrounded by a group of soldiers and people; somebody important, the commander in charge of Shali. His lower lip was shot away, probably in the last war, and a doctor had done a crude job of patching it together. We ignored our guide who warned us off, and we muscled our way into his presence. He was surprised to see outsiders.

"How can we get to the front?"

"Do you want to go to the front?"

"Of course."

"Do you dare?"

He talked with his men. They shrugged and let us pile into his big sedan. It felt good to sit in a plush car after all the tiny hard, cold Ladas. I thought we'd be in for an interesting time until I noticed that the commander wasn't actually coming with us. Instead, he sent two-gray haired fighters to chaperone us. Khampash followed in his car.

We drove east past the market a few yards, turned left, and then stopped on a side street. The fighter in the passenger seat radioed the front line. The only word I recognized in the exchange was "normaal?" But it was phrased as an uncomfortable question rather than as a statement. I reassured myself that they just didn't want to get journalists killed. Or were they worried about their own security? There was a more urgent exchange on the radio.

I heard the question "normaal?" not once but many times. I assumed it meant the same in English. He waited, listening carefully to the radio. Again he asked, "normaal?" This time his question was more urgent, as if saying the word would make it so. There was a response from the other side. The fighter in the passenger seat flicked his head forward with grim resolution.

"Normal?" I asked. They didn't answer. We drove forward. Before I could settle in and relax for what I thought was going to be a long ride to the front lines we turned left, right, and then drove out into an open field. Two minutes after we'd gotten in the car we were on the edge of town next to a yellow field of cut wheat. The sun was setting behind us and threw an intense yellow light across the rural scene. Our driver had a tight-lipped, intense look I'd learned not to like here. He spun the wheel back and forth as we slid sideways through the mud.

I tried to hold on to my sense of direction by using the giant black pillars of smoke and the setting sun as my guides. I was having a hard time believing my estimations. We hadn't traveled more than a kilometer from the town center, and we were just ahead of the advancing Russians. Some peasants were stacking yellow straw into a red horse-drawn hay wagon off in the distance. This didn't seem right. This was a Constable painting, not the front lines. I wondered if this was what had happened to the other journalists when they were kidnapped. Our driver stopped, rolled his window down, and scanned the sky. Gunships? I tried to see through the tinted windows but it was blurry and dark.

The driver listened, scanned the sky for gunships again, and drove faster and faster. As we slithered through the edge of the stubble field I noticed that there was only one other track in the slippery mud. He was really staring at something. He spent more time looking out the cracked window than on the road in front of him.

"Gunship?" I asked. "Russkis? False alarm?" He didn't answer.

We took a sharp left along the edge of the stubble field. A tiny head popped up above the brush on the side of the road. Russians? No, Chechens. The driver slowed down, relieved. A cluster of fighters hid under the cover of a tree as we pulled up. The commander there barked at his men. They crawled out from under the trees and sauntered toward a ditch twenty feet wide and sixty feet long that separated the two fields. I could see why they'd picked this spot to make their stand.

Hills made from the piled up dirt were at either end of the trench. The machine gunners sat on the hills, where they had an excellent field of fire. It was an excellent spot for killing tanks. The steep angle would expose the tanks and slow down the wheeled BMPs, and the trees would give cover to the fighters when things got too hot. Or was this simply another suicide battalion getting ready for their last defense? The only supplies I could see were a black plastic bag with some rolls bought in the market.

The fighters dutifully set up with their guns and looked fierce for the camera. But something was odd. They were here to defend Shali, but they were staring at Shali. As they posed for pictures, someone said "gunship!" They motioned to us to get down into the trench. It wasn't a gunship. It was bigger, deeper, and not in the air. We could hear the metallic clanking and grinding sound of tanks above the low thrum of the massive engines. The commander grabbed his binoculars and stared at the next ridge, one thousand meters away.

The second in command was at the top of the left ridge. He shouted something that was translated as "tanks. Lots of tanks." He indicated that they were coming directly toward us on our left and right.

"How many tanks did he say?" I asked Khampash. I held my fingers up, "One? Two?"

He held up both of his hands.

"Ten?"

He flashed his fingers three times.

I thought he was repeating himself. I asked again, "Ten?"

He shook his head, smiled, and rolled his eyes.

Finally it sank in. Oh fuck. He meant thirty tanks. There were two divisions of Russian tanks approaching from where we had just been. The slow, steady rumble droned on like the low, steady beat in a horror film. I looked at the line of defenders. They had one grenade launcher and two machine guns; the rest had AK-74 rifles. There weren't even any extra ammo boxes. It didn't take a military analyst to guess the outcome.

The last sunlight glowed with a lustrous golden hue as the older fighter came down from the hill with his binoculars. He squeezed his eyes as though he couldn't believe what he'd just seen. The hay wagon was gone. We got ready to go.

The short ride back seemed like the longest ride of the trip. We were driving faster than when we'd arrived, but every foot took us closer to the approaching Russians. Only a small ridge of broken trees separated us from the tanks. When we turned onto the side streets of Shali we started breathing again, as though we'd been underwater too long. We traveled down the main road to the town square, which looked exactly the same as when we left.

Based on my calculations, we were now a good kilometer behind Russian lines. We stopped to buy food. Khampash left me alone in the car with strict orders not to stick my head out. He gave me his short AK to keep me company. Before long, men in long leather coats began peering in the car and walking back and forth aimlessly. I rolled down the window, smiled at one of them, and waved the gun. He smiled and walked away.

We were taken to a safe house only five meters from the front line we'd just left. They used the term *safe house* because kidnapping was still their major concern for us. The night brought a different perspective. Everything around us was more frightening, less sure, less human. The muddy streets and puddles were frozen and slippery. Every light was suspect, every sound a hidden threat. The battle started. The sounds of the machine guns were pathetic against the massive, ear-crushing explosions of the tanks. Then the rockets descended, so close and fast that the detonations of the first and last rockets in the barrage were indistinguishable. We discussed our options. The Chechens said, "Let's eat."

Khampash took out his car battery and connected it to a portable VHS player and a television set. We crowded around the tiny TV and watched tapes shot by fighters in the trenches while we ate dinner. The Russians on the tape repeatedly sent in bombers against the wrong hill, pounded the wrong positions, and lounged on their armored vehicles or in their transport helicopters like sitting ducks.

We had an Iridium satellite phone and I'd promised to call some news organizations if I got into Chechnya. We were so close to the Russians now that the radio operators probably wouldn't send a rocket barrage homed in on our signal. If the Russians captured us they would steal everything we had, confiscate our tapes and films, interrogate us, accuse us of being spies, and then hand us over penniless and stripped to an NGO. The Chechens counseled us to say we'd been kidnapped if the Russians captured us so they'd play us up instead of beating us.

We went outside, found a weak signal, and started to dial the glowing green numbers. Sedat wanted to file first. I thought Sarah should since this was her first war. Sedat got his way.

Sarah was nervous and then angry about filing her stories. She kept writing and rewriting the story and reading it to me. Sedat had been telling her not to call until she got back. Why give away her information to a news agency for pennies? But Sedat continued to borrow the sat phone to file reports. Then it dawned on me that he got paid each time he filed a story, and he wanted a scoop. I told Sarah to call whoever she wanted and tell her story. She tried NPR. The producer there told her that her story would be considered unusable because she was there with a Chechen guide. She asked if they would have preferred that she'd had a Russian guide to get into rebel-held Chechnya. Frustrated, she called more news organizations. They had never heard of Shali. They said they already had people in the region. By region, they meant Russia. She called the CBC, which disheartened her by saying that she could go ahead and file her story, but they might or might not use it. When I came outside she was sitting and sobbing on the porch. She didn't want to call back but I urged her to do so, to think of what she'd seen and imagine if no one knew. She called again, and she was giddy afterward. They liked her report and would run it. AP Moscow told me there was really nobody there, to take my story and could I just fax a report in? Sedat continued to file for CNN Turkey like clockwork.

The battle went on for at least two hours. Jet fighters came and dropped bombs. After a while we couldn't hear small-arms fire, but the Russian tanks and rockets still pounded the fields. I wondered whether the Chechen fighters were dead or if they had escaped. The odds weren't in their favor. I asked Khampash if we should leave now. He said sure, but why not come to the harvest dance first? There was a celebration at the next house. Young women shucked the corn and danced with the men to the sound of hand-claps in the candlelight. There was no electricity or music.

I stood on the porch of the house until midnight and talked to Ibrahim, who was nineteen years old. His mother sat by the stove inside and told me that Ibrahim was her favorite son; her older son Moslem was lazy. Ibrahim was studying the Koran and was intensely fascinated by his new guests. He attached himself to us, and I felt a great connection with him. His world was falling apart, the Russians were coming, and the thing that seemed to concern him most was whether or not we were comfortable. Were we tired? Would we like to sleep? Were we hungry? Please eat some more. Did we need more tea?

We spoke in our respective languages and used sign language to communicate, but he wanted to learn English so he could talk to me. A cruise missile streaked by and landed a few kilometers away. The deep boom shook the ground.

"Argun," said Ibrahim.

Two more missiles came. The time between the sight and sound of the impact was fourteen seconds. "Grozny," I said. Ibrahim nodded. The yellow kerosene lantern flickered with each rocket or bomb blast.

I started to teach Ibrahim English. He delighted in constructing simple sentences from the handful of words he learned. He showed me the damage to his house with just the words *wall, window, door,* and *roof.* A gunship had attacked a tank at his front gate during the last war. But these two wars were one and the same, and when they were over the scars would be identical. I asked Ibrahim through Khampash if he would stay or leave when the Russians arrived. Ibrahim spoke thoughtfully. When he was done, Khampash turned to me and gave his translation.

"If my family needs me I will stay. If they do not I will fight."

I looked at his mother through the window. She cradled her face in her hand as she stared into the fire. Two wars in one lifetime was too much.

◆ ◆ ◆

The Russian tanks were now firing just a few streets behind the house in what may have been a last stand for the fighters on the front line. There had been no return fire for quite a while, and it wouldn't take long for the Russians to figure out that the city had been abandoned. Khampash cheerfully told us that it was normal for a handful of Chechens to take on a few thousand Russians; their favorite expression was, "If we die, we win."

The bombardment was getting uncomfortably erratic. Khampash had assured us that the commanders would radio us if they abandoned Shali. Now rockets were flying over the house. Then there was silence. I had an urgent feeling. We had to leave. Now. As in Grozny, the silence meant that the Russians were entering the city. As usual, Ruslan was busy sleeping. We packed, quickly exchanged gifts, said our goodbyes, and left. Leaving nothing to chance, our hosts had even packed food for us.

There was no one on the streets. No cars, no people, no lights, no sound. Not a good sign. A Gaz jeep came from the opposite direction; that road must be open. We flagged it down but the driver almost passed by in his hurry. He backed up. The conversation with Khampash was frenetic, urgent. He'd tried to escape but he had to turn back because the bombardment on the road was too intense.

We cruised the streets of Shali. The town square was empty. The jeeps were no longer outside the commander's house. The kerosene lanterns that lit the homes were extinguished. Khampash drove slowly toward the southern road, well past where the tanks were yesterday, as we probed nervously for Russians. Khampash stopped, turned the lights off, and listened. There was no sound from the road ahead.

The pitch black night lit up to our right as a fiery object streaked toward the heavens. It stopped at the top of the arc, seemingly fixed in place. Suddenly we were lit up. The light was bright, too bright. Shit . . . Russians. Fifty meters down the road another flare rose, then another, and another, until a long line of illumination flares outlined the Russian front lines. We could see the tanks and soldiers under the ghostly light. Russian infantry advanced at a steady foot pace toward the road.

We discussed our next move. We decided who would get out which door if the rockets began. But these were mostly tanks and APCs with heavy guns, and there would be no time to get out of the car if they decided to shell us. My only hope would be to roll out the back. I hooked my finger on the rear hatch release and wondered how death would come.

Khampash said, "At this point only Allah will decide whether we will live or die."

He put the car in gear and started to move forward. There was no moon and I couldn't see the road. As we picked up speed, the angle of the road took us closer to the front line. We saw the spark of a rocket motor being ignited to our right. I instinctually ducked, but the rockets weren't for us. I could hardly stand it as we got closer and closer to the front line. Why don't they open fire? I asked myself. Why can't they see us? Sedat held his flak jacket against his window. Sarah squeezed my hand.

We were now only one hundred meters from the Russians. More rockets took off, but we were spared again. Then, mercifully, the road turned away from the front lines. We picked up speed. We had to get to the border as quickly as possible before the Russians stormed up the road or sent paratroopers up ahead.

Just past Duba Yurt, the last village overlooking the plains, we had to cross a river where a cruise missile had taken out the bridge. We got out to see if Khampash could climb the steep embankment. He got lost in the riverbed somehow and when we found him, we discovered that the Lada's left front suspension strut was broken, sheared straight through. Khampash's new expression after our miraculous deliverance from the Russians was, "Robert no problem!"

Khampash said we'd have to walk back to the village of Duba Yurt. A friend there would help him fix the car. We were self-sufficient, with food, stove, water, tarp, and sleeping bags, so I suggested walking out, but the others weren't thrilled with the idea of a hike through the mountains in sub-zero temperatures, and we returned to the village on foot. We could see and hear the battle raging around Shali in the clear winter night. Three tanks blazed like dull orange funeral pyres. We could see traffic on the road. Battered Russian-made military vehicles, some with anti-aircraft guns, were heading south at high speed, many empty. It was easy to determine the difference between civilian and military vehicles: The fighters drove fast and recklessly, while the civilians drove slowly. It was obvious that there were no fighters to stop the advance.

We were forced to spend the night in Duba Yurt, a few kilometers from a strategic crossroad that the Russians wanted. We walked up and down the icy roads of the hillside village. It was comforting that all the houses seemed occupied. Khampash's friend lived at the very top of the hill just below a radio tower. He called out for his friend, and soon an old lady came out carrying a lantern. She invited us in. They lit a fire in the square steel stove, prepared beds in the next room, and made food and tea. Once again, the *adat* of hospitality humbled us.

We were bombed the rest of the night, or so I was told; I slept deeply. The next morning I was awakened not by the bombs but by snoring. I dozed as the sunlight streamed through the white curtains, warm and lazy under the heavy quilt.

A big bang finally got me up at 8:30 A.M. The jets were coming over the hill behind us and bombing the small village. From the window I could see the village below me, the Argun River gorge, and Grozny beyond. It was another beautiful day and I had an impulse to go for a walk and explore, but here blue skies meant intense bombing and good hunting for gunships. They told us that there had been forty direct hits in this village of thirty five thousand people, including SCUD missiles.

Sedat was in a foul mood. He kept telling us that things were bad, that we would be captured, probably jailed and tortured. Ruslan was tired of his constant doom-mongering, and went off into the other room to play "Bomb" on my tiny handheld computer. Undeterred, Sedat continued with his dour forecasts. "We must destroy our film and cameras," he said, "we must tell them we've been kidnapped. Then they'll keep us alive, to show that the Chechens are evil." Sarah was nervous but took comfort in Khampash's constant good nature.

I went outside to put my boots on. When I'd taken them off the night before, they were clumps of mud from the hike to the village, but now they were spotless and clean. Our hosts had cleaned all of our muddy boots as a sign of respect. Khampash wanted to interview us for his television show. I didn't know how many people in Chechnya had electricity, let alone a television. But that wasn't the point. It was more important just to do it. We went up the hill behind us to the radio tower.

Life seemed normal up on the hill. Men were gathering wood into a truck, and smoke drifted up from the chimneys in the red brick houses below. The twisting, howling sound of the artillery shells flying overhead were the only evidence of the war. The Russians seemed intent on pulverizing a cement factory a mile or so below us in the valley. The unseen shells just cleared the top of the hill and created white puffs as they hit the concrete walls of the factory. Khampash pointed his camera at us and asked us to describe what we had seen. There wasn't much to add to what the people who lived here already knew. The Russians were killing their own people. The Chechen infrastructure, villages, and people were being slowly and methodically destroyed under the pretext of hunting down terrorists. I had yet to see the Russian side. I knew I was shown the things I was allowed to see. And I felt like the minister of propaganda. But I also knew the truth in what I saw, whether it was executed Russian paratroopers, mutilated children, destroyed farm villages, or captured spies, and the pattern that all these stories created was a picture of intrinsic truth.

The sound of a jet pass interrupted Sarah as she was being interviewed, and a bomb landed a few hundred yards behind us, then another. The Russians were bombing something in the woods. Or were they bombing our little cluster on the hill? It was hard to tell if they were being deliberate or just casual. We went back to the house and waited.

I wanted to be with the people, to soak up their courage. But we were shooed inside the steel gates like chickens because of kidnappers. As soon as Khampash turned his back I went out in the street again.

It was Friday in the village of Duba Yurt, the day of rest, and it felt like a Sunday in America. Men stood around and talked, women went house to house to vist, the children played with homemade toys. The only thing that was out of place was the fact that a Russian jet flew over and dropped bombs about every fifteen minutes, usually two at a time. I was close enough to watch the bombs detach from below the planes as they started their long descent to the ground. Some bombs were close, some distant. This time the observation plane appeared after a bomb run instead of before.

The villagers told me that they'd bombed the graveyard, cars on the road, and even the hills around the village. When I asked to go see the impact zones, they told me that it wasn't safe, so I waited. At the sound of jets, the men looked up and watched the planes. Oddly, the women and children paid no attention unless the plane was right overhead or low. Once the bomb hit, the women went back to their business of laundry, cleaning, and cooking. The kids squealed out loud when they saw the mushroom cloud of gray smoke from the bombs. I was shushed inside a house because a crowd had gathered around me again.

While I was waiting in a small room I heard what sounded like a classical chorale. More of a dirge. I was fascinated. It couldn't be a recording because there was no electricity.

I ventured outside again. Some women motioned to me from across the alley. I went inside a large roofed area where about a hundred men in tall lambskin hats, leather jackets, and leather boots walked slowly in a circle, singing a cappella. Their eerie, rhythmic chant rose up with seemingly random guttural grunts, high-pitched wailing, and sweeping tenor tones. It was a zkhir—ancient Sufi ritual meant to create a trance. Some of the men kept a basso profundo beat. An old man sang in high falsetto. They shuffled and stamped their feet until the hard concrete floor resonated. It was a funeral for an older woman.

The chant went on for a long time, slowing and fading, then speeding up and building in a communal expression of sorrow, of belief, of life and death, uninterrupted by the bombs outside. As one of the crowd I could feel the inner strength of these people radiating outward as they sang to Allah to forgive the sins of the departed. This was why the Chechens endure.

The sun was setting by the time the Lada's suspension rod was repaired. The bombing stopped at around 10 P.M. and we took off down on the main road, where large convoys of civilian and military vehicles were escaping south from Grozny and Shali. The fighters no longer waved and yelled their takbirs; they were intent on getting the heavy weapons and trucks into the mountains before daylight. As we drove around, the town seemed calm until we assessed the effects of the day's bombing. Eerie views of wrathful destruction were illuminated by our weak yellow headlights. There were shattered houses by the road; farther on, an entire village bombed into matchsticks. It occurred to me that during the entire time I'd been inside Chechnya I'd never seen a military target that had been hit. We passed the bombed graveyard and the destroyed car. The road back had been made worse by bombing and heavy missile hits. We slipped and slid in the mud across a makeshift bridge replacing the one destroyed by the cruise missile.

Khampash couldn't find the way to the gorge but made liberal use of his new motto, "Robert no problem." We made our way through slowly despite the wide craters, blown bridges, and rockslides.

A glowing oval of flickering light floated high above us in the sky. It was too big to be a flare, too high to be a bomb blast. I wanted to get out of the car to take a picture. Ruslan said no. From the back of the car, the blue tint on the window made the light appear to change colors, from blue to yellow. I forced my way out of the car to get a better look. Our driver had never seen anything like this before. It took me a while to understand what I was looking at. The mountains were on fire.

The Russians were trying to destroy the last lifeline to the outside world with SCUD missiles, which exploded and burned on impact. As the fire spread southward, the incineration of trees created a jagged, oval ring.

We got back into the car and started driving. There was nothing we could do now. Once again our future was in someone else's hands. We were now twelve kilometers from the border. The winding road had been blown into a narrow, precipitous path. The craters were twenty feet deep in some spots, and the hills above had been hit, sending tons of rock down onto the road. At one point the road narrowed to a mere ridge between two giant craters. Somehow there was just enough space to get by. The air was full of smoke from burning pine trees. As we rounded a bend we could see that two more mountains were on fire. The flames climbed up the steep side of the mountain and seemed to drip down into the valley below. Not content with trying to kill women, children, and even the dead, the Russians were now attacking the mountains.

As the walls of the canyon rose up, the road turned into a thin ribbon of flat dirt cut through the sides of avalanches. Then the car slithered down into the icy river. There was no longer a road, so we had to drive through the river. We felt no concern about land mines now, only the need to get into Georgia before the next missiles struck.

Finally we saw a crudely made road that climbed out of the river. The towering black cliffs blocked the stars on either side and provided us some sense of protection. We had finally reached the camouflage bunker that served as the Chechen border and the door to the outside world.

Commander and former deputy prime minister Turpalov Ali Atigirov was arrested by the Russians in October 2000 and received a prison sentence in April 2001 for his part in the 1996 raid on the border town of Kislyar. He is currently in Lefortovo Prison in Moscow.

Commander Abu Musayev, Sultan, Commander Aslambek Ismaelov, and many others were killed in the retreat from Grozny in February 2000, when they were caught in intense shelling and had to cross a minefield. Basayev lost the lower part of his leg leading the men through the minefields.

Khampash is in Turkey seeking asylum.

Officials found Russian Interior Ministry General Gennady Shpigun's decomposed body in April 2000. They determined that he had escaped from his kidnappers and died from exposure.

On April 12, 2001, Adam Deniyev, the man blamed for the murder of the Red Cross workers and the kidnapping of journalist Andrei Babitsky, was blown up on live television. He was reading the Koran on the roof of his studio in Avtury.

French journalist Bruce Fleutiaux, who was kidnapped on October 1, 1999, and released June 12, 2000, committed suicide in April 2001. He was thirty-three. His wife said he was never the same after his experience inside Chechnya.

Aqil walked out of Grozny one week after it was surrounded. He is now a bounty hunter in Arizona specializing in international and difficult cases.

Joel was last seen on the front lines of Grozny by Aqil, and is presumed dead.

Sarah is a currently a senior editor for *17* magazine.

Sedat Aral never handed over the tapes of the trip. He was offered more money to return. He tried to reenter Chechnya again but the rebels would not take him in.

NTV, the last independent non-state-owned Russian television network, was taken over by state-dominated OAO Gazprom in April 14, 2001.

The Russian government said it had killed 15,500 Chechen rebels since August 1999. They insist that "one hundred peaceful Chechens are killed by rebels every day." The official death toll of Russian soldiers is around two thousand. The Union of Committees of Soldiers modestly estimates 10,500 soldiers and security people had died.

Russian doctors in Vladikavkaz, eighty miles south of Grozny, have estimated that they have performed more than ten thousand operations on Russian soldiers. They also believed that the Chechen rebel estimates were correct; Fifteen thousand Russian soldiers had been killed and sixty thousand wounded.

Vladimir Putin is still prime minister of Russia.

Fighting continues in Chechnya with an average of five to ten Russian soldiers dying every day. According to the Danish Refugee Council, the population of Chechnya now stands at 793,437 people. Of that total, half are displaced from their homes; 70 percent of the displaced are women and children. The Russians estimate that five thousand civilians have been killed. The Chechens estimate three times that number died. Nobody will ever know how many people have died except those who were there.

AND HEAVEN

And Heaven

AND HEAVEN

AND HEAVEN

We all have an idea of heaven. To some it filled with angels and light; to others it is a place of well-being or a land of eternal peace. Perhaps to others it is a tropical paradise. One of the longest-running wars on earth is taking place in a paradise, or more specifically Me'ekamui—the "holy land" in Nasi Oi, the dialect of Bougainville. Bougainville is a tiny island in the Bismarck Archipelago in the South Pacific, southeast of Papua New Guinea and north of the Solomon Islands. It is a mere ten thousand square kilometers and has a population of 160,000. The island of Bougainville is about as close to the idea of paradise as you can come without inventing one. It has steep mountains, massive boulders, a smoking volcano, crystal-clear cascades that stream down steep moss-covered slopes, coral reefs, sheltered bays, and a race of shy people who speak softly.

But Bougainville is no longer heaven. The island was cordoned off, the people had been moved into concentration camps, and a group of ragtag rebels are fighting government troops for independence from Papua New Guinea and the control of a massive open pit copper mine. Although casualties from the fighting were low, it was estimated that up to 20,000 residents might have died from starvation and sickness. A number of peace talks were held, but a core component of the Bougainville Revolutionary Army was holding out in the misty, isolated interior of the island. How did an idyllic South Pacific island that had enough wealth to provide a third of Papua New Guinea's income fall into such a condition? How did the peaceful islanders turn into bands of armed rebels and manage to survive a decade of constant onslaughts by a military with superior training and materiel?

In 1998 I decided to find Francis Ona, the leader of the rebels on Bougainville. Ona was a mine surveyor and truck driver turned revolutionary, a leader of the Bougainville Revolutionary Army (BRA), and president of the Bougainville Interim Government (BIG). He had survived a decade of battle with the Papua New Guinea government.

I say "find" because not many people had met Ona. He hadn't been seen for more than a year and it seemed that he didn't want to meet any outsiders. The word was that he wasn't happy with the portrayals he'd received from the handful of journalists who had braved gunships and open-water crossings in small boats. But Francis wasn't getting much information from the outside world because the government of Papua New Guinea had placed an embargo on Bougainville for eight years, and he'd been a little paranoid about outsiders for a while now, especially since the government had supposedly tried to ambush and kill him after he'd returned from peace talks the year before. After that, they hired a band of mercenaries to take control of the Panguna mine and to "cut off the head" of the rebel leadership.

Francis and I had an interesting nonrelationship. A sympathetic group had given me Ona's fax number. We'd never met, but I'd sent faxes for five months. Most of the faxes never transmitted, but occasionally my polite request would slide through. I never received a response. Later I would find out that Francis had a nice fax machine that kept running out of paper or wearing down the car battery that powered it. Nevertheless, he really didn't care too much about outside opinion or meeting with journalists. But that wasn't why Francis didn't want to meet with me. I would find out later that Francis and his people were convinced I was a white mercenary sent to kill him . . . not the best way to kick off a friendship.

I originally wanted to meet Francis because he was an ordinary man thrust into an extraordinary circumstances. He and his people shut down the Panguna mine on Bougainville, which provided about 45 percent of Papua New Guinea's revenue. It was just one of several planned mines that were set to rip into the pristine environment of Bougainville. The story of a small group of black-skinned natives who had held off not only the forces of Papua New Guinea but also a mercenary army had a nice PC ring to it. Furthermore, the press wasn't covering the story because nobody could figure out how to get in. Or maybe it really didn't matter what happened on a tiny flyspeck island in the South Pacific.

The historical information and photographs I was able to gather indicated that the two hundred kilometer-long island of Bougainville was lush, dramatic, and unique. It rose from coral reefs to gentle hills and had seven dramatic volcanoes at its center. Bagana, the largest at 5,740 feet, was still active and had erupted twenty-two times since 1842. Bougainville's stark topography was dotted with caves and waterfalls to the south. Villagers could sustain themselves just about anywhere on the island, and they viewed any damage to this tropical paradise as sacrilege. Here the land was all-important, all-giving, and irreplaceable, and it contained deep rumblings of discontent.

The first Westerner to see the island was Captain Alvara de Mendana, a Spanish explorer who sailed through the Solomons in 1568 and returned in 1594 to look for gold. He became ill and died on the island. The inhabitants of Bougainville saw the next outsiders in July 1768, when Louis Antoine de Bougainville sighted the island from his ship *La Boudese*. The islanders came in their boats to greet him. Then they tried to attack him. The next European contact came in 1792, when another French ship attempted to trade goods for fresh foodstuffs and the peculiar wooden head-bashing clubs the islanders made. Although Bougainville never actually landed there and France never claimed it, the island was named for him.

As a result of arbitrary European colonial diplomacy, the island was determined to be within Germany's possessions in 1866, and the German New Guinea Company took charge. A subsequent agreement between Germany and England in 1899 separated Bougainville from its ethnic and geographic neighbor, the northern Solomon Islands. The Solomons were to be ruled by Britain while Bougainville remained under German control. During this time Bougainville's value to Europeans was its cheap labor—so cheap, in fact, that it was free. Queensland and Fiji needed workers for the sugarcane plantations, so a practice called "blackbirding" flourished throughout the South Pacific. Enterprising men like Dr. James Murray would sail to Bougainville and invite locals on board his ships to visit or to trade goods. Once on board, he would kidnap them.

The first people to take the island by force were the Australians, who

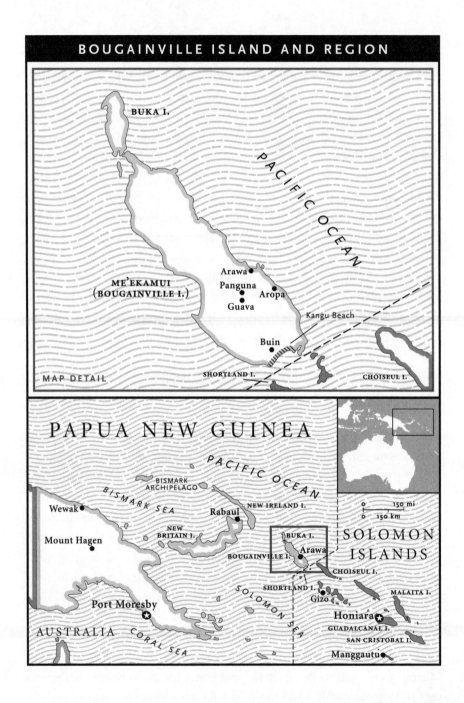

BOUGAINVILLE ISLAND AND REGION

landed in the ersatz German territory in 1914, and again after the Great War. The island was then put under Australian administration by the League of Nations as part of New Guinea. Bougainville was taken by force again in 1942 by the island-hopping Japanese as part of their Greater Southeast Asia Co-Prosperity Sphere. Bougainville and Guadalcanal nearby were battlegrounds during World War II. As after World War I, the island was put under Australian administration, this time by the United Nations.

Australians considered Bougainville to be a remote tropical island until copper was discovered on Nasi Oi territory in the early 1960s. Australian-based companies began prospecting in 1963. The Panguna mine forever changed the lives of the Bougainvilleans who lived around the small village of Arawa and above in the mountains. Oddly enough, the Bagana volcano erupted on May 30, 1960. It's easy to understand how the people here could be superstitious.

Conzinc Riotinto of Australia moved in to secure mineral rights and build the mine. CRA was a division of Rio Tinto, an ancient and massive mining company based in Australia. Bougainville Copper Limited (BCL), a Papua New Guinea company listed on the Australian Stock Exchange, was to run the mine.

BCL carved a modern city out of the pristine jungle. More than ten thousand outsiders descended on Arawa to build the mine. It took almost a decade to complete the infrastructure, including a port and housing in Arawa. At the time the local people felt they'd had a windfall. They enjoyed the modern conveniences and company housing, and the influx of outsiders at first intrigued them—though it would soon come to concern them.

BCL tore down or relocated entire villages, built roads, and installed an electrical system. They promised to take care of the people in exchange for letting them build their mine. Bougainvilleans knew the value of land handed down through matrilineal ownership from mother to eldest daughter, but they didn't grasp the difference between the surface of the land and the value of the mineral rights that lay below. Many of the Nasi Oi tribespeople did not know how to negotiate for their rights or even understand compensation. The Australians also planted seeds of dissent by registering the men as the landowners instead of the women. Many couldn't read or sign their names. When men were employed and became wage earners it began to destroy the matriarchal Nasi Oi culture.

The value of the land was based on simple factors like loss of growing space and the need to reestablish a homestead. The payments averaged around $600 and ranged from $103 to as much as $60,000 per year. In the new economy, those who worked in the mine became well off, earning good salaries, living in company-built houses. Those who didn't work for the mine, however, instantly became marginalized. Once this discrepancy became clear, a chorus of dissent rose from the people.

The mine began production on April 1, 1972, exactly eight years after the first geologist from CRA had landed on Bougainville. Four thousand people worked around the clock producing 130,000 tons of rock to be smelted into copper for sale to Japan, West Germany, and Spain. It was to be one of the world's largest open-pit mines. In its final state, the mine was six kilometers wide, four kilometers long, and half a kilometer deep. If the Empire State Building were put inside, only the antenna would be visible above the rim. To cross the mine at its widest point would require two Golden Gate Bridges. In April 1972, the Bagana volcano sent up continuous plumes of gas-charged ash that was visible from space. Something had awoken.

At its peak, the mine provided 44 percent of the export income of the government of Papua New Guinea and 17 percent of the government's internal revenue. The government was also a 19 percent shareowner in the joint venture. Bougainville's people were the most educated and sophisticated of all the islanders. The roads were paved, money flowed; it was the last place anyone would expect a war to break out. But the undercurrent of resentment toward the mine threatened to boil to the surface. Although the mine produced three hundred million dollars a year for Port Moresby, only about four million dollars made it back to Bougainville.

Many Bougainvilleans felt they had not been consulted on—or even told—what was about to happen. Of the four thousand workers, only a third were from Bougainville. The "rusties," as Bougainvilleans described the lighter-skinned mainlanders, had little in common with the natives. A lot of money was being made by the two hundred or so businesses that sprang up, but only half of the shopkeepers and support personnel were locals. The extraordinary wealth generated by the mine passed the

Bouganvilleans by because they lacked first-world skills and investment capital. At the same time, new arrivals from Port Moresby—a thousand kilometers away—were visibly enriched.

But the Bougainvilleans also became concerned by the scope of the operation and the destruction it wreaked on the island. The mine turned a green mountain full of animals and plants into a hot naked scar on the landscape. Entire rivers changed course and turned green because of the tailings. The exposed ore oxidized and created an acidic leach that turned the fresh water into a vinegarlike poison. The ocean turned brown and sterile from the poisonous runoff. It is estimated that the mine dumped a billion tons of waste and that the tailings covered an area of 480 square kilometers. As the destruction of their pristine island became evident, many Nasi Oi felt that they would lose their entire world.

Bougainville had changed from a peaceful, interlocked tribal society that lived off the land to an angry industrial wasteland populated by outsiders. As BCL identified other mine sites it became obvious that Bougainvilleans would lose their country as it was dug up from underneath them and shipped overseas. While the locals watched their island being dynamited, crushed, and washed away, they looked for a way to voice their grievances.

As happens on many faraway islands circled on maps, the Bougainvilleans were never asked their opinion about foreign control of their destiny. But they always reminded foreign guests that the island belonged to them and nobody else. In 1968 the Bougainvilleans demanded secession, but the government of Papua New Guinea simply ignored them. Two weeks before Papua New Guinea became independent from Australia on December 16, 1975, Bougainville again declared that it was autonomous and that it had an ethnic affiliation with the Solomon Islands. That year, Papua New Guinea installed a two-year provisional government.

The revolution in Bougainville was always there. The link between the people and the land was unbreakable until outsiders literally began carting their island away. The man who was to lead the revolution was neither a firebrand nor an ideologist.

Francis Ona was born in the village of Guava, in Panguna Valley in 1951. The site of the village provided a spectacular view of the ocean below. Its remoteness didn't stop him from attending the Deomori Catholic school. The Marists, or Catholic Society of Mary, had established a mission in Taboroi. The goals of the American-based mission were to bring civilization, education, and Catholicism to the clans and tribes of Bougainville.

After leaving Rigo High School, Francis Ona began working at the mine in 1976 at the age of twenty-three as a surveyor. His family had received few benefits from the mine. His uncle was a landowner and received a small payment. Later on he began driving one of the massive dump trucks that traveled in endless chains from the bottom of the mine to conveyor belt. During this time he began to realize the final scale not only of the Panguna mine, but also of other mines planned for the island. He worked at night on a cleaning crew in order to photocopy documents and learn more about the actual income and scale of the operation. He also began to calculate just how little the original owners were being paid in comparison to the money sent to Port Moresby.

Like most Bougainvilleans, Ona had never really accepted foreigners in his land. The locals had responded to outside plantation owners by simply boycotting the foreign-owned plantations and starting their own. They viewed their colonial protectors with some cynicism. They had seen Germans, Japanese, Australians, Americans, and New Guineans come and go. Each made claims and demands on their land and people. These were met with simple requests to train and finance Bougainvilleans to do it themselves. After all, it was their land, wasn't it?

The questions of independence, secession, and ownership had never been resolved to the Bougainvilleans' satisfaction, since they had never been conquered, they had never agreed to be ruled, and they had never accepted various foreign claims to their small island. Their only allegiances were to their families, their chiefs, their villages, and their wontoks—a complex system of relatives through many layers of marriage.

The revolution began in August 1987 in the form of a small group of Nasi Oi villagers led by Francis Ona and his female first cousin, Perpetua Serero. As the new leaders of the Panguna Landowners' Association, they formulated the idea that both the younger and older generations had claims to the proceeds from the mine. When they didn't get satisfaction from the contract landholders, Ona, who was still an employee of BCL, simply demanded ten billion kina from the mining company. In addition, his group made demands for half the corporate profits, local ownership within five years, and strict controls on the mine's environmental activities. They wanted compensation for the environmental damage to their land. It appeared that the Marists had educated Francis too well.

A group of Bougainvilleans created a militia in 1988. They, too, began protesting the actions of the massive copper mine that had displaced twenty-four thousand villagers and wreaked havoc on the pristine environment. One of Francis's jobs was to survey the site of the seven-kilometer long drainage tunnel that would keep the mine dry. It was suspected that the mine would be much larger than originally presented to the landowners. In 1988 Francis began to network with other Bougainvilleans and share his information. The people soon realized that the ultimate damage was much greater than just the actual hole. The water, the land, and the tailings would poison huge sections of the land and oceans.

Sam Kauona Sirivi remembered the last meeting between the Landowners' Association and the BCL mine. A New Zealand company gave a presentation that showed the damage that the mine was doing to the land, but their final conclusion was that the mine was not to blame. Francis was furious. He called the government, the mine, and the provincial government liars, and said that he was going to take it up personally as a revolt. He began recruiting young men to join the fight the next day. Shortly thereafter, dynamite was stolen from the mine's storage areas. Ona quit his job at BCL in November 1988, and using his intimate knowledge of the operations, he and a group of others began to sabotage the mine. They used the dynamite to topple the supports for the vital power lines that fed electricity to the mine. The minor acts of sabotage turned into a full-fledged conflict when the government sent in troops.

Sam Kauona was trained as an officer in the PNG army in Portsea, Australia, and had graduated as a platoon commander and instructor. In January 1989, he was asked to prepare munitions to be used against the Bougainvilleans. When he spent a weekend in Bougainville to see his fiancée, who lived there, he attended a meeting of Bougainvilleans who had gathered to oppose the PNG's heavy-handed tactics on the island. Kauona's commanding officer told him that people had seen him at the meeting and that he would be court martialed when he returned. Kauono chose to stay and train the rebels, and joined Francis in March 1989.

At a meeting in July of 1989 in the village of Orami, the fighters of South and Central Bougainville chose to name themselves the Bougainville Revolutionary Army. Francis Ona became the commander in chief. Sam used his military background to quickly change the BRA's tactics. Formerly, the youths fought with rocks, slingshots, and even bows and arrows made from conveyor belt rubber stripped from the mine. Sam taught them how to use explosives, how to ambush, and how to operate the M-16s that they captured. The rebels had no outside support, and were housed and fed by the villagers. The PNG military controlled the towns while the rebels controlled the bush. Most of the fighting took place around the Panguna mine and village.

Ona didn't follow a specific ideology in his revolution, but he had progressed from demanding compensation to sabotaging BCL to sending outsiders home. During 1989 the BRA continued to damage the power pylons and attack workers. The government brought in more riot police to suppress the locals, but the mine was finally closed in May 1989 due to the security problems. Now Francis and his small band of unemployed youths had escalated a tiny rebellion into an islandwide cause. A month later the prime minister of Papua New Guinea declared a state of emergency on Bougainville. The government of PNG was now faced with a drastic loss in revenues from the closed mine.

The government went from house to house in an effort to eradicate the rebels. If no male was in the house, it would be burned and the family moved to a concentration camp for their protection. It is estimated that sixteen hundred houses were destroyed this way. In July 1989 the Australian government supplied four Iroquois helicopters to transport police with strict prohibitions against combat use. These were converted into gunships by the government of Papua New Guinea however, and on St. Valentine's Day, 1990, the Papua New Guinea Defense Force used them in a massacre. During the raid, five people were dropped from the helicopter. The island was ready to explode. By March 1990 all Australian citizens and mine employees were evacuated. The government forces were defeated in a number of skirmishes, and then the PNGDF was pulled out.

Francis had simply shown the people documents that convinced them that the mine was not telling them the truth. The government insisted the BRA was a group of "rascals" who had broken out of jail and formed a sham rebel army to give themselves respectability. Somehow Francis Ona had liberated Bougainville for Bougainvilleans. Ona said that Bougainville should no longer be named after a foreigner, and declared independence for Me'ekamui, which means the holy land in Nasi Oi. But now that they had won the battle, they were about to lose the war.

No longer under direct threat from the PNGDF, splits began to form in the BRA. Sam Kauona, the military commander of the BRA, created the civilian administration called the Bougainville Interim Government. Ona was the president and Joseph Kabui became vice president. But the BIG had little synchronization with the more militant BRA under Ona. His attempt to set up a traditional council of chiefs was doomed by the lack of unity.

In March 1990, Sam Kauona signed a peace treaty with the commander of the PNG Defence Forces on the HMS *Endeavour*. The idea was to provide peace, but also to divide the rebel forces and conquer them. Conditions on the island were chaotic. The PNG forces armed Bougainvilleans in order to hunt down the rebels. The Bougainvilleans trusted the outsiders, but the PNGDF used the time to gather intelligence and try to assassinate Francis and other leaders.

The government of Papua New Guinea then placed an embargo on the island; even medicine was forbidden. The result was that Bougainville went from being the most affluent and progressive part of Papua New Guinea to the least. For seven years the Bougainvilleans lived off the land, using native medicines and fueling diesel trucks with coconut oil that they had distilled. The ingenious natives even pulled generators out of the mine equipment and generated electricity from mountain streams. Still, even these measures couldn't compensate for the effects of limited medical care and poor diets.

In September 1990 factions within the BRA allowed the PNGDF to come in to the city Buka to restore order. The PNG government took advantage of the splits and created the Resistance Forces to counter the part of the BRA that was led by Ona and his partner, Kabui. In April 1991

Papua New Guinea's new government directed the PNGDF to invade Bougainville in an effort to eliminate the rebel factions once again.

The island descended into anarchy. Many fled to or were forced into "resettlement centers." By the middle of 1994, a third of the 150,000 islanders lived under terrible conditions in concentration camps. The people were resolute in the areas around the mine and in the city of Arawa, but many islanders not affected by the mine saw no reason to resist.

A cease-fire was declared in September 1994 but the embargo remained. When the rebels boycotted the Arawa peace talks in October of that year, the PNG government arranged for Theodore Miriung to represent the rebels. A series of peace talks resulted in the formation of the Bougainville Transitional Government (BTG). It signaled a wider schism between the hard-core rebels and some of the more pliant Bougainville chiefs.

In January 1996 rebel spokesperson Martin Miriori's house was burned down. The single most important military action was the repulse of PNGDF forces in July 1996 by the BRA, when Operation High Speed II forced out a large group of PNGDF troops. In September a dozen PNGDF troops were killed on Kangu Beach. When the bodies were discovered they had been mutilated. A month later, BTG leader Theodore Miriung was assassinated. There was little chance of a peaceful or military solution.

By 1997 the government of Papua New Guinea had run out of options. Prime Minister Julius Chan decided to hire a team of mercenaries, and turned to Sandline International. Tim Spicer was charged with leading the assault on the rebels on Bougainville. When Spicer showed up for a meeting with Brigadier General Singirok, he was arrested. Executive Outcomes' men were sent home and Spicer was kept behind to face charges. When he was finally released it appeared that the only solution was political. In October 1997 an Australian-led Truce Monitoring Group was sent to the island to maintain the peace and to facilitate a number of reconstruction programs. Francis Ona then said he would shoot any white man who set foot on is island.

To get to Bougainville I had to enter illegally from the Solomons by way of Sydney. I love Australia, a land of ugly cars and beautiful women. I lived there briefly in the mid–1970s, in the slums of Newton. These days Australia is hip in a funky sort of way; it has the charm of 1920s England mixed with the glitz of Southern California.

In Australia I met with a small group of human rights people who worked diligently to keep the events in Bougainville in the public eye. When I arrived in Sydney, Rosemarie Gillespie called. Rosemarie was a fifty-something lawyer who handled a lot of immigration cases, a flower power gal who harbored a little anger for governments and a lot of sympathy for the voiceless people of color. She'd supported Francis Ona from day one. She saw the fight not only in terms of human rights but also as a mirror of the events in Australia's past—the complete destruction of cultures and landscapes in the name of colonial progress.

I'd been calling her for three months, trying to get a straight answer on whether Francis and his rebel group, the Bougainville Revolutionary Army, had green-lighted my trip. But after dozens of lengthy, rambling conversations the truth was slowly sinking in. I had a suspicion that her contacts in the Solomons hadn't been passing her messages on to Francis. There had been shifts and splits inside Bougainville; as an outsider, it appeared, she was no longer part of the struggle. A white woman who spoke her mind could be a liability in the backroom deal making that forged the promise of a cease-fire on Bougainville. There was talk of peace on Bougainville, but not from Francis. His second in command and an outside group based in the Netherlands were working with the New Zealand and Australian governments to create a quasi-legitimate peace treaty that would allow unarmed Australian troops to land on Bougainville to maintain the peace. It didn't have the backing of all the chiefs on Bougainville, however.

Rosemarie and I discussed the ever-shifting politics of the conflict. Instead of flatly winning independence, the moderate group had negotiated a bland framework for reconciliation. The UN wasn't involved, and there were no concessions or even a discussion of reparations. The PNG government had simply lifted the embargo and Australia sent in observers.

Ona was deeply suspicious, as he should have been. A number of attempts had been made to kill him. It had been the stated goal of the former PNG government and the mercenary groups they hired to "cut off the

head" of the rebel movement, either virtually or actually. After the first
peace talks, Francis and the BRA leaders were attacked by Hueys armed
with guns on their way home. Things had been very quiet lately and no
one had talked to Francis in a long time. I asked Rosemarie if Francis was
still alive. No one seemed to know.

We discussed some odd connections. One of the contributors to *The
World's Most Dangerous Places* was asked by Executive Outcomes to pose as
a journalist and bring in a backpack as a gift. The backpack would have a
radio transmitter that would be used to guide the mercenaries directly to
Francis. The contributor refused. After the last round of peace talks the
leaders of BRA were given gifts as a token of the government's sincerity.
The gifts? A backpack for each leader.

Rosemarie was intrigued that I seemed to know about the skulldug-
gery going on and wanted me to meet Francis to confirm that the mercenaries were planting bugging devices in his backpacks. I explained that
although I was somewhat sympathetic to the rebels' cause, I couldn't be
supportive. I was just an interested person who wanted to see what was
going on in Bougainville firsthand, and had brought along an ABC film
crew. We'd simply document what we found.

This reminded her of my traveling companions. Rosemarie was very
concerned that I was bringing a friend named Rob Krott, a nice Catholic
boy who had served in the U.S. Army as a Green Beret and had done some
military and journalistic adventuring between tours of duty in Korea, the
Balkans, and Somalia. I thought that Krott's background as a Green Beret
would provide some insight into the tactics that had allowed this small
band of natives to defend itself against well-equipped troops with helicopter support and communications.

Rosemarie was quick to brand him a mercenary. Wasn't Krott a German name? Was he really a South African? She continued to ask question
after question about Rob. Finally I said that even if we were dyed-in-the-
wool mercenaries, the BRA could probably deal with a couple of white
guys and a two-man film crew wandering around the jungle.

But she continued to pester me on the subject, and would eventually
tell Jay Anania—the ABC producer—that he had a duty to tell everyone
that I was bringing a mercenary to Bougainville. So much for peace, love,

and understanding. I encouraged her to talk directly with Rob, but she had made up her mind.

On my last day in civilization, Rosemarie called to tell me that Ruben Sierra of the Bougainville Interim Government, Ona's group, didn't want us in Bougainville. Come back in a couple of months, he said. I asked if she'd spoken to Francis. She said no. I told her pointedly that if the BRA had been fighting for independence and recognition for eight years but now they wanted to prevent me from hearing what the people had to say, then that would be the story I told.

Rob Krott and I flew from Sydney to Brisbane to catch an overnight connecting flight to Honiara, the capital of the Solomon Islands. The flight was light with returning shoppers and a sprinkling of tourists and expats. You could tell the expats by their gaunt looks and faded clothes. Going native wasn't pretty here.

Every visitor's first introduction to the Solomons is the Central Africa–style airport and bone-jarring potholes on the way to town. The people of the Solomons are ethnically related to the Bougainvilleans. We pushed through a sea of black faces and dilapidated cars to find a taxi into town. Honiara was cool at night, and there was no moon. It felt like we were in a third-world African war zone even though we weren't in the third world, Africa, or a war zone.

The next morning Rob and I met the TV crew in the lobby of our hotel. They'd been hired by ABC News in New York to document the trip. Jay Anania was a forty-something filmmaker from New York, and Bob Woodruff was a lawyer turned ABC News correspondent who bore an uncomfortable resemblance to actor Tom Cruise. They'd just come from doing a story about the vine jumping on Vanuatu. I barely had a chance to sit down and say hello before Woodruff started asking me questions about the "real" purpose of my trip in full view of the hotel staff and passersby. He was acting on Rosemarie Gillespie's tip. I answered him politely, but there's nothing quite like being asked such questions by a complete stranger. His style was pure *60 Minutes,* but he'd forgotten that investigative journalists usually don't play their hand before you've even had a chance to shake hands.

But I forgave Bob. He was just doing his job, and hopefully he wouldn't interfere with me doing mine. Still in the lobby, he asked me how we were going to sneak into the Solomons. This was TV to him, not real life.

When day broke, it was dull and raining. We looked like an aging college football team as we strolled down the muddy streets of Honiara, the largest city on the island of Guadalcanal. Most of the locals we met seemed to accept our ridiculous cover story of being four white men sent to do a piece on the beauty of the Solomons. Eventually we would be branded as four bad men who had come to do no good.

Our timing was poor. The local newspaper reported that a large shipment of weapons had arrived at Honiara from America that morning. It was destined for the Shortlands, a small island next to Bougainville. The article was filled with suspicion, not because the arms would presumably be funneled to the BRA by the sympathetic border patrol, but because somebody had diverted a lot of money on the deal. Although the government of the Solomons had reportedly paid $3.5 million, the paper said the invoice for the aircraft, machine guns, and ammunition was for only $800,000. Oops. It looked like somebody had pocketed the difference.

Honiara was pure third world. People walked slowly or sat and watched the passersby. Chinese merchants sat in the back of their unlit shops with grim expressions on their faces. Scabby dogs ran through traffic; the most popular car was a double-cab Toyota pickup truck. The locals got around on the beds of trucks. Nothing was quite shiny or straight.

We visited a faded, dusty museum and learned about the history of the Solomons. Headhunting was big. A number of weapons were labeled USED TO KILL HUMANS. The shop sold nice re-creations that suited tourist budgets or luggage rather than historical accuracy. Only tourists carried head-bashing clubs these days.

At dinner, within earshot of curious expats, Woodruff started asking Rob where he had worked as a mercenary; he wanted to get this over with because he had to get back to cut another piece. The trip could have ended sooner than he thought. And it promised be a lot of fun, if we didn't end up in jail first.

The next day I made a number of phone calls to set up contacts, but no one was home. Instead of waiting around, I decided to see Father Norman Arkwright, whom Rosemarie had recommended I speak with. He understood the Bougainvilleans because he ran a small camp for refugees who had come here to escape the fighting. We drove up a muddy overgrown track to his house, where he was in a meeting. He came out to talk to us. He was a polite, wiry, and graying man who listened intently and said little, and although he'd been in the Solomons for thirty-four years, he looked as though he'd left England just yesterday. He wasn't thrilled to have us interrupt his day. The gist of his message was that if we had three months or so to spend waiting, we might get to where we wanted to go. A truce had been declared on October 11, and the cease-fire was scheduled to go into effect on April 30. The PNG government had also lifted the "dead or alive" bounty on Francis Ona, but we didn't know if anyone had told Francis this.

A dark-skinned Bougainvillean came out of the house to listen. When he found out we were a film crew, he smiled and said nothing. A massive deluge interrupted our conversation so we promised to come back on Monday. I found out later that like Rosemarie, Father Norman also phoned ahead to warn that we were on our way to Bougainville.

An aircrew appeared back at the hotel, fresh from peacekeeping duty on Bougainville. They were stranded on the island for a couple of days when their Hercules C-130 broke down. We could identify the Australian and Kiwi aircrews by the large green cases of Victoria Bitter beer they carried under one arm and by the large coolers full of beer and ice that they dragged into their rooms. They were with a party of PNG soldiers, including one unsmiling member who never took off his sunglasses. The Kiwi aircrew chatted and joked with us, unlike their PNG or Australian counterparts. They were here to supply the eight hundred or so Australian soldiers on the island who were working to rebuild the place and maintain the peace.

There was also a tourism seminar later that night at the hotel. A group of thirty or so panpipe players performed in their skivvies. It was a sort of Zamfirfest combined with a Kenyan hotel warrior culture show. The music sounded suspiciously like country and western, only played with flutes. The lead man was dressed in a bark loincloth and carried an electrical bullhorn, a curious traditional instrument. I sidled over to the director of tourism, Wilson Maelua. Instead of a car salesman's handshake he gave me a look of deep suspicion.

"Why are you here?" he asked. "Where are you from? Do you have permission from the government? What hotel are you staying in?"

Not exactly the warm greeting I expected.

He eyed me up and down as I filmed the panpipe band. Then the director of tourism for the Solomon Islands said something quite startling: "We don't like people like you running around our islands making videos. We've had problems before with people like you."

I recalled an article in a local tourism magazine that said that the Solomons wanted to increase the annual number of visitors from six thousand to forty thousand over the next ten years, and make the Solomons a mecca for the discerning ecotourist. Good luck.

He was very concerned that we hadn't set everything up in advance and told me that we didn't have enough time to see the Solomons, even though he had no idea how long we would be staying. Every time I asked him about going somewhere, he told me that it would "take a long time" or that it was "very difficult." So much for our cover of filming a documentary about the Solomons. Which was technically true; it just sounded so damn silly. I'm sure another phone call was made the next day, like Father Arkwright's call and Rosemarie's before it.

The Solomons were no stranger to war. In May 1942 the Japanese established a seaplane base on the island of Tulagi off the main island of Guadalcanal. By August of that same year the Americans launched an invasion, securing the island by February 1943. Guadalcanal was where Colonel Fox invented the foxhole in 1942. It was the land of the famous marine Chesty Puller, and where John F. Kennedy ran the PT 109. Hundreds of ships and aircraft lay silent under the green-blue waters of Iron Bottom Sound.

There was a small World War II museum in Villa. It cost S$10 to get in and S$220 for a "television camera." Four Japanese 104-millimeter guns stood unblemished, rust-free and in perfect condition. There were also Grumman Wildcats, P-38 Lightnings, and PBY Catalinas. A Japanese group offered one million dollars for one of the guns, and an American group offered to trade a brand-new Grumman and half a million dollars in cash if they could get their hands one of the few original Hellcats left. The planes were corroded and in bad shape. Small skinks darted in and out of holes like hyperactive tour guides. Lilly, the proprietor, said that they did-n't have a financial value and that they needed to stay here so that no one forgot how many people fought and died here.

We spent some time visiting Edson's Ridge, also called Bloody Ridge. It was the scene of some of the fiercest fighting in the South Pacific. We slithered and slipped up the muddy track in our little Mazda micro-car. The villagers came out to view our charge up the hill. After backing up and attacking the hill a few times we made it, to the astonishment of the local boys who ran up after us, making engine and whining tire sounds. We talked with a man named Gideon, who lived at the top of the hill. He had a spectacular view of the soft rolling hills beyond.

The rain had been coming down hard. The river flooded the villagers' crops of yams, taro, and bananas. Gideon said it would be hard for the village to survive. I talked to him about the history of the island. He said that not much had changed in twenty years. He found a lot of grenades and bullets left over from the war. He liked to throw them into a fire and run away as fast as he could. The kids who watched us charge up the hill showed up. They waited to sell us bullets and an old rusted Garand rifle they'd found.

The old American landing pontoons from the assault on Guadalcanal were slowly rusting away in the angry surf of Red Beach. The three young kids, all with biblical names, showed us the Japanese war memorial that commemorated an attack at Hell's Point. Here, eight hundred Japanese had died in a suicide charge against the U.S. Marines. The isolated gray granite monument had an inscription that called for an end to war. All over the island there were American and Japanese monuments to the thousands of men who died in the fighting.

Many soldiers' bodies were abandoned here because their commanders couldn't retrieve them. Japanese families came here to collect the bones of their dead and take them back to Japan for burial. Others came to lay flo-ral wreaths on the ocean near the spot where the ships went down. It is easy to forget how quickly paradise can be turned into hell.

That night our little foursome headed down a muddy lane and through a high-swinging fence to Herons, the main nightclub in Honiara. The cover charge was S$70, and once inside, it looked like a Shriners' convention. It was only 9 P.M., but the locals were already staggering around bombed out of their minds. The locals shuffled to nonstop reggae that was so loud you had to shout to be heard. A Gilbert Island girl asked me to dance and found it funny that our entire group appeared to be named Robert.

I learned a little more about the islands. People from Malaita and Manggotu were considered to be aggressive. Usually this type of comment would be from someone who lived somewhere else, but it was actually the precursor of a nasty little war that would break out in a few months. We also learned that some of the locals liked to go to the Heron to "hosepipe" or "purse" the foreigners. The locals promised to be your friend in exchange for beer. A night's escapades started at another bar called the Yacht Club because it was the cheapest place to buy beer. Then they'd head off to Herons to hosepipe the expats.

In Herons, if you didn't keep an eye on your beer after you set it down, someone would steal it. We got all sorts of advice from people there. One local gave us a word of caution—it was fashionable to have a mixed baby, so the local lasses were extraordinarily friendly to foreigners. But if her brother or family caught up with you they could demand S$2,000 for "spoiling" the girl and threaten to "bash you up" if the cash wasn't forthcoming. If you got the girl pregnant, the family would show up in a group to demand that you marry her, but only after you paid her dowry with new cars, bikes, and appliances of the family's choosing.

The Heron Club looked like the perfect underground place to see if anyone knew how to get into Bougainville.

People who introduced themselves as one thing suddenly become another as they warmed up to us. One young man who introduced himself as marine engineering student later tore me away from the conversation. He yelled over the loud music into my ear: "I am a drug dealer and the women your friend is talking to are a policewoman and a prostitute. Be careful."

Badger, a graying man who had introduced himself as a journalist, said that he would arrange everything for me. I assumed he meant transportation to Bougainville, but instead he brought over a woman whom he introduced as his thirty-two-year-old kindergarten-teacher niece. Instead of a pimp hat, Badger wore a tattered baseball cap with a Puma logo. Badger was about fifty years old and alternated between English and pidgin depending on how much grog he'd had.

Throughout the night, the locals dragged us from one group to another to say, "Stay away from those people, they are no good." Occasionally, we ended up on the dock in the outdoor VIP drinking area, where we were the only VIPs. When we got rained on, we went back into the club and were shuffled from one "bad group" to another.

The evening was full of half-drunken descriptions of life in the Solomons. These cultural discourses were continually interrupted by the reappearance of Badger, who insisted that I must enjoy myself and have a good time, even though I was having a good time already. I got the point when he repeatedly brought over his niece. He even resorted to telling me that I could "break her in." He explained that this was a common courtesy extended to visitors. I couldn't quite figure out if Badger's offer was mercenary or fueled by drunken hospitality.

I reminded Badger that his niece was thirty-two years old and probably didn't need to be broken in. His answer was "Jesus Murphy By Bloody Christ, It's True!"

I packed it in around 3 A.M. In a chivalrous gesture, Badger rode in our car from the bar parking lot to twenty feet outside the gate "to protect us from rascals." I was getting a sense of who the rascals were.

When the others asked "What's the plan?" I answered, "There is no plan. We just need to find one more grain of sand to tip the scales in our favor." There was no specific way to get from the Solomons into Bougainville. You needed the assistance and goodwill of the people.

Finally, the balance tipped. Back at the hotel Badger was sitting with Clement Base, the premier of the western provinces. Clement was a soft-spoken, shy man with a large Afro. Clement also had the distinction of being born in a town called Paradise on Bougainville. I asked him if there was a big sign outside his village that said WELCOME TO PARADISE.

"We don't just welcome anyone," he said.

We discussed my trip to see Francis, and Clement seemed happy. "You couldn't have picked a better time," he said. It was a sharp contrast from the "you couldn't have picked a worse time" we'd been getting from everyone else so far. We would fly to Gizo, where we would catch a boat to Bougainville. I asked what preparations we needed to make for our trip.

Although the blockade on Bougainville had been lifted, we would be going into a very primitive and remote area. We needed cooking materials, pots, food, sleeping bags. We also needed gifts. Tobacco, balloons, and chocolates were ideal. The other requirements were airfare to Gizo and back for our fixer and money for a boatman.

I asked Badger again if we would see Francis, and told him that I wasn't going on a wild goose chase. He said that we would absolutely see him, so I handed him S$50 for pocket money. We planned to meet up in Gizo.

We arrived in Gizo the next morning. The skiff that brought passengers from the island airport into the main town of Gizo was empty. No Badger. It looked like I'd been "hosepiped." In Gizo we were told to talk to "the bishop," so I walked over to the church and asked for the bishop. It turned out that "the bishop" really was the Bishop John Zale, but he was nowhere to be found. It might have had something to do with the cameraman and the talking head who followed my every step. This was something of a disappointment since the bishop was one of the folks with connections who could have approved our trip to Bougainville.

But I decided to push on without his approval. There was a Twin Otter that flew to Choiseul and the Shortlands at the northernmost tip of the archipelago, closer to Bougainville. The plane took off in two hours, so I bought a couple of weeks' provisions at a Chinese grocery.

The Twin Otter carried about twenty passengers and it was full. The pilot told us that the wings were corroded away and that they needed to be replaced. The first stop was the tiny eighty-square-kilometer island of Mono, home to one thousand people. The airstrip was simply a gash that bisected the jungle island. They unloaded our luggage and were ready to take off when I commented to the pilot that our luggage was still sitting on the ground. After a minor delay we took off for the Shortlands. At one time it was the smallest international airport in the world.

As we taxied toward the tiny graffiti-covered shed that served as a bus-stop-style airport I noticed a round-bellied white man talking to a large man in a cop uniform. I remarked to myself that it was odd to see an Australian this far out. The Australian slinked away. The large black islander stood by the door and waited for it to open.

I got out and was ecstatic to find that our luggage and supplies had made it with us. The big man towered over me, blocking my way from the plane. When I stood up to face him he was smiling through red betel-stained teeth. To make small talk I asked him about the human tooth hanging from a string around his neck. It turned out to be his father's tooth. Jay asked politely if he could videotape him. The man said no. Jay taped anyway and captured a very large, smiling man with a human tooth around his neck telling us to get back on the plane. I had an overwhelming desire to ask the big man if the tooth was the only part he spit out.

The Australian in the too-small hat had disappeared. My little crew was being arrested and then deported. It was obvious that there was nothing to discuss, since the big man with the human tooth had told us specifically to return to immigration in Honiara. I thought we should do the opposite and go back to Gizo. The pilot didn't really know what to say. I told him that I had a one-way ticket, and that it didn't seem fair that he should have to fly us all the way back to Honiara, so I suggested that he just drop us off at Gizo.

Although defeated, it felt good to be back in Gizo. But before we could take the boat back to town, the boat captain wanted to wait for a plane from Honiara. Rob and I were killing time at the dock wondering about plan B, our little misadventure, and how the locals didn't want us to get to our destination when who should appear strolling down the wooden pier from the airplane but Badger.

Badger was in fine spirits. Literally. He strolled unsteadily down the pier carrying a battered little briefcase. He smiled and waved as though he always intended for us to meet this way. When I remarked on his condition, he said that he tried to bring a couple more beers on the plane but they wouldn't let him. We humped all our gear and the two heavy boxes of food I'd bought in the morning back to the "PT-109 Hotel." Calling it a hotel would be something of an overstatement, but it was cool and a fresh breeze came off the water.

When Matthias the bellhop showed me to my room, he explained,

"Here is the fan for cool breeze, here is the bed for sleeping, and after dinner we look for *tikki tikki*."

"*Tikki tikki?*" I asked.

"You know," he said, "*tikki tikki*." I thought he meant women.

He made the old finger-poking-the-hole gesture. Yes, I was right. But no *tikki tikki* before dinner.

Back at the bar, Badger had now become our best friend again. He limited himself to two beers then—just before he went for a walk to set things up—he asked for a little pocket money. Badger intended to go chat with the bishop. He added in an offhand way, "I will bring three nice girls." The locals seem to never separate business from pleasure.

Badger reappeared that evening, not with women but with a young man who worked in the boat shed next door. Peter joined us during dinner and spoke so quietly I could barely hear what he was saying. I found out he was a boat mechanic and a skipper who'd taken three "fellas" I knew across to Bougainville. The three fellows were Dom Rotheroe, Alex Smailes, and an Italian photographer who snuck in a few years back. They'd described their trip as "interesting." They were shot at and lost in a storm. Things got so dire that their boatman was forced to throw all the smuggled beer overboard. They made it to Bougainville, barely.

In his overly friendly way, Badger invited Peter to sit down. Peter refused not once but twice. He said he'd been working late fixing outboard motors and wanted to sleep. He grimaced when I told him I wanted to meet with Francis.

His opinion was that the commanders of the BRA lived isolated lives in their bush camps, and that we should talk to the "little people." He told me that hundreds of journalists had gone across during the conflict, but he'd never seen any articles. He was exaggerating slightly, since only a handful had come this way. But I got his drift. He didn't like outsiders. Obviously Peter wasn't going to be one of the most helpful people we came across. Later I found out that it was Badger he detested, not us. Nevertheless, he gave us a lot of useful information in our quick talk.

He said that instead of heading straight in, we should cut wide and then land on the central part of Bougainville. The north of the island was very dangerous because of the PNGDF. He left us with a bit of advice: "The closer you stay to the ground, the more you will learn."

Rob and I discussed our options: Stay and try again, or leave and come back another time. Then things started to happen on their own. The phone rang in the hotel while Rob and I were having breakfast. It was the police chief in Gizo, who told us he would like to talk to us at 9 A.M. For a lark, we showed up at 8:45.

The chief, resplendent in his dark Ray Bans, was not amused. He pointed angrily at the clock over our head, brought himself up to his full height, and barked "I told you to come at nine o'clock! Come back at nine o'clock!" Rob and I decided to kill some time. The government offices were across the street, and who should we meet but the premier of the northern Solomons, Clement Base, our dinner guest back in Honiara. Strangely, he was happy to see us and asked how our stay had been. We politely told him that it was interesting, that we would have an audience with the police in a few minutes, and that we were probably going to get the bum's rush out of the country.

We came back at 9:10 and were brought into the presence of three men—local immigration officer Eddie Kipling, a police staff officer, and Chief Superintendent Aloysius Ora. The police chief was now incensed that we were late. There was no pleasing these folks. He started his tirade.

"Yesterday you went up to Mono, Ballalai, and Taro, and you were directed to return," Ora said. "There is some concern over your activities. You have been talking to people and information has come from all around the islands about you. It appears you are Vietnamese, er ah, Vietnam soldiers or rather ex-military Vietnam vets and you have the whole islands in an uproar. The people at Shortlands are very scared. Four white men arrive in our islands and we are very nervous."

We laughed at the description of our activities. Still, if I put my analyst hat on, Jay did look like a CIA man with his straw hat and military air. Bob the ABC correspondent could pass for a clean-cut neutral government man along for the ride. And Rob and I looked like the business end of a very sanitary, American-style covert op.

They told us that people from all over the islands had been calling in with descriptions of four large white men walking around with guns in holsters, ammunition pouches, and heavy military gear in large green bags.

We laughed again. I explained that they were welcome to check our bags. They'd find dirty socks and film canisters. I showed him my "holster" and pulled out my "gun"—a small video camera in a belt pouch. My "ammunition pouch" was full of soggy paperwork and my passport. The large green bag, which we called "el gordo verde," was Jay's overstuffed duffel loaded with water, video gear, and clothes.

For good measure, I turned my video camera on and held it three feet from Aloysius's nose as he interrogated us. The proceedings were quite comical. The immigration man wanted to see our passports and was concerned about how we represented ourselves when we entered the island. I told him the truth: We were visitors traveling with a film crew that was taping our trip. I told them that I hadn't set up preparations in advance because I didn't like to see all the hotels and restaurants. I liked to travel with regular people in far-flung regions.

Strangely, the chief warmed up when I asked about the people on Bougainville. He explained that he had family in Bougainville and that when the colonizers drew the borders in the region, they didn't care that there were families on both sides. Sensing that this might be an opening, I asked him point-blank if we could go to Bougainville.

He smiled painfully. The immigration man explained that they didn't allow people to go to Bougainville. The implication registered slowly. We'd been a little too vocal in our desire, a little too obvious in our approach, and Rob Krott's image as a mercenary, along with the ABC crew, had left our chances at slim to none.

We decided that since neither side wanted us to go to Bougainville there was absolutely nothing to do but relax for a while. Rob and I went diving, visited the island that Kennedy swam to after his PT boat was sliced in half, and sat in the bar. We carefully explained to the bartender why he shouldn't allow Badger to charge drinks to our room. Rob and I commiserated about how this trip was not to be and the fact that Francis Ona and the people of Bougainville would have to sit in the jungle, waiting for publicity that would never come.

Back in my hotel room I thought about failure. What was different?

This time I had spent three months trying to get official permission. I had done what I was told, met all the right people, even offered major exposure to the rebel group on American prime-time television. I had a plane to catch back to Honiara where they were waiting to arrest me. As the day passed, I decided to do it my way.

I walked out of the hotel past our piled-up luggage to the boat shack where the Bougainvilleans hung out. This time I was alone with only my small camera, the way I like to work. I walked aimlessly around the rotting boats, canoes, and World War II debris and struck up a conversation with someone. I walked into the shade where three other men were sitting and offered them cigarettes. "Are you from Bougainville?" I asked.

They raised their eyebrows upward in the curious Solomon Islands way of saying yes.

"Are these local canoes? How far can they go? Do they go all the way to Bougainville? Are people going to Bougainville?"

Same answer. Then a man stepped out of the dilapidated building and asked me, "Do you want to go to Bougainville?"

I gave him the Solomons eyebrow raise.

His name was Giles and he was a boatman. When asked me my business in Bougainville, I cut straight to the point. "I want to meet Francis Ona."

I showed him pictures from when my friends Dom and Alex had met Francis. He recognized and named each gun-bearing rebel in the photos. When he got to Francis Ona's picture he said, "Dat 'im."

Giles told me that he could take me tomorrow morning but first he had to ask the bishop. I thought I was right back where I started. But it seemed that the bishop was not a villain in this story, but a good guy. I told Giles I would be back at my hotel.

Jay Anania and Bob Woodruff came to Rob and me. They told us that they'd decided not to go to Bougainville. Although they were supposed to be shooting a segment for an adventure show, the professional news crew thought that it might be too adventurous to sail across the strait and enter rebel-held territory. I was glad in a way, because their presence made it difficult to talk to anyone. People had difficulty confiding in us when two filmmakers stood behind me.

I expected a knock on the door and the police wanting to know why

I wasn't on the plane I said I would be on. I decided to sit in the bar, where Badger had become a fixture. A young black-skinned man came to find me, pulling me away from Badger. We went to sit behind a rotting World War II–era Dodge truck. He talked quickly. He'd been sent by the brother of a BRA commander to take me to Bougainville. He said he couldn't be seen talking to me because he'd spent six years in Bougainville and two years in jail for running people across the water.

He slapped me on the back with a maniacal laugh. "I have two eighty-horses on a small canoe," he said as he made S-waves with his hand. "Bishop Zale is alive because of me." He formed his hands into pistols and made rat-a-tat sounds. "Nobody can catch me," he said.

I asked him how he knew me, and he said that Bishop Zale sent him to me. I explained that not only had we been bounced from Choiseul but we'd also had a heart-to-heart with the top cop.

He looked at me and said, "You want to help, don't you? You must come to Bougainville."

To make everything look normal he walked back to the bar with me. Just before we entered he pulled me into the women's bathroom. With a big smile he told me that we wouldn't speak to each other until everything was ready, and that he would tell everyone that we were going to his village to snorkel and fish.

There were a couple of promising developments in the bar afterward: He bought his own beers, and as he left he told me not to hang around with Badger.

By now, I'd become accustomed to the barley breath of the permanently inebriated Badger. I told him that I would be flying back today, so for the rest of the day he tried to figure out how he would keep his bar tab going. Sensing that his SolBrew-soaked ride was coming to an end, he got more creative. First he invited strangers into the bar and asked me if I would buy some "capital fella" a beer. Of course he always included one more for himself. His next trick was to pull up chairs around my solitary table and then invite his comatose friends one by one to enjoy a round on this capital fella Robert.

Yet another talk with the bartender put an end to that. Then he tried to put the final squeeze on me. "Robert, I have worked very hard for you, and have come a long way now that you are going home. But what is to become of me now?"

I reminded Badger that he was home now. His original story was that he needed money to get home—which at the time was Gizo. So technically, he was home. This stemmed Badger's display of sorrow momentarily. He returned to the table with his collection of drinking buddies, now passed out in the afternoon heat. After emptying their beers, Badger collected his crusty briefcase and disappeared.

That night Peter, who ran the outboard repair shop where the Bougainvilleans hung out, came in for the four beers that he customarily drank between 6 and 8 P.M. He usually sat quietly in the corner, but that night he wanted to talk to me. I left Rob to fill out postcards, and talked to Peter. With Badger gone, he was a little more talkative than the last time we'd met him. He warned me against taking a Solomon Island boat. We may get to the island of Bougainville, but we might not meet Ona, who was still in the bush camps. He told me the specifics of getting across.

It took 180 liters of gas to get from Gizo to Taro in Choiseul, the place we were apprehended. Gas for the outboards cost S$2.20 per liter, and you needed four drums to get to central Bougainville. Each drum held two hundred liters. Add to all that between twenty and fifty liters of spare fuel.

The canoes had two 40-horsepower engines, and the trip took seven hours on a good day. We needed to bring along some extra gas for the local people who would hide us in their small dugouts and sneak us around the checkpoints on Choiseul. Once we were safely past the last checkpoint the boatman would let us out. Then it would be a long ride up the coast of Bougainville to the town of Aropa.

Since there were eight hundred Australians and New Zealanders on Bougainville restarting schools and getting the infrastructure going again, our chances of getting around unnoticed on the island were slim to none. Assuming we made it to see Francis Ona, we would almost certainly be deported to Port Moresby, the capital of Papua New Guinea.

Doing the math back in my room, I realized that I'd run up against another problem: our budget. It cost $880 just for the fuel to go to Bougainville and back. Peter didn't tell me how much the boatman got paid for taking us there, waiting, and then making the return trip. There was another charge just for journalists. Even though I'd overcome the legal barriers, or was prepared to ignore them, the locals had thrown up their own barriers to our mission. The best way I could figure it was that if Rob and I were to leave the next morning we would end up inside Bougainville with no way to get out, and if we were captured we would have some serious problems. We had already been told to leave the Solomons, they didn't want us in Bougainville, Francis didn't want to meet us, and everyone was suspicious that we were on our way to kill him. A press release went out:

BOUGAINVILLE: SOLOMONS AUTHORITIES DETAIN FOUR FOREIGNERS

THE HAGUE, The Netherlands (March 8, 1998—Bougainville Interim Government)—The Secretary of the Bougainville Interim Government (BIG), Mr. Martin Miriori, has praised the swift action taken by Solomon Islands authorities for clamping down on four foreigners who planned to cross illegally into Bougainville from Taro island last week.

The four men—who have been identified as Robert Pelton, Rod Krott, Rod Woodruss (all believed to be Australian citizens) and J. Anania (suspected US citizen)—were spotted at Choiseul Bay by Solomon Islands police and immigration officers while acting on a tip-off from Bougainville Interim Government/Bougainville Revolutionary Army (BRA) authorities in Bougainville, and were forced to return to Honiara where they are now being held for questioning.

It has been alleged from reliable sources that one of these foreigners, Mr. Rod Krott, was involved with foreign mercenaries on the Sandline issue last year, which the former Papua New Guinea Prime Minister, Sir Julius Chan, had allegedly hired and wanted to use against the population of Bougainville.

The report said that the trip for the foreigners was planned and coordinated with the help of Ms. Rosemary Gillespie who is now blacklisted by the BIG/BRA leadership and the people of Bougainville for her involvement in dubious activities, desperately trying to encourage continuous divisions among the people, and consequently undermine the current peace process.

It is understood that Ms. Gillespie herself also tried to fly into Solomon islands with the group, but the airline authorities in Brisbane refused to allow her to board the plane.

"Solomon Islands authorities must be congratulated for their quick reaction to stop these type of foreign elements who seem to be working against the spirit and intentions of the current peace process on Bougainville," Mr. Miriori said.

Mr. Miriori said: "Our people can no longer tolerate the likes of Ms. Gillespie and others of her close allies, who may have their own hidden agenda in Bougainville while exploiting the situation, and operating in connection with unknown corrupt regimes and individuals to destroy Bougainvilleans in our present struggle to achieve lasting peace and freedom for all our people."

To say that the current situation was delicate would be an understatement. The government and military of Papua New Guinea didn't want us here. The government of the Solomon Islands didn't want us here, the Australian and New Zealand peacekeeping force didn't want us here, the odd collection of emaciated expat do-gooders we'd encountered didn't want us here, and we even had a specific unvitation from Francis Ona's secretary. And of course the elements of the Bougainville Interim Government didn't want us here. We had yet to find anyone who did want us here.

We'd flown more than seven thousand miles. We'd been told to get lost by the do-gooders, the moderates, and the hard-core, the tourism people, the police, the immigration officials, the missionaries, the locals, the politicians, and the Australian military. We were even sent back from an ill-fated flight to Choiseul. Now I had managed to find three people who were willing to take us, there but there was still no invitation from Francis. If Francis wanted to stay in the jungle and let his cause to go the way of many other good ideas, so be it.

Back in air-conditioned Brisbane, I flicked on the TV to catch up on the news. There were more peace talks on the Bougainville situation, this time in Canberra.

I called Rosemarie Gillespie from the Novotel in Brisbane. I was feeling somewhat hostile to her since all I'd gotten for my troubles was a true-
life Monty Python script. I told Rosemarie that the story that would come
of this trip would be about blundering cops, cowardly superstitious politicians, and a paranoid rebel leader isolated from the world in his jungle camp
playing Greta Garbo. I unfairly egged her on, saying the Bougainvilleans
were fools and the Solomon Islander officials were like Keystone Kops.

She'd been inundated with calls from various people wanting to know
what was going on and who we were. The fact that we'd spent three months
telling them who we were and what we wanted to do didn't seem to phase
these people in the least. The rumor mill was working overtime on both
sides of the pond as well as in Europe. She'd been officially blacklisted and
had had to deal with a phone call from the rebel HQ asking why was she
helping to send in mercenaries. Miriori's press release had done its magic.

She offered to have Max Watts—another BRA rep—talk to me. I
politely told her that I was no longer interested in talking to white people
who explained what Bougainvilleans wanted. I left my phone number,
thanked Rosemarie for all her help, and packed my bags for a trip to
Afghanistan.

The phone rang. It was Max Watts. First of all Max wanted to know
what we were doing on the island, and he wanted me to know that Rosemarie had been working very hard on our behalf. Max had also been
working to get me into Bougainville, but he cautioned me about my
reception.

Max spoke slowly and eloquently as he lay in bed with an open stomach. He had just returned from having his kidney and other plumbing
removed and was still trying to figure out his morphine drip while he
talked on the phone.

He asked me about Rob and the others. He had been around long
enough to avoid throwing simplistic labels on people. After all, Max was
the man who'd had his girlfriend stolen by Fidel Castro, and had turned
Jane Fonda on to politics in Paris when she was married to Roger Vadim.

Max told me that Krott was marked as a mercenary from the get-go and
the other two people who showed up confused the situation. I found it
funny, since a real operation would have a much better cover, and told him

I wouldn't be too smug about islanders discovering something that never existed. It was time for the rebels to be big boys and speak for themselves.

Max called back. He'd called Moses Havini, who said he was too busy preparing for the peace talks, so he rousted another Bougainvillean, Martin Miriori, and told him to expect my call. Martin answered at his hotel room in Cairns. He was pleasant, but it quickly became apparent that I was talking to a politician. When I explained that he'd taken an opportunity to present the Bougainvilleans' case in front of twenty million Americans and turned it into a sideshow, he didn't really care.

And so went the Solomons. My journey to find a visionary hidden in the deep jungle was thwarted by people with dark designs and circuitous reasoning. Francis and his cause was the only flickering flame in this murky quest. And then it hit me.

Martin was keeping Francis isolated from outsiders. Ona's only source of news and information was the radio and sat-phone links via Martin and his people. The longest and most righteous war in the Pacific was being turned into a sellout. Another press release went out.

GILLESPIE REJECTS BOUGAINVILLE ENTRY CLAIMS
  CANBERRA, Australia (March 9, 1998—PACNEWS)—Australian civil rights lawyer Rosemarie Gillespie has angrily rejected claims that she helped four foreign nationals who tried to enter Bougainville illegally through the Solomon Islands.

  Gillespie says it was she who alerted the Sydney-based National Coordinator of the Bougainville Freedom Movement, Vikki John, about the entry attempt and this led to Solomon Islands police preventing the four men from crossing the border into Bougainville.

  Gillespie, a vocal supporter of Bougainville independence was appointed Research Officer for the breakaway Bougainville Interim Government in 1995. She entered Bougainville four times during the war, carrying medicine and other humanitarian supplies and did much to publicize the plight of the Bougainville people to the outside world.

  In a statement issued Sunday, Gillespie says she was approached in January by an American writer, Robert Pelton, who wanted to interview rebel leader Francis Ona for a new edition of his book, "The World's Most Dangerous Places." She said she repeatedly told Pelton and his three colleagues that the time was "not right" to visit Ona and that they should not do so unless they were invited.

She said she was concerned when she learned that one of the men, Rob Krott, was a former member of the U.S. Special Forces and had served as a mercenary in several countries.

"I raised the alarm when they would not take notice of me," she said.

Gillespie said allegations made against her by the Secretary of the Bougainville Interim Government, Martin Miriori, and others were non-sensical and defamatory and she is threatening legal action.

And so my first attempt to meet Francis Ona resulted in a fiasco. Still, Ona's steadfastness impressed me. He refused to abandon his goals, and he cared little for the publicity most rebel groups would kill for. Francis had reason to suspect outsiders, and he absolutely had reason to suspect a fair-haired mercenary who was to accompany me as a cameraman.

I would try again in 1999. But in one of those lazy, circuitous circles that seems to connect not just once but again and again, my path was to intertwine with that of Francis Ona's archenemies. In the summer of 2001 I learned about other actors and events that operated on Ona's periphery. It was a story about guns, money, and power.

The man who sells peace has ten puppies by his two chocolate Labradors named "Grenade" and "Pin." The tiny chocolate bundles tumble with glee out of their whelping pen. They spread out in a mob of reddish brown, nipping at pant legs and tugging at shoelaces. A tall man in his mid–forties with short-cropped hair directs his young blond girlfriend as she chases after the puppies relieving themselves in the backyard. I am visting Michael Grunberg, a successful accountant, not to discuss money but to discuss war. Michael has done well in the business of peace and lives comfortably as a tax exile on the isle of Guernsey.

Guernsey is a self-governing island of sixty-four thousand people and seventy banking institutions located in the English Channel, thirty miles from the coast of northern France and eighty miles from England. Technically not part of the United Kingdom, the island is an idyllic escape from reality. Although its main export is wool, Guernsey is inhabited by people who don't seem to have an identifiable source of income. Nor do residents seem eager to advertise any indication of their occupation or wealth. Guernsey is a separate country with its own money and flag, and its wealthy citizens live lives of calm and serenity. Its location between France and England made it a perfect center for wealthy privateers in the 1600s, then a haven for well-off French during the revolution, and now a haven for tax exiles. The air is crisp and clear, houses are kept neat and conservative; there is no crime, no urban blight, not even a hint of the kind of conditions in the countries that Michael is used to doing business in—Angola, the Congo, Sierra Leone, Uganda, Papua New Guinea, and other troubled nations.

Michael Grunberg, born in 1956, is a chartered accountant, financial adviser and a tax expert. But you would be hard-pressed to find any mention in the media of his financial successes unrelated to warfare. It is for this reason that some would suggest he is in the business of war—a driving force behind the concept of private armies for hire to acceptable customers, be they first or third world. Currently he officially acts as the business adviser and main spokesperson for Sandline International. He served in a similar capacity for Executive Outcomes, and despite his calm assurances that his interest is strictly financial, he has been on the scene during key negotiations and times of crisis in the affairs of these two mercenary firms. Nothing sneaky or even underhanded. In fact Michael's clear and consistent recounting of events and motives has weathered the criticism leveled at his clients.

Michael was an accountant with BDO Stoy Hayward from 1981 until 1994. He left in June 1994 as a partner to focus on his own clients and interests. There is no doubt that the man is intelligent; and speaking with him, you are convinced within minutes that he has done nothing rash or foolish in his entire life. If you doubt his talents as an accountant it will suffice to say that his total tax bill for last year was 64 pence, or one U.S. dollar.

Michael would just be one of thousands of responsible, financially astute accountants if it weren't for his choice in clients. He has deliberately put himself on the front lines of a battle raging over how to bring peace to troubled nations or failed states. Grunberg champions the idea of offering private armies to international customers who need untidy little rebellions taken care of—or need large swathes of countrysides retaken from nihilistic rebels. Such services have of course been provided for centuries by nations wishing to protect their interests in oil, strategic minerals, and geographically critical countries by directing or changing governments, through covert or overt means. The payback for governments has always been a stronger financial interest and protection of vital resources and strategic regions.

Michael does not deal in the high minded or hypothetical. Within a few weeks, and with a appropriate down payment, his clients can have an army complete with gunships, tanks, artillery, soldiers, light arms, and aircraft in place and ready to fight. Ostensibly the goal is to train and support, but past experience has shown that the employees of EO and Sandline have been the sharp tip of the spear. There are two criteria: You'd better have the cash, and Michael and his clients have to want to work for you.

Sandline International—the name comes from the expression "line in the sand"—isn't really a corporation in the normal sense. There are no smiling secretaries, no lunchrooms or staff picnics, no polished logo above the door. It is less than a handful of now ex-military men from the United States and the United Kingdom with special forces backgrounds who can draw up plans on an ad hoc basis using mostly freelance talent and contract vendors.

Their mission statement sounds innocuous enough—"Sandline is a Private Military Company (PMC) focusing on conflict resolution. The company works worldwide and is resourced by professionals with many years of operational experience at senior rank within first world armies." Their generic Web site is the only physical manifestation of their existence.

Even compared to the old-line purveyors of military expertise, the world of Sandline International is not that grandiose. While estimates of recent contracts given to Sandline and their subcontractor, South African–based Executive Outcomes, sound impressive—$10 million (Sierra Leone), $35.2 million (Sierra Leone), $36 million (Papua New Guinea), $40 million a year (Angola)—they pale in comparison to military contracts handed out to civilian providers of military equipment and skills blessed by traditional governments. And collection has been a little tough for Sandline and EO. The $10-million Sierra Leone gig, for instance, brought in only $1.5 million in actual cash. Contrast that with Dyncorp, a $1.8-billion-a-year company, and you begin to see the benefits of keeping your head down and lunching with the Pentagon.

But until Executive Outcomes hit the radar in 1993, no private military corporation brashly offered to simply go in and fight a war on behalf of a client nation. EO, and now Sandline, made war a service industry.

Michael is not the sole focus of interest when it comes to creating or even promoting the brave new world of mercenary armies. There is another man—one of Michael's associates and the chief alchemist behind the idea of war for hire. A close neighbor whose lavish taste in possessions and activities contrasts markedly with Michael's conservative choices and actions: Tony Buckingham.

Michael was introduced to Tony in 1993. They began a close partnership the following year when he left Stoy Hayward. Michael has served as Tony's business adviser and partner in many of his efforts since then. They make an interesting partnership, Michael every bit as patient and calculated as Tony seems to be impatient and audacious.

Just down the hill as you look out Michael's front picture window is a conservative, solid-looking house, one of Tony Buckingham's homes, with a commanding view of the windswept ocean. It's exactly the kind of place you would expect to find someone like Tony, talking on his portable phone with associates half a world away, a drink in one hand and a cigar clenched between his teeth. Taking in the view and loving the game.

Anthony Leslie Rowland Buckingham was born in 1952. He is now a very wealthy man, even in that rarefied world where wealth is measured not just by money but also by reputation, the length and age of your yacht, and more telling, the number of important people in your Rolodex. Tony is by most accounts a gregarious, self-made man who according to even some of his friends still can't resist regaling the less fortunate or wealthy with stories of his adventures, conquests, and wealth. Tony is also described as a fast friend, a fearless sportsman, and a smart businessman with a Teflon-like disdain for public opinion. All are necessary attributes in the business of doing risky things in the more ragged regions of the third world.

Although he is rarely interviewed or photographed, Tony is not a recluse. He can be spotted sailing his navy blue Farr 40 yacht, *A Bit of a Coup,* or driving in international rallies in a 1964 Aston Martin DB5 with friend Simon Mann, or just hanging out at the Monaco Grand Prix. Surprisingly visible for a man who doesn't talk to the press. Tony seems happy to let others invent and polish while he enjoys life. In the world of small-cap stocks, racing, and resource deals, men with daring and money do well.

Buckingham's military background is said to be 21 SAS. He achieved the distinction not by running up and down fog shrouded Scottish moors, but by essentially coming out of the reserve. Inquiries about his past are met with the same winks and obfuscation accorded all members of that organization. There are plenty of rumors about quid pro quo with Her

Majesty's secret service, very James Bond, very cocktail party chatty—if indeed there was any such service. What is known is that he made a lot of money in the oil business. His first known career was as a commercial diver on oil rigs in the North Sea during the 1980s. That and his love for sailing and the ocean have led some people to assume he was a member of the Special Boat Squadron, or SBS—the wetter version of the SAS.

Buckingham hit the business radar in the late 1980s as a director of U.K.-based Sabre Petroleum. He resigned in July 1991 and founded Heritage Oil and Gas the next year. Buckingham's break into the oil business came about via his personal relationship with Jack Pierce, at that time the head of Canadian-based Ranger Oil, and the powers-that-be in the Angolan government of President José Eduardo Dos Santos. Tony approached Pierce with the opportunity to exploit a production-sharing contract with the Angolan government oil company in the North Sea's shallow-water Block Four. Ranger won the lucrative offshore concession and began drilling in 1991. Buckingham was given 10 percent of Ranger's cut, and used this to form Heritage Oil and Gas. Oil and money flowed in 1992 as Tony also enjoyed a 49 percent stake in Ranger Oil. Buckingham also got involved in mining in Uganda in late summer, 1994. Michael later accompanied Tony to Angola to see the alluvial diamond deposits, and began to look at diamonds as another good bet in risky regions. It didn't take long to realize that no company could safely invest in hostile regions without appropriate security. Typically this security was provided by the government or by privately hired security firms. The threat was not isolated theft or sabotage, but wholesale attacks by hundreds of rebel soldiers.

Buckingham built up and invested in a number of companies and holding companies, most administered in Guernsey. Through these and other companies he invested in resource projects in Iraq, Namibia, Nigeria, Uganda, Congo, Oman, Sierra Leone, India, and Angola—all what might be politely described as failed states; countries where the government is a temporary affair and large swaths of territory belong to someone else.

As with all the truly wealthy, there is no way to accurately break down the size or success of his endeavors. By 1995, however, he revealingly told a potential client that he had invested more than two hundred million dollars in high-risk ventures related to mineral resources in Africa. Even given

Tony's penchant for bringing in equal partners, this is a large amount of money.

He likes to use OPM—Other People's Money—and trades on his relationships with leaders and local knowledge of mercurial African politics. He is a good student of foreign politics. He does business with President Dos Santos of Angola and the son of Kenya's president Arap Moi, he prospects for gold in Uganda, and explores for oil in Lake Albert. This high level focus on natural resources and patronage means Tony can get the big shots on the phone to close the deal for either himself or his partners. It's no coincidence that Buckingham can show up on a private jet to discuss selling mercenaries to a government like Papua New Guinea—then be found at the Monaco Grand Prix rubbing elbows with Europe's elite. Among movers and shakers Tony is an all-star.

His deals are structured loosely and usually benefit his partners equally. He's sometimes listed as a "consultant"—for example, he received a hundred thousand dollars for serving as a consultant on the PNG/Sandline International deal. But Tony has also consulted, helped, and invested in a variety of projects, not all of them related to mines or mercenaries. He knows the value of access to favor and knows how Africa works. Making sure everyone from the leader on down to the local chiefs is happy is paramount to doing business on the business frontiers of this world.

If ever there was a man who saw the need to offer peace or its sister, war, it would be Tony Buckingham. And if ever there was a man who saw the need to sell peace, it would be Michael Grunberg. Or is it the other way around?

Although it is accurate to say that Michael and his clients sell war, from Michael's perspective his products and benefits are peace and security—the building blocks of struggling nations. Governments often find that these fundamentals come with too high a political price tag to provide overtly or quickly enough to make a difference. EO's and Sandline's major calling card has been the threat of all-out warfare dispensed by dispassionate outside killers using the same methods as those who are threatening governments and investors in failed states. In the world of warfare this is the ultimate weapon, and if used in time the ultimate vaccine. Even the threat of bringing in Sandline can not only serve as a sort of blood transfusion to hemorrhaging third-world rulers, but also provide a major financial bump on the world's small-cap mining markets. No one wants to invest millions in a mine to have it overrun and looted a few months later. Michael sells security and a chance for struggling nations to stabilize long enough for development to take root. And—he is quick to remind—he sells it at a substantially lower price than the UN or proxy forces can offer.

Private armies are not unusual. Militias, mercenaries, security details—anywhere you can find trouble and guns, you can find private armies. Private armies are not bad or good; they are simply more sophisticated weapons. They are also a deterrent to violence, whether via a security guard protecting a mine from pilferage or the threat of Hind gunship attacks against rebels who are intent on gaining control of diamond concessions.

Oddly enough, the genesis of the modern private military company came from the mind of a "horse whisperer." If you ever visit an American-style western dude ranch in South Africa, you might run across a blond man with one green eye and one blue eye named Luther Eeben Barlow. You would be hard-pressed to guess this genial man's former occupation. In fact, Barlow invented the modern private army available for hire or rent, a concept that was to change history and force the military to rethink how small countries fight wars.

Barlow was born in South Africa in 1956. At age six, he and his father, a railway station master, moved to a farm in Waterberg, Nylstroom. His father tried to make ends meet by working for a mining company on weekdays and then raising cattle and growing corn on the weekends. Barlow was drafted at age seventeen and soon joined the 32 Buffalo Battalion. The Buffalo Battalion looked for officers with a penchant for daring, and Eeben fit the bill perfectly. He was quickly promoted over the seventeen years that he served.

He also was in the Civil Cooperation Bureau in Western Europe (Region 6), where he reportedly worked for South African intelligence. Some publications claim that he was in charge of the surveillance and assassination of two ANC-related residents, as well as of disrupting the group's activities in Western Europe. He says that his work for the CCB while based in Knightsbridge, London, was mostly disinformation. He was officially the South African DCC directorate of covert collection.

The man who started Executive Outcomes in 1989 had bigger ideas and a certain style that would garner him much attention, most of it negative. Executive Outcomes' logo was a horse—more specifically a paladin or knight chess piece. Executive Outcomes parlayed the skills Barlow and his other military friends had gained in their years of intense intelligence gathering, training, and combat with communist forces in Angola, Namibia, and other regions. The Buffalo Battalion was unusual in that it consisted of a small group of white officers with mostly black troops from northern Namibia and Angola. Their specialty was to insert well behind enemy lines for extended periods to track, harass, and kill the communist groups threatening South Africa. They fought against SWAPO, the Cubans, MPLA, and other groups. They also trained pro-Western groups like Joseph Savimbi's UNITA. Officers had to enjoy long-range hunting, be able to work with indigenous tribesmen, and stand up to the intense rigors of being hunted themselves in the vast open lands of Angola and Namibia.

As a fledgling company, EO was doing tiny jobs like teaching the security divisions of mining companies how to infiltrate organized crime groups and gather intelligence that would predict attacks on mine equipment or facilities. It could rely on an impressive list of résumés and skill sets from the underpaid and downsized elite units of the South African army— a place where a typical solider might make two hundred dollars a month.

In late 1992 the rebels of UNITA were making great gains in their war against the communist regime of Dos Santos. They attacked and captured the important oil port of Soyo on January 20, 1993. In that port was an eighty-million-dollar computerized oil pumping control unit that was costing Tony Buckingham twenty thousand dollars a day. His people approached the rebel group UNITA and asked to be allowed to remove it. UNITA said no. Tony then explored his options. His close friend Simon Mann—a former SAS troop commander and intelligence specialist—introduced Tony to Eeben and his tiny company Executive Outcomes. Eeben, Tony, and Simon met in London in January 1993 to discuss what could be done.

The Soyo job was the first major EO operation for a foreign government, and it was described by those who were there as being pretty hairy. The idea was to have white 32 Battalion vets go in, push out UNITA, and then hold the oil center until the Angolan army (FAA) could enter and hold the region. There followed a single attack using standard 32 Battalion tactics—intel gathering, pinpointing mortars on escape routes, and very aggressive sustained fire upon contact. There are few groups that could withstand a 32 Battalion frontal assault. Fewer could escape the deadly accurate mortar fire that shreds the remaining fighters and escapees with shrapnel. Although one insider described the Soyo job as a "close one," the job got done. In the end Tony's equipment—along with other oil companies' equipment—was removed, but there were casualties. Reports in the press alleged that mercenaries had reappeared in Africa—a sensitive subject in Angola after the CIA's debacle from hiring and using British mercenaries against the Angolan communists in the early 1970s. Ultimately UNITA retook Soyo from the Angolan army.

One week after Soyo, the Angolan presidents' people called Buckingham from their London embassy and told him that Dos Santos wanted to meet him. Buckingham looked at his calendar and proposed a date. The caller said the president's private jet was waiting for him at Stansted airport. Buckingham flew down to Luanda the next day to discuss how Angola could use EO on a bigger scale to train the troops and defeat UNITA, which had a tight grip on 60 percent the country. Specifically they discussed how to free up the diamond producing areas that provided critical income to the rebels.

As expected, Buckingham, Mann, and Barlow did not think small. A proper army had to be at least six hundred men, tanks, armored cars, helicopters, both transport and attack, intelligence gathering, medical evac, and even a press contingency. Missing from this forty-million-dollar-a-year plan—and from all EO's and Sandline's official contracts—was the aggressive attack plan that is the companies' hallmark. Most of the terms cover equipment and training; expectations of violence against countrymen are not spelled out. The government paid for the Soyo job from the funds of the state-owned oil company and the second plan from the state coffers. It made perfect business sense to spend the money on training their army to regain back the oil and diamond areas. The odd thing is that Buckingham and Mann were in Luanda the day after the Angolan embassy phoned, and not Barlow. Apparently the dogs of war had someone holding the leash.

Mann promptly called Tim Spicer, a Scot's Guardsman he had worked with during the Gulf War, to see if he wanted the job of training and commanding a battle-group-sized unit of Angolan troops. Spicer passed. The task was directed to Eeben and Executive Outcomes. Eeben had to quickly put together six hundred men to train and support an army capable of pushing back UNITA, the formerly CIA-backed army that 32 Battalion had trained in the apartheid era. The initial mandate—to train Angolan government troops to defeat UNITA and push them out of the oil and diamond areas—changed very early from support and training to conducting the actual combat. EO's efforts resulted in not only tens of millions of dollars flowing into the EO's coffers, but also getting the rebels to the negotiating table where they signed the Lusaka Protocol.

A former member of EO remembers, "When EO first got the big Angola contract they put on a big recruiting drive. They had to get six hundred men; we only ever had around three hundred. The ads attracted all kinds of losers. We used to get all types of strange résumés and videotapes. We used to share the funny ones. There was one guy stark naked with a plastic toy AK. The first part was ten minutes of posing and then him telling us that he was baddest motherfucker in the world.

"In the early days of EO they had to fill the ranks. They did PR. One time they had a TV crew from Carte Blanche, a South African television show. We get the word that they are taping, and one guy figures it's his big break. He gets dressed up in the whole battle dress—knives stuck everywhere, camo, webbing, headband. Then he blacks up his whole face and tells the crew that he has been selected by the group to be our spokesman. He was sitting there dripping black facepaint, putting it on as fast as it melted off. That's the image of a mercenary that people think of."

On this sunny day playing with puppies in Michael's backyard, his products and services seem as benign and healthy as the clear air and slow pace of his chosen world. It is important for me to understand Michael and his world because both good and bad things have been said about the use of mercenaries to resolve low-intensity conflicts and prop up teetering rulers. I am in the presence of a man who knows how to make money from the private sale of war but personally distances himself from the company ownership. Michael's vociferous pit bull-like defense of the concept of mercenaries and private armies leads me to believe that there is clearly a benefit. Direct or indirect. Monetary or not.

I want to get beneath the hundreds of strident articles I've read about minerals and mercenaries and get to know the motivational forces behind this trend. Although Michael has been very vocal through letters, correction demands, and legal threats about mistakes made by the press, he has rarely provided interviews. The media have been typically negative about the activities of Executive Outcomes and Sandline. This intrigued me, and the fact that Michael's client had been hired directly or indirectly to kill Francis Ona and his people made the meeting imperative.

My first meeting with Michael was not so relaxed or welcome. On my way through London to Afghanistan I thought I would say hello. He invited me to meet with him in his Mews home in the upscale part of downtown London. Michael had decided to meet with me to discuss Executive Outcomes and Sandline, I think more out of curiosity than anything else. He was aware of my book profiling EO and Sandline, and even had it displayed prominently on his bookshelf.

We chatted politely about my interest in doing a book and documentary on his company. During his rapid-fire briefing between cigarettes, Michael's point of view became clear. Small, struggling postcolonial countries didn't have the military skills to protect themselves from attacks by small rebel groups. Most of those attacks were against the few producers of income, usually mines or oil installations. Since foreign governments wouldn't come to their aid, rulers were left with few options. Sandline and EO would work only for recognized governments; the entire media fascination with mercenary companies working for mineral concessions was fantasy. Sandline worked for cash, and there was no link between their business and the interests of mineral companies. Grunberg's office was decorated with clippings and cartoons from the "Arms to Africa" event. This incident began when Sandline was accused of illegally sending weapons to Sierra Leone during an arms embargo, and ended in acute embarrassment for the government of Tony Blair and Foreign Secretary Robin Cook. An Australian cartoon showed Sandline as thick-lipped African thugs with machine guns sorting out the most mundane problems by force.

My questions were wide ranging and Grunberg was quite specific in his answers. He could machine-gun dates, names, figures, quotes, and stories too fast to keep up with. Michael never lies, he simply provides dates, numbers, and documents to show his point of view. Most of the media coverage focused on one fact: The major deployments of EO or Sandline troops were in countries where major mineral or oil concessions were at risk, and where Tony Buckingham's companies did or had done business. Michael refuted this by saying that resource-rich countries are the only clients who can afford a private military corporation's services. Most articles made factual mistakes or incorrect corporate connections—although, stepping back, it was apparent that the same people show up in both resource- and military-related activities. Still, it was easy to see that there was small group with similar self-interests. He was mildly combative in our discussion but polite and insistent in setting the record straight as it related to Sandline International and Executive Outcomes.

Then—noticing my black briefcase on the floor—he interrupted his answers, got up from behind his desk, and moved the bag so that it did not point at him. It appeared that he was used to dirty tricks. He was polite and attentive, but I could see that he saw no benefit in sending a message to Francis Ona on faraway Bougainville after his client worked diligently to provide the gunships, mercenaries, and skills required to kill him. He did say that I should mention that it was because of the attention and backlash from mercenaries that peaces talks had been accelerated. "Tell Francis to thank us for the peace talks," he said, smiling.

That was the beginning of a beautiful friendship. After corresponding for more than two years, Michael invites me to his Guernsey home for the weekend. There is no separation between Michael's personal and business life. At home he spends a good part of his time answering emails to Sandline and taking calls from prospective clients. Even a very familiar name from Sandline's past calls to talk about a upcoming project. Over morning coffee he sits in front of sleek titanium Apple G4 laptop and answers business inquiries and the much more numerous inquiries from hundreds of ex-military men who want to be mercenaries. He chuckles at some of the inquiries. The most men Sandline ever sent to the field was about twenty. The rest came from Executive Outcomes' database. Part of the attraction of Sandline International is the myth and mystique.

As for Grunberg's early association with EO it is again, quite simple: "Money. The Soyo deal was a loosely structured event. The larger training deal began without a contract but I was brought in by EO to professionalize their contractual arrangements and make sure they not only made money, but that they got paid.

"They did get paid the first year. I helped them the second year. It's very simple," he repeats for emphasis, "money."

Michael comments, "Tony Buckingham's style is to provide whatever the government needs to get the job done. In Sierra Leone they needed security, but in Uganda they needed water. In Namibia they needed money to fund an election. He doesn't do it the French way and just hand them money."

Michael puts Tony into perspective. "Tony has introduced EO to various governments because their involvement enhances the security situation in countries where he has or had interests. This works to the national advantage and to his as a businessman because a secure environment facilitates economic growth. In other countries the problems may be a lack of water or medical services, and the introduction of this help enhances relationships with the state. Beats bringing in a suitcase of cash, which is what less subtle Western businessmen might do."

There is a continual speculation about the simple facts of his clients' ownership, income, and purpose. Michael insists the purpose of EO and Sandline is simply "to make m-o-n-e-y"—as if I am overlooking the obvious purpose of any for-profit corporation and digging too deeply into moral or social implications. "Sandline's and EO's ownership are not secret; the information is simply not made available in the public domain. It is like asking who the holders of major nominee positions are in the world's largest public companies, and then saying that there has to be some suspicion because the banks or lawyers fronting these nominee holdings won't disclose the information."

He disagrees that the goal of EO in Angola was to capture the diamond areas.

"The goal was to push the rebels out and recapture the towns. Were there diamond areas there and were they secured? Of course. You go for the towns because that's where the civilian population is." He repeats for emphasis, as if I am an errant schoolboy for asking, "Civilian populations, not the mines." But they are often one and the same target.

Sierra Leone in 1999? "Sandline was there not just to assist ECOMOG, not just to supply weapons, while the Kamajors were going to provide intelligence."

I am trying to consolidate a number of differing explanations of the same event. None of the people I am talking to is lying. It is like the film *Rashoman*—each person's story is correct, but they all tell a different story. From the top, the use of mercenaries is a simple financial necessity, to protect large projects, to ensure that the mine is still around throughout the mercurial security conditions of the country, and in a certain sense to make sure the president who signs the deal is still around to collect his cut. Is there bribery involved? Of course. Influence? Absolutely. Evil intent? That is the question that remains to be answered.

There is no one set pattern or modus operandus for mercenary groups. In EO's Angola job, Diamonds were the lifeblood of Joseph Savimba and UNITA. UNITA had brought nothing but warfare and misery to the people under its rule. The Sandline deal in Sierra Leone was at best a thinly disguised attempt to shift Rakesh Saxena's promise of ten million dollars in private funding to a mercenary group, in order to restore an exiled government and gain concessions. The enemy was an evil mixture of rebels and renegade soldiers that overcame an outside peacekeeping force. Bougainville was an attempt to shore up a democratic ruler's control and quickly fix a festering problem. The negative aspect of successfully fighting a mercenary war in this scenario is that the complaints of dissidents might be quickly dealt with to their detriment, and to the benefit of the corrupt and small group of people who created the problem in the first place. In all cases EO and Sandline had done the "right thing" but should you expect mercenaries to "save" countries? This is asking too much of a mercenary company.

"Fixing countries is not our job. We provide security so that others can do what needs to be done. Once rebel groups are disarmed and peace is enforced, the government, businesses, and aid groups can operate without fear," notes Grunberg.

With all the focus on round numbers and the concept of mercenaries, there is another impediment to their ultimate success. Grunberg likes to point out the limitations and unattractiveness of EO as an investment. "In Angola, for instance, let's say EO was paid around forty million dollars a year. So let's assume that 30 percent is profit—so you only make nine or ten million a year. Then you have your expenses, overhead, and other items. You are talking about a few million dollars a year." This is reason enough to show why Buckingham and the bigger players do not need or want to get involved with future Sandlines. "Why would Tony get involved? Tony is looking for big deals. Not one million here, two million there."

The odd thing was, the business of mining and oil in the third world links all the players together—whether socially, in the few expat bars, or in deals that require inside knowledge and savvy partners.

The point that Grunberg makes is that Tony Buckingham—like Americans such as Jean Raymond Boulle and Robert Friedland and a host of less scrupulous European, Israeli, and African investors—not only works directly with government officials of the countries he invests in but also curries favor by ensuring that the projects have adequate security once they're in place. In other words, the offer of investment comes in one hand and the offer of security is clasped in the other hand. In Angola and Sierra Leone, the mercenaries came before the investment. This is the fundamental problem I am dealing with. From the mouth of Michael comes pure business logic, but from the annals of history come conflicting facts and the beginnings of a moral dilemma.

Sandline International was created over a dinner between Tim Spicer, Simon Mann, and Tony Buckingham at an Italian restaurant in Chelsea in October 1995. Although Eeben Barlow had registered Executive Outcomes in the United Kingdom, there was just too much baggage from apartheid-era Koevoet police, Ovambo trackers, and 32 Battalion soldiers. Part of the reason EO had to drop their Angolan contract—in addition to successfully driving out the UNITA rebels—was pressure from the United States to hire an alternative American group of military trainers. What was needed was a politically correct U.K.- and U.S.-staffed private military corporation. The heavy lifting could be subbed to EO and contracted individuals, but the big dollars were through less controversial relationships.

Tim Spicer had retired from the military and was working as an account executive with Foreign and Colonial. Spicer was also a former lieutenant colonel in the Scot's Guards and delivered daily press briefings during a four-month period for General Michael Rose in Bosnia. The original idea for Sandline came from the concept that shaped Executive Outcomes. The people behind that idea were Eeben Barlow and a small group of like-minded South African ex-military and ex-intelligence vets who saw the need for military skills to be used in a more aggressive military environment than pure static security. Simon Mann, another former Scot's Guardsman, was the link between Tony and Eeben. Simon Mann, a friend of Tony's and ex-SAS, was born in 1952. After his service he chose a career in software, specifically secure computer software and systems. He was a director of Meridian (holder of QDQ Systems) until November 1986 and then Data Integrity until 1989 and then Highland Software between April 1990 and October 1993—the year that EO hooked up with Tony and Michael first met Buckingham. As a former Scot's Guardsman, Simon knew Tim Spicer from his time with General Peter de la Billiere's group during the Gulf War. Simon was good friends with Tony Buckingham; the two skied, sailed, and even went on car rallies together. He also brought his friend Tim Spicer into the world of mercenaries.

Before EO, France, America, and Britain had been covertly creating mercenary armies via individuals and front organizations in Nicaragua, Angola, the Congo, and other hot spots. But no one had specifically created a private army in order to generate a profit. With EO, war had a brand name and a brochure. Now it needed a proper British face.

Executive Outcomes had a Web site, a video, and a brochure, but the owners and crew carried political baggage that made it hard to sell to traditional governments. When Simon Mann, the ex-SAS and Scot's Guard, hooked up Tony Buckingham and Eeben Barlow, the business of mercenary armies went big time. There was a deliberate attempt to distance Sandline International from Executive Outcomes, but it was very difficult when key documents—such as the original holding companies for the Papua New Guinea job, a temporary corporation called Castle Engineering—bore the signatures of EO's Eeben Barlow, Lafras Luitingh, Anthony Buckingham, and Simon Mann. The account was quickly closed, and a new Sandline Holdings account was created. The corporation was repurposed and names changed. It seemed blatantly obvious to everyone but Michael Grunberg that a small circle of people kept showing up in the same places. Still, Michael worked diligently to keep firewalls between Tony's oil and diamond interests, Eeben's aggressive investments, EO's military activities, Sandline's more mundane activities, and eager clients and governments.

There was the major political liability of directly offering so many South African ex-military men, especially with the top officers being apartheid-era, anticommunist commandos in foreign countries. There was also legislation pending in the South African government that would make the act of supplying mercenary armies illegal. At the end of 1998 Executive Outcomes closed down, even though the alumni are very active in other pursuits.

The solution was to create a politically correct private military company that would be deployed into low-intensity conflicts—wars that did not attract direct government involvement due to the political and media fallout but would be blessed as appropriate responses. Executive Outcomes had demonstrated absolute success in Angola, Sierra Leone, and other more secretive activities—a track record Sandline very much wanted to trade on. The hardheaded South Africans vets had simply focused on sorting out the problem, laying into untrained African rebel groups with massive firepower and a complete understanding and acceptance of African warfare. But there were bigger opportunities if a company could embrace the more subtle needs of larger more politically sensitive conflicts.

Tim Spicer says in his autobiography *An Unorthodox Soldier* that Tony Buckingham was willing to back Sandline as a business venture. Spicer provided combat experience, press savvy, and contacts within the military. By February 1996 Tim was working full time to drum up business. Within a month Defence Systems Limited (DSL)—another U.K. private military company—referred an inquiry from the government of Papua New Guinea to buy helicopters for a police special unit. DSL was formed by ex-

SAS members in 1981 to provide security to foreign companies in hostile countries. They "didn't get involved in other people's wars," as founder Alastair Morrison says. But Sandline did.

In April 1996 Tony Buckingham and Tim Spicer flew to Australia to discuss the PNG government's inquiry. They met with the PNG minister of defense, Mathias Ijape, Defense Secretary James Malagepa, and Brigadier General Jerry Singirok in the Cairns Hilton coffee shop to discuss an internal problem and a need to purchase equipment. Singirok pointed out that the Australians had been supplying helicopters, but only on the condition that they were not to be used for military purposes. The helicopters Singirok wanted were to be used in Bougainville, home to a tiny festering war in the South Pacific that had killed between ten and twenty thousand inhabitants through disease and violence. These same helicopters were used to shoot at rebels as they brought supplies and fighters from the Northern Solomons in long canoes with outboard engines. The helicopters were also used to land troops for attacks on mountainous villages and sometimes they were used by the Papua New Guinea Defense Force to throw captured rebels into the ocean from high altitudes. The government's only goal was to regain control of one the country's major sources of income, the copper mine in Panguna.

Grunberg and Spicer were to present the initial thirty-million-dollar plan called "Project Contravene" toward the end of April 1996 while Singirok was in London to buy used patrol boats from J&S Franklin. Singirok showed the plan to Ijape, who in turn showed it to Prime Minister Chan. Chan was less enthusiastic and chose a homegrown plan entitled Operation High Speed II.

Well after this meeting, an enhanced form of "Project Contravene" requested an additional six million dollars. On August 1, 1996, the link between Sandline International and Buckingham's interest in doing business in Papua New Guinea became abundantly obvious, as evidenced by just one fax sent to Papua New Guinea's Minister of Defense, Mathias Ijape:

> I know you have been talking to Tim about the PM's view of the military situation. . . . Coincidently, I have today had a meeting with the financial institutions with whom we have invested into Angola, Sierra Leone and

other clients. To date these investments total some US$200,000,000. All of this investment has been into the extraction of mineral resources (oil, copper, diamonds, gold) and all have involved high risk security/military situations. These investments and the military land, sea and air operations that have gone with them are, as you know, a matter of public record. . . . Making these investments will not be straight forward given the fact that large western mining interests already hold key concessions. . . .

> With Best Regards
> (Signed Tony)
> A L R Buckingham

Later, Spicer drafted a letter on Plaza 107 stationary suggesting that the government of Papua New Guinea "form a joint venture with Rio Tinto to reopen and operate the Bougainville mine once recovered." The message was that maybe Rio Tinto would assist in funding Project Contravene and that there was a shared interest by Sandline and Buckingham in reaping the benefits of freeing up the Pangua mine. The project was pushed forward by Deputy Prime Minister Chris Haiveta, who invited Spicer in November to visit Papua New Guinea. By December, a contract to create a commander's plan was agreed to for $250,000.

One minor problem was that Sandline didn't technically exist. A corporation was set up in Bahamas (#89683). Michael provided space in his Plaza 107 office in Kensington on Kings Road and Sandline was in business. But the PNG government was a little hesitant to write a check to a brand new company, so one of Tony's corporations was used for the transfer.

Spicer flew to Bougainville in mid December 1996 to conduct a reconnaissance operation. He flew over the mine and determined that it was important to get the people of Bougainville on their side and convince them to turn against the rebels. He did not seem to understand the complex energies and angers that existed in the jungle below. He put together a complex thirty-six-million-dollar plan that intended to resolve Bougainville's nine-year-old crisis in four months.

The enhanced Project Contravene included intelligence gathering, psychological warfare, and the ground troops from Executive Outcomes. Michael had worked carefully with Tim to work up the costs and the contract. They had learned from EO's experience in Sierra Leone, and needed an ironclad document if things went south. A dozen copies of this plan were presented to the PNG government on December 31, 1996. In January of 1997 Spicer and Buckingham flew to Port Moresby to present their by-now $150,000 plan, and it was accepted. The only changes that Singirok requested during the final contract negotiations was that the proposal not include transport helicopters; he intended to source these from J&S Franklin. It was later discovered that Franklin was putting money into Singirok's private account in London.

The plan was complex and multinational: Eastern European weapons, Russian, Spanish, and American aircraft, American and South African pilots, Angolan, British, American, and South African officers and troops. The equipment list was impressive: two Russian Mi-17 transport helicopters, two Mi-24 gunships, a Cessna twin engine, a Casa 212 aircraft, and a collection of weaponry that included hundreds of rockets, machine guns, and grenades. The dirty work was to be done by the men of Executive Outcomes—essentially the same people who had worked for EO in Angola and Sierra Leone. They would also toss in a hearts-and-minds package that would call the locals to a meeting at which demonstrations of firepower would persuade them to give up. Spicer believed that the natives were superstitious and that this attraction to magic and the supernatural could be used against them. A SkyShout system would broadcast messages in pidgin to assure the islanders that everything would be fine. Electronic monitoring of radio broadcasts, hiring informers, and offering bounties would hopefully lead to the exact locations of Francis and other rebel commanders. Spicer would then use special forces and the rapid mobility of gunships to swoop down and "cut off the head" of the BRA. This was a new type of nonmilitary guerrilla warfare, one without uniforms, training, or even hard tactics.

The men of Executive Outcomes were used to fighting in Africa against Africans. One successful rescue mission been carried out in the Irian Jaya side of New Guinea using a decoy Red Cross helicopter, but this was fighting a protracted guerrilla war in extraordinary terrain. Spicer may not have known that several of the PNGDF's finest troops had been defeated by children with slingshots. The children hit armed soldiers in the eyes with pebbles, forcing them to drop their weapons in pain and allowing villagers to run up, club them, and grab their new American-made weapons. He probably scoffed at the idea that Japanese World War II weapons had been dug up and made functional. He might have seen the shotguns fashioned from pipes and nails, but he probably didn't see the deadly accuracy that allowed rebels to shoot Singirok in the arm while he hovered in a helicopter. He probably underestimated the competitive financial, ethnic, and moral forces that would lead to his downfall and embarrassment.

The government of PNG sat on the proposal as events worsened. Singirok tried to show that he could deal the rebels in Operation High Speed II, but it ended up in a horrible massacre on Kangu Beach. The other barrier was Singirok's relationship with British-based military supplier J&S Franklin, which was proposing the purchase of armored vehicles and other equipment. Finally, with Australia and the outside world staying out of the internal conflict, Chan made his move. The elections were coming up in April 1997, and the four-month plan was running out of time.

The project was confirmed on January 31, 1997, and the process of paying eighteen million dollars to an account in Hong Kong began. It isn't known where the money came from, but it was very difficult to not only find but also convince other PNG government officials to make an eighteen-million-dollar wire transfer to mercenaries. The government of PNG is supposed to bid on any goods and services that exceed half a million dollars. In order to avoid this illegality, the payment was made in multiple, simultaneous transfers of $480,000. There was already deep concern that the hard-pressed government could not afford thirty-six million dollars for a military action. This came on the heels of discussions with Jardine Fleming and RTZ-CRA to sell its investment in the Panguna mine. In Februrary the long-dormant stock of RTZ-CRA shot up ten times. On March 2 Chan announced publicly that the government of PNG would buy the 53 percent share held by RTZ-CRA. The down payment for the military action and materials to end the war in Bougainville and eliminate Francis was officially presented as the investment cost to buy back the mine.

✦ ✦ ✦

Around forty South African mercenaries arrived in February with eighteen pilots, their ground crew, EO's Nic Van den Bergh, and Mike Borlace. Borlace was formerly with Gurkha Security Guards and had experience in Sierra Leone. The weapons and supplies landed in four flights on a leased Antonov 124 cargo plane. The first two arrivals of this mammoth aircraft alone sparked the attention of the local Australian military attaché, not because of the plane or cargo but because a senior PNG officer in civilian dress was supervising the unloading. The attaché then contacted journalist Mary-Louise O'Callaghan in Brisbane. Within days the story was out: Mercenaries were coming to Papua New Guinea. The Australian government was livid that PNG had flown in mercenaries to put down a revolt of its own people. On Sunday, March 16, in the course of his preparation, Tim Spicer was invited to a meeting with Singirok. When he arrived he found himself roughed up and held captive. He was now the hunted and the target of "Operation Rausim Kwik." Spicer was locked up, charged with having a Makarov pistol, and shuffled between a barge, the military barracks, and prison at Boroko Police Station.

Tony Buckingham, Michael Grunberg, and a Sandline employee, American special forces veteran Bernie McCabe, worked from a Hong Kong hotel to secure Spicer's release. Finally the British high commissioner, Bob Lowe, was tasked to come to Tim's rescue. The weapons charges were dropped, and the mostly South African mercenaries were gone by March 21. The mercenaries still joke in the bars of Freetown and Washington about being PNG—Personae Non Grata. Tim Spicer's and Sandline's first outing as mercenaries had ended in a debacle. The government of Papua New Guinea came close to being overthrown. Brigadier General Singirok was fired, and for a week riots against the government and their use of mercenaries provided speculation that there might be a military coup. On March 26 Prime Minister Chan resigned, along with Haiveta and Ijape. By all accounts the event was a failure . . . except of course for Francis Ona and his rebels on Bougainville, who hadn't lifted a finger during the entire event.

Grunberg credits a series of bribes by rival J&S Franklin to Singirok's London Visa account as one of the reasons for Spicer's arrest and imprisonment. Others say that Singirok had wontoks on Bougainville that provided him with information on EO's fighting style, and Singirok didn't want to see his countrymen killed by South African mercenaries. Singirok's reason is that he simply wanted the money to be spent on his men and didn't want outsiders fighting inside his country. Singirok alleged that all the main players inside the PNG government had received payments from Sandline, although he was the only one convicted of receiving payments from J&S Franklin. When Spicer finally returned to London, Michael Grunberg walked across the hall with a fax from a fugitive banker Rakesh Saxena in Vancouver British Columbia. Saxena was contacting security firms about security and protection of some assets overseas. Something about Sierra Leone and getting mining concessions in exchange for reinstating an exiled president.

Things are quiet on Guernsey in the evenings, so he keeps a library of three hundred DVDs in a glass-covered bookcase carefully lined up alphabetically and cross-indexed by title, actors, year of issue, and genre. I peruse his library and try to judge his tastes. Nothing surprising, nothing odd, nothing to indicate his personal tastes or pleasures. I mention that I am surprised that he doesn't own the mercenary film *The Wild Geese* or even the classic 1981 film *The Dogs of War*. The latter is a fictional movie based on the Frederick Forsythe book about mercenaries hired to take over a mineral-rich West African country. In the end they disappoint their evil corporate taskmaster by assassinating his puppet ruler and hand the country over to an idealist ruler. When Michael says "Never heard of it, what's it about?" I believe him.

Despite his polite, friendly manner, Michael is not someone you would want to cross. He has taken on the British government in the "Arms to Africa" scandal and come out a winner, albeit with a few financial scars for the effort. He has taken on the world by defending a very politically incorrect concept—that private military companies can bring peace and stability to less developed regions of the world. His major focus is trying to get politicians, pundits, and journalists to actually focus on what they see and not what they fear. Executive Outcomes has defeated two major rebel groups in two different countries when left to their own devices. They did it quickly, cheaply, and within a comparatively humanitarian environment.

Michael says, "Ask anyone in Sierra Leone if they want Sierra Leone back and they will resoundingly say yes." He points to the waste and cost of the UN and other misguided peacekeeping efforts as a reason to include Sandline in any potential military peacemaking or peacekeeping projects. He has made his point once in Sierra Leone, and despite setbacks he is waiting for the phone to ring. Another dictator or government will call, and once again Sandline will come to the rescue.

With Michael's help I am snapping all the pieces of the puzzle together. There are some pieces that look like they match, but I am warned not to make the easy fit as most journalists have. Grunberg is adamant about the lack of connection between Buckingham and EO, and good-naturedly threatens me with legal action if I say that Tony and he made any serious money from the activities of EO.

"Tony's relationship with EO and Sandline is that of a patron. There is no financial connection."

But there is that shadow, the footprints, the circumstances. There is the undeniable evolutionary chain. Without Buckingham there would be no large-scale military armies for hire. Without the Soyo job EO would still be a tiny private security consultancy. Without Buckingham's meeting with Dos Santos EO would not have expanded into a forty-million-dollar-a-year company. Without the resources, experience and team in Angola, there would have not been a combat ready team in Sierra Leone in 1995. Without Sierra Leone there would have been no LifeGuard, no helo pilots, no seasoned ground troops. Without the successes of EO there would have been no Sandline and without Sandline there would be no plan to kill the rebels on Bougainville and secure the mine for reopening by investors who seem to be related to the interests of Tony Buckingham. More disturbing is the secondary effect—using outside military forces can create a completely unexpected outcome, in this case the fall of the government, abandonment of the mine, and an accelerated independence process for the Bougainvilleans. But as I am tempted to complete my mental jigsaw puzzle, I am given more insight into this world that suggests I shift my focus a bit.

Michael tries to help me understand the mind-set of the international resource investor. Often people are not there for the long term, since the money is made in the rapid stock appreciation on small-cap Canadian markets. The money made is often unrelated to the actual value of the mine or the volume of resources extracted from the ground.

Michael explains and contradicts. "There are great risks in dangerous countries. Investors are there for the long-term since it takes a long time to recover their very significant front-end investment. It is the multiple of the profits as reflected in these companies' share prices on, say, the Canadian or Australian markets—just like the stock prices of any profitable business—that is the true reflection of the wealth created. This is directly related to the volume and associated cost base per ounce/carat/tonne of the minerals extracted from the ground. To protect these investments you need to ensure that they are secure and that the physical environment of the country in which you operate is stable and safe. Without this rock solid foundation there will be no investment, no wealth creation for the investor, no economic return for the indigenous population and no value created out of the assets in the ground."

"If there are pirates or mercenaries, they would be the financial market investors who make their money by acting quickly on whispers and rumors. These are the real mercenaries tracking the major players—the people who know the basic elements to create a successful venture." In a somewhat teutonic tone, Michael reminds me that investments like Sierra Rutile need a ring of steel around their investment to be successful.

All perfectly logical until you realize that if you think eighty South African mercenaries taking on five thousand rebels is the epitome of boldness, then it may be more daunting to learn that Michael took on the government of Papua New Guinea with a small team of lawyers and came back unbloodied and victorious with Sandline's eighteen million dollars plus penalties, the unpaid half of the PNG contract. Grunberg is also contemplating taking on Sierra Leone for the twenty million dollars still owed and promised to Executive Outcomes in 1995. Michael wages war on many fronts; with money, contacts, and ideas; on the ground with private armies, in the press, and behind the scenes. To some who have seen the wars that Sandline is brought in to end, those who have not met the men of EO, or taken the time to understand the powers that hire them or the people they have protected. Some may find that Michael may be the ultimate mercenary.

Michael provides more insight, "Sierra Leone originally hired EO for $1.2 million a month for twelve months. For the first nine months Executive Outcomes did not receive any payment for their efforts. The first formal contract was drawn in December 1995, and both sides agreed that there was an arrears of $13.5 million. In April 1996, EO's payments were settled at $1.2 million in a renegotiated contract once Kabbah had taken up the Presidency. They were arbitrarily cut to $700,000 without notice in August and, after further negotiations, were reset at the correct level of $1.2 million again with one-quarter of this sum being added to the arrears and the rest paid on a monthly basis with a promise to pay the arrears over three years with interest once the contract ended."

Despite fighting a war for nine months using the profits from the Angola job, EO remained in Sierra Leone. Michael clarifies. "The December 1995 contract we had was signed by Maada Bio, in his then capacity as Strasser's Chief of the Defence Staff (CDS). Kabbah was to take power in April 1996 as a result of the elections held in November 1995 and he was skeptical about the need to continue to retain EO once he was in place, so in March 1996 it was proposed to him that EO—who one insider joked might ensure Kabbah's Presidency being listed in the Guinness Book of Records as one of the shortest in history—would be prepared to stay on in April 1996 to cover Kabbah's first month in power. Then if Kabbah and his democratically elected government felt they needed EO, there would be a new contract. There were two contracts—December 1995 and April 1996 (signed in June of 1996), plus the letter of termination sent from Solomon Berewa (Kabbah's Attorney-General) giving EO one month's notice in December 1996 to wrap up by January 31 of 1997. At the insistence of the rebel leader Foday Sankoh, The Abidjan Accord of November 1996 called for the confinement to barracks of EO personnel until the arrival of the promised UN Monitoring Team in early 1997.

"The termination was a little premature—perhaps to save a couple of million dollars (despite the fact that EO had reduced its fee from January to reflect the government's increasing financial pressures), and EO was required to withdraw prior to the UN team, which in the event never arrived. This gap facilitated the successful rebel coup in April and May of that year.

"Executive Outcomes did not come to me until December of 1995. They weren't getting paid and I was able to help them sort out the problem. In Christmas of 1995, I vividly recall a final financial settlement meeting held in the CDS's office at Cockerill Barracks with about five ministers, the financial secretary, the Governor of the Central Bank and Uncle Tom Cobbley. The new contract was signed a day or so thereafter and then the Strasser, and subsequently Bio, and subsequently Kabbah governments honored their financial obligations to the best of their ability.

"The plain fact was that, until EO had finally asked me to get involved no one had even met with anybody at the Ministry of Finance—they had relied on assurances from Strasser as head of state, assuming that there was some semblance of order and organization. When I pitched up on my own to meet with the Minister of Finance he gently said to me: 'I wondered how long it would be before someone from EO was going to come and see me.' It was just plain bad commercial management and this was because the company was managing a war and had forgotten to manage their business."

Michael pointed out the financial realities of doing business in Sierra Leone. "There are no secret links with Branch Energy, allowing the two to forget about payments because they were going to make zillions out of diamonds, etc. Tony's Branch Energy invested twelve million dollars before the 1997 coup and made zero dollars. If there were direct links why didn't EO stay behind instead of hiring a twelve-man group to guard the mines? All this about Branch effectively funding EO is such rubbish. EO left Sierra Leone in January 1997, but everyone who had valuable assets to protect, from the Italian-owned Salini constructing the hydro dam at Bumbuna to the U.S.- and Australian-owned Sierra Rutile in the south turned to Life-Guard because they were the best and the only credible source of security."

Michael carefully pulls out the original paperwork to prove his point, including then-secret attachments. It is apparent that the goal of Executive Outcomes was to push back the rebels for money, but it is also clear that EO used the profits from the Angola job and fought a war without payment for nine months, and to a lesser extent afterward. In Michael's earnest efforts to show that this war is just business, stretching the timeline further shows that there were other reasons to be in Sierra Leone.

In January 1997 EO left Sierra Leone. In June 1996 Robert Friedland's Carson Gold merged with Buckingham's Branch Energy to create DiamondWorks, a Canadian-based company that is traded on the Toronto Stock Exchange. One month later, in July 1996, Kabbah and his government ratified Buckingham's year-old Branch Energy diamond concessions. One of the two prime leases is a renewable twenty-five year lease on the four-hundred hecatare Koidu diamond fields in Kono. Koidu is the site of two kimberlite diamond pipes with an estimated 2.67 million carats of diamonds. These mines were protected by former employees of Executive Outcomes, who were re-formed into a company called LifeGuard. Once again the links were there.

When DiamondWorks filed its ownership and options on February 18, 1997, Tim Spicer had a security consultancy agreement along with the option to purchase 20,000 shares for $2.72; Tony Buckingham and other directors had options for 125,000 shares. But this story did not have the classic ending. DiamondWorks suffered economic hardship; Buckingham and Grunberg severed their ties to—and, it would be assumed, their investments in—the company. DiamondWorks stocks were suspended from trading, taken over by other investors, and then re-listed. So it is clear that in this brave new world, the endings are not perfectly scripted.

Still, I am finally seeing the picture. In a world of plausible deniability, suspicion, and myth, the storm swirls around a vortex—a calm, invisible force that sends other elements swirling in destructive and productive energies. Buckingham is at the center of the vortex sitting calmly unattached or connected. But his actions send a stream of people and money into the world of war and resources. Amazingly undocumented or interviewed, he has adopted the skills of the Kamajors, the mystical hunters of Africa who believe they can become invisible in battle. When the attacks start, Tony can become invisible by waving his personal talisman to deflect bullets. Michael Grunberg is Tony's personal talisman—a cutoff to shut down or deflect criticism, a lightning rod to attract anger, a invisible shield in some cases and a calming force in others. Whenever the media get curious about Tony, Michael is there to throw cold facts on the fire of speculation. Neither Michael nor Tony invented the business of mercenary warfare. They didn't start the wars they provide solutions to, they didn't create the cultures that demand patronage and payback, but they work effortlessly in regions that terrify most. And they profit from their courage. They don't seek to run the countries or make the laws. They simply seek to create a profitable partnership with the government, investors, and ultimately the people who receive whatever benefits come from the mines, oil wells, and other ventures. While they come to the table with only cash and a hearty handshake, they bring the promise of a private army.

EO and Sandline (and their patrons and advisers) didn't invent the idea of using mercenaries to sweeten business deals or gain favor. But each person has made a unique contribution to the business of war and offering solutions to security. Tony and Michael can be credited with inventing the modern PMC, private military corporation. A private army that can be used as you please . . . if you have the cash, of course, and only if they want to work for you. They insist that they only work for recognized governments, even if they have to do a little contractual shape shifting to change Rakesh Saxena's money into Sierra Leone government's money, or even if EO worked for coup leader Valentine Strasser. Their ultimate benefit is offering something other than chaos and anarchy. It can argued that some countries have sold far more than just mineral concessions to helpful governments that have intervened on their behalf. On the other side, there have been major political changes in Angola, Sierra Leone, and Bougainville. Faced with complete anarchy and the most brutal rebels since the Khmer Rouge, EO quickly brought sanity to Sierra Leone. Even the subsequent investment by Tony's partners can only be considered a positive force. In Bougainville the attempt to defeat the rebels and resuscitate the Panguna mine was misguided, perhaps as a result of a lack of intelligence and the lucrative nature of the military contract changed the South African model.

Michael shows me around Guernsey in his sport utility vehicle. Like everything he owns it is spotless, modest, and new. There is something bothering Michael as he drives me around on a scenic tour of Guernsey. He pulls over and searches around the car. Michael is a careful man who knows what a death threat is. Is it a bomb . . . a tracking device? No, a small stone stuck in the tire tread that makes an annoying *tick tick tick* sound as we drive. Michael doesn't miss anything. Later that day we are having dinner in downtown Guernsey. Over dinner we discuss the economics of private military companies—not so much the profits as the economic and cultural realities of doing business in Africa.

It is important not to judge Michael's business in the stolid dull context of Western Europe. You have to view it from the perspective of the people and countries he does business with. Bribery is no more than the ancient custom of patronage, multimillion-dollar contracts can be a few simple pages and have secret addendums, billion-dollar deals are made with handshakes, promises can be convenient lies. There is only one constant, and that is that nothing is constant. Michael explains that corruption is a matter of fact in the third world, whether it's the "small small" demanded at the airport or the gifts like a new laptop or airline ticket that ensure a quick and enthusiastic meeting with a foreign minister. "There is nothing new, wrong, or illegal with the granting of big chunks of concessions for diamonds as personal favors.

"Being helpful to a government is appreciated and brings its rewards. It also generates a feeling of warmth and appreciation which may—or may not—be reflected in receiving better treatment when seeking to acquire the rights to a mineral concession or the like. This is the way of the world: why do western businesses have corporate entertaining budgets? Why do they offer free technical appraisals which might just lead to the sale of their equipment? Why does supplier X introduce company Y to help client Z fix a problem? It is all done to further cement their relationships, conduct more business, and produce a growing return for their shareholders. There is no mystique to this nor is it unique, it is simply the application of age old trading customs to the environment of Africa as it is today."

It is this odd dilemma that dogs Michael and the companies he works for. The popular belief of journalists is that bankrupt governments simply pay for mercenaries to fight their wars by handing over mineral concessions or diamonds or oil as payment. Michael as an accountant finds that idea ridiculous. "You can't fight a war, pay soldiers, buy weapons, or even make a phone call with dirt. Diamond mines, oil fields require millions of dollars of further investment; soldiers have salaries; gunships and bullets all have to be paid for.

"A mining concession is not an asset, it is a liability: You need to invest millions of high-risk dollars before you can even confirm that there is an economically viable asset in the ground and millions more before you start producing Dollar One."

Both EO and Sandline not only started working on multi-million dollar projects, but their clients—Sierra Leone and Papua New Guinea—were in arrears by millions of dollars. Sandline was smart enough to not start the PNG project until the first eighteen million dollars were in the bank before they were unceremoniously hustled out of the country. They did collect however, and Michael is still looking for a customer for two well-preserved gunships.

Michael is wiser for the experience. "In this business you must get payment in advance because after the war has been won or the conflict resolved the motivation to make those payments suddenly diminishes."

But if the question is turned around, it becomes a little less solid. Did a number of the major and minor players end up with choice mineral concessions after the fighting subsided? Yes, I have seen the proof. Like a shadow following a low-flying gunship concessions follow mercenaries, even if not lockstepped by cause and action. The linkage is vague, offset by a few months, even years, coming into focus then retreating in a blizzard of paperwork and legalities. But can mercenaries fight wars in exchange for concessions? Not at all. Is this simply "diamond fever" caught by ex-military men who see a better future in get-rich mining than in fighting? Or is it a carefully calculated approach to get ahead of the larger, more powerful resource companies? Probably both.

From the pilots who flew the gunships to the men who introduced Sandline to presidents, most ended up as owners of diamond or mineral concessions—but they had to find investors and had to work them. Some, like Saxena, ended up emptyhanded for their efforts. Sometimes EO found itself stiffed by contract reductions, or simply nonpayment, or—as in the case of Sandline—bundled into an aircraft heading home. It could be the small riverback plot near Bo in Sierra Leone owned by Cobus Claassens and friends, or the DiamondWorks mines in Angola and Sierra Leone. Or it could have been the completely worthless Panguna mine, crippled by destruction and plummeting copper prices.

To add another layer of reality: Tony is no longer interested in diamonds, DiamondWorks virtually shut down on the Toronto Stock

Exchange, and the realities of copper have made the Panguna mine almost worthless. But for a brief time the idea of combining a private army with the possibility of riches was strong and bright.

Yes, the connections are evident but offset, like the sprouting of seed months after being planted, or—as the media will always see it—as something negative, like the dark stain that is left after a body is removed from a hot African road when a journalist is too late to see the actual deed. But what about the future of mercenaries as an army for hire? With the principals having gone on to other things, was it just a bright flash of hope in a dark world of violence? Michael explains that the future of Sandline will be in relatively small training jobs providing expertise. Still, Grunberg would like to see a different role for mercenaries, or Private Military Companies, as they are becoming known. "Unless the United Nations can see that private military companies can be a valuable extra string to their bow and can be used effectively and professionally to bring an end to conflicts in the darker reaches of Africa where the international community is not prepared to send its own troops but recognizes its moral responsibility to care.

"Every five years a big job will come along, and it will make money. It will not be from PR or careful sales. It will be some ruler of a small third-world country who will call . . . but he won't make that call until he hears the AK fire just outside his window."

PART THREE

I had tried and failed to enter Bougainville. As bits and pieces of news came out of the island, I noticed that Francis Ona was still an enigmatic holdout in the misty mountaintops around Panguna. Then one day a letter appeared addressed to me.

Dear Sir

We have received your letter by fax from Rosemarie Gillespie. We did not respond at the moment of recieving your request because at that time we put on a policy to strictly ban all media from meddling in our affairs. The 9 years desparate struggles against monsters have taught us invaluable insights. We do not trust any foreign media. They were only making millions from the blood of both Bougainvilleans and Papua New Guineans.

The letter went on to compliment me on my intentions and requoted entire passages from the fax I'd sent. Then it listed ten items I should disseminate verbatim to the world's press. Finally, Francis's secretary wrote:

I can assure you that what ever you publish in your preliminaries will gain you access to Bougainville to see our President Mr. Francis Ona. I will eventually introduce you to him to accept your coming over to Bougainville.

The game was on again.

This time I would enter from the north instead of taking the circuitous route through the northern Solomons. It was forbidden for outsiders to fly into Bougainville. Things were very tense, and the peacekeepers on the island kept a firm hand on any information coming out of the island—anything but sweetness and light. They were working with the rebel leaders, whom they had connived to enter peace talks. Money and other benefits were also involved. It wasn't a very moral stance, but it was workable. It was not so much the reality of peace as the appearance of peace that was needed.

I entered Papua New Guinea through Port Moresby with cameraman David Keane. On first impression, Port Moresby looked like an armed camp. Homes were surrounded with concertina wire and high fences. Security guards blocked the driveways; windows had steel bars. Large numbers of men had drifted into town looking for work and now sat around staring listlessly. At night many of the men become *raskols,* or bandits. There were forty thousand unemployed youths in Port Moresby and eighty-four illegal squatter settlements. According to the Institute of National Affairs, 98 percent of the people cited crime and theft as the biggest single obstacle to business in Papua New Guinea. The occurrence of property crime was twice as high as in Australia, and violent crime was nineteen times as high.

Statistics only hinted at the state of siege that the whites felt. A female expat in the airport said she didn't even get off the plane in Port Moresby when flying home. She used to wait in the airport, but someone had once stolen all her baggage, so now she just waited on the plane until it took off for the connecting flight. It was simply too dangerous.

Despite the bars, guns, barbed wire, and fear, Port Moresby was surprisingly modern, almost too modern. The only clue that we were in a remote region of the world was a colorful mural of painted faces in the customs area. I went from the airport to one of the nicest hotels in town—an ice-cold, very modern Travelodge with a view overlooking the city.

A group of noisy Australians from my plane was in the bar. They ordered beer and noted very loudly that Maggie was our local bartender. I was surprised at the number of jibes she ignored. One rude Aussie remarked on her dark skin and large Afro-style hair. "You're one of the local ones ayh?" he said. "Thaay gaave you a good job eh?"

Maggie pretended not to hear and got their beers as quickly as any other bartender I'd ever seen.

The Aussie paid for his beer and took a sip. "Yeeh caaan't taste the bee-tel nut in this stuff," he said.

I scanned a local paper called *The Wontok*. The headlines made sense if you read the pidgin phonetically. Easter was "Ista"; Jesus was "jisas." Us was "yumi"—for "you-me." Although I was in an English-speaking country I had a lot to learn.

The next day we flew to Buka, the last scheduled stop from Port Moresby. Along the way we could see the jungles and serpentine rivers of New Guinea. We weren't allowed to travel from Buka on to the island of Bougainville. If I'd told immigration that my final destination was Bougainville, I would have required special permission, which would have been refused. I decided to fly to Buka and wing it from there. Technically I was supposed to check in with a new peace group run by the rebels, but I also sensed that this was just another way to keep people out. Not every-one was invited to the Holy Land.

When we got to the tiny one-room airport in Buka we discovered that a new air service to Arawa on the island of Bougainville had just started up—a Twin Otter from Hevi-Lift, the same company that supplied Sin-girok's military helicopters. I asked two Australians who were waiting to travel to Arawa with the Ausaid group how we could get on the plane, and stood next to them when I bought tickets for the last two seats. Within a few hours we were loaded up and on our way.

The flight to Arawa provided a dramatic introduction to Bougainville. What had been a purple silhouette from Choiseul in the Solomons was now a grand tableau. There were mountains with vertical slopes, waterfalls, a smoking volcano, and coral reefs. When we landed at Arawa we discov-ered that there were no hotels or restaurants. The idea was to find a guest-house and pay for a room. All four of us jumped onto the back of a Toyota pickup truck to go to Teresa's guesthouse, which cost 60 kina a night, including meals.

The guesthouse was in a plot of former mining housing. When the mine employees left, other people moved into the breezy two-story houses to protect them from looting. It seemed oddly suburban; a man was cut-ting his grass with a lawn mower across the street.

There were once forty thousand people in Arawa, but now that number had fallen to 10,000. War, starvation, and sickness had killed fifteen thousand of them. According to the Red Cross, the PNG-imposed blockade killed two thousand children in just the first two years. But people were starting to come back because they sensed there were more opportunities here. I discussed various scenarios for Bougainville with the aid workers as we sat on the balcony overlooking the street. Not all of them had a happy ending. There was to be a referendum soon but either way, the result of the vote wouldn't create true autonomy.

The people here were traumatized. Teens watched silently with dark expressions. People had come here to brutalize and kill them. They would need trauma counseling. One odd result of the tenuous peace was a Ponzi scheme going around. Locals put in two thousand kina and were supposed to be paid off every six weeks. So far the Ponzis had been paying off like clockwork. One scheme called Uvistrek paid off 50 percent in two weeks, 100 percent in four weeks, and so on. The longer you kept your money in the scheme, the more it paid off. The schemes had been going for two years. Teresa, our host, insisted that people were getting rich.

"The locals are chartering F-28 helicopter to go to Port Moresby and driving top-of-the-line Land Cruisers," she said. "The man who runs the Ponzi scheme lives in Siwai and even the woman next door has made twenty thousand kina."

The locals were cashed out when they reached a million kina. Teresa continued to try to convince me that the scheme worked. "Nearly all the local businessmen have reached a million kina. Then you give a chance to other people. They are opening branches of Uvistrek in Leh and Buka. People are taking their money out of all the other banks and putting it into the schemes."

I tried to explain how a pyramid scheme worked, but Teresa was adamant that everyone came out ahead. The candle slowly burned down as we talked under the star-filled night. At one point the second-story home started to sway back and forth roughly and the ground trembled beneath us. We were sitting through an earthquake, a common occurrence here.

Bougainville is the easternmost island in Papua New Guinea before you hit the Solomons. The people on Bougainville are unlike the Melanesian "rusties" from the mainland: Their skin color is pure black. The only people as black as the Bougainvilleans are some tribes found in northern Uganda and the southern Sudan, and perhaps the people of the Andaman Islands off the Indian coast. The Bougainvilleans are very proud of their skin color and their history. Some will tell you that they are from Africa, or that they are the children of Solomon, the Chosen People.

There are more clues in their conduct. Their habits are very similar to those of the people of Sudan. Social miscues are easy here. They speak very softly, as if embarrassed, and will talk at length while staring at the ground. They are shy and gregarious, suspicious of outsiders and extremely hospitable, peaceful and warlike. They live in heaven and in hell.

The next morning David and I went to see the deputy commissioner. A new military Land Rover passed by us on the road. The driver turned around and said, "G'day, mate."

The Australian military had found us. I started a polite preamble about shooting a show for the Discovery Channel when the driver said, "Oi, we want to be on the telly. Get in." We sensed that declining their invitation would make them suspicious, so we agreed. We jumped in the back of the canvas-covered truck and were whisked to the converted school that served the peacekeepers' base.

We were shown to the public relations woman, who immediately wanted us to interview the brigadeer in charge of the peacekeeping operation. I interviewed the brigadeer. He had absolutely nothing to say other than that things were fine. Then they sent us with a crew to see the island. The Aussies were cheerful but found the post mind-numbingly boring. Their biggest problem was that the locals drank a homemade wine called JJ, or Jungle Juice.

Loloho served as the main base for the Australians. It had once been a giant complex where the ore came down from the mountain and was loaded onto ore ships. There was a PX with chilled soft drinks, radios, candy bars, and personal items. They were providing medical care for the locals and the soldiers in tents. When I filmed the examination of an injured kid, an Australian officer chewed me out; we should have asked permission, he said. I found it odd that we were being chaperoned by a PR person and yelled at for filming a good deed.

The peacekeeping mission was supposed to be a multinational affair but it was primarily Australian. The Aussies were kept inside the base and the Vanuatans and New Zealanders went out into the villages, but only when they were invited. The troops were prohibited from giving gifts, fixing potholes, or doing anything for the locals. They could chat with them but couldn't offer any aid, because it might appear that they were favoring one village over another. They had a travel curfew of 21:30, or they could stay overnight in villages.

There were two no-go zones. One was a large red area around the Panguna mine, the other was the village next to it. I asked why.

"Well, we have been asked not to fly there and it's something sacred."

I asked nonchalantly about the road to the mine. They told me that the road up the mountain to the mine was blocked by checkpoints. In addition, there were snipers in the hills and even a helmet on a stick to mark a dead PNGDF soldier. Another Australian soldier upped the ante by telling me that the marker was a skull on a stick. I asked if they had been up to see the mine. Judging by their expressions, I guessed that they hadn't.

The next day the Aussies drove us around on an aimless tour. The destroyed town of Arawa is a macabre education. We crossed a ravine where the BRA had ambushed a PNGDF force by putting mines under the road. They blew up the first vehicle and killed half a dozen. (When pronouncing the number six, the Kiwis said "sucks," and the Aussies "sex.") We passed the golf course, the tennis courts, and the police station where the PNGDF had lined the rebels up against a green cinder-block wall and shot them. The peacekeeper tour guides gave us lots of trivia as well. "Over there," our driver said as he pointed to a sparkling bay, "a fisherman thought he caught something big, but it was an Australian submarine."

There was an odd detachment between peacekeepers and the locals. They waved at every single local we saw, but they weren't allowed to give the locals rides. Their rationale was that the people might become dependent on the peacekeepers.

That night a neighbor stopped by for a visit. Chris was a former BRA fighter who now worked for Oxfam New Zealand. He joined us for dinner and brought some Mason jars of local hooch—Jungle Juice—from down the road. The JJ was made from pineapples and could be up to 80 proof. Chris used to work in Panguna as a personnel officer.

"Of the three thousand people who worked at the mine, a thousand were expats. Their outside influence did change things. Bougainvilleans like heavy-metal bands. They like Levis because they think they match their black skin."

Chris was a member of the Bougainville Resistance, the group that was set up by the PNGDF as a countermeasure to the BRA, or Bougainville Revolutionary Army. He was a military intelligence officer. He could testify to the extrajudicial executions. They were responsible for the Kangu massacre.

"The resistance kept the BRA in shape," he said. "A platoon was massacred along with some policeman. They used to switch sides depending on conditions."

Even though there were two sides, most islanders could point to blood relations with one leader or another. Joseph Kabui was Chris's cousin. He compared the fighting to NGOs fighting among each other, then remarked that the M-16 was hard to clean, and that he could shoot pigeons with it. I realized that the JJ was kicking in.

He tried to think of famous Bougainvilleans. He thought a long time and came up with William Takaku, the director of the PNG National Theater and the man who'd played Man Friday with Pierce Brosnan in the movie *Robinson Crusoe*. I mentioned that maybe Francis Ona might be the most famous Bougainvillean, but Chris had a different view of Francis's history.

"Ona worked in personnel in the mines. Francis was also a surveyor and was demoted for marking some surveys wrong. He is simply an angry man. He listens to outside people too much. He is a bit superstitious. Maybe he believes in magic."

Chris tried to explain how people felt here. There was the evil eye. People could kill you just by looking at you a certain way. The concept of payback was strong. If you slighted someone on the mainland, they'd send a little man with an ax from Mount Hagen to fix you. Payback.

Chris looked around at the Western-style building we were in. "We didn't build these places, the foreigners built them. We also have a right to destroy them. We believe we are owners of whatever we sit on.

"The whole idea of NGOs is going to change when I get going. Funded on an as-needed basis. My people are not deprived. They should be left alone. We don't want free gifts. What is free means that they have bought you. A bit like whoring. PNG is politically independent but it is a beggar. This place here is a paradise. I would place a moratorium on mining until all Bougainvilleans are educated."

The Australians trained him to fight against the BRA. "We were in uniform and carried a lot of ammunition. I would come back and shoot the rebels in their houses. The rear and forward scouts were resistance fighters. Our recon unit was trained by the Rangers." He described his journey from BRA rebel to government informer.

"As rebels, we fought empty-handed, as a self-defense measure. Our job was to come down here to the village, grab the arms from the soldiers, and run back into the mountains. But one day when we got here they killed our operational commander and we stayed.

"I joined the government faction because I was beaten very badly." He demonstrated where and how he was beaten. "They got me from the side with a gavel, then they put me in a concentration camp. First it was one-to-one interrogation. Then one, two, then three. Then there was a blinding light. Next time I realized. Then I put up my hand and grabbed the head of the gavel. After all this bullshit they told me, 'Bougainvilleans are the best boxers in the world. We like a good fistfight.'

"When they beat me I was angry. I am not a violent person." He broke off his story to look in the Mason jar of clear JJ. As he rotated his glass the clear liquid formed a small vortex. "Good JJ has a white tornado in the middle," he said.

Even though Ona was his mortal enemy, he made light of his politics and called the rebel leader on the hill behind us "Cranky Franky." The joke going around town was that the Australians should turn Panguna into a national park and make Ona the head ranger. Then the war would be over.

One of the reasons Kabui split with Francis was his use of outside advisers like Rosemarie Gillespie and Max Watts. "There is too much meddling. Kabui did a background check on 'Crazy Rosie' and found that her father was an intelligence agent during World War II. The BRA used to complain, 'why do they let Australians in?'" said Chris. He knew I was trying to get up to see Francis, and I asked what he thought of my quest.

"You are a very lucky to go up . . . He needs an ego boost." He lit a large, locally made cigarette with newspaper print on the wrapper and took a deep drag. "You can forgive but you can never forget."

For the people around me, my meeting with Francis had an odd religious connotation. I would be ascending to the Holy Land in the clouds to see a phantom. Francis's wife was a Papua New Guinean, and he had seven children. The children went to school in Arawa. Francis had been up on the hill for so long that nobody remembered what he looked like. Maybe he was dead. Maybe he lived in town. Nobody knew.

While I waited for a ride that could take me up the mountains, I talked to Teresa. The women were in charge here. They would throw a feast for their husbands' families, but only after ten years, and only if the husbands proved themselves and they had good healthy children. The clans made many of the decisions about who married whom. Ona was one of the title-holders of property around the mine. His cousins were also titleholders. There were rumors that he was doing well with Maybank, another pyramid scheme. Teresa knew that a helicopter landed there once and that Francis did communicate, but only through intermediaries.

Other women came over to talk with me. I gave them my recipe for French bread and they copied it carefully. I asked why they were so intent on learning my recipe. Teresa said that the women were very jealous with recipes here; when they shared them they usually left one ingredient out. Their ovens were made of forty-five-gallon drums. They turned the drums on their sides, covered them with stones and earth, and set the fire below.

Teresa had been to Sweden to represent Bougainville as the head of a women's rights group. "The women there are very pretty," she said. "I was looking for ice cream but couldn't find it." She went there in the winter. She had also been to Cambodia with the UN. Her husband was from Papua New Guinea and had fled before the crisis. When she went to visit him after the crisis she discovered he had a new wife and family. The women sitting across from her had the same story. There was a commotion as a wife cussed out her husband across the road. He was lazy, no good, and drunk. The other women joined in the humiliation of the drunken man.

Dave and I had a daily ritual of walking to town to visit the main center. Some kids were playing a bizarre form of cricket: They stacked up mackerel cans and then knocked them down with a ball made of plaited fronds. If the children knocked the cans down, their next target was whoever tried to reset the cans. I talked to three girls in a completely destroyed Mobil station. They had never seen television, but they had heard radio. Their favorite group was the Backstreet Boys, and they wanted to know if David was married. They had also seen movies, and their favorite was *Rambo.*

The banks and squash courts had been turned into rudimentary stores and restaurants. The small shops had neat stacks of tinned goods. Outside, men with sunglasses and dreadlocks glared at us. The town seemed to be in a time warp, and the feeling was intensified by the slogans on the buildings. A Coke sign told us, YOU CAN'T BEAT THE FEELING.

Idle teens dressed in grubby L.A. Laker T-shirts came in from the villages to sit and watch.

"What are you waiting for?" I asked.

"For the sun to go down," one of them replied.

"Then what?"

"Drink JJ and wait for tomorrow. Then come into town and hang out."

They had no money, no jobs, nothing to do. In the hills they had gardens and chores. I suggested that maybe they could offer to clean up around the stores and ask for twenty kina. "Maybe," he said. The PNGDF drove by in their camo Land Rover.

The next day I bumped into Tony the boatman, the man who was going to take me across the channel from the Solomon Islands. He staggered through the market in Arawa in full camo military gear. He was staggering because he was stoned, drunk, or both. He stared at me through bloodshot eyes and said that was no longer running journos and aid workers. Only beer now. He bought SolBrew brand beer for 90 kina a case in the Solomons and sold it here for 140 kina a case.

+ + +

By now most people knew that we were going up the hill. The villagers watched us differently, more respectfully. Something of great importance must have been happening for Francis to see outsiders. His enigmatic game playing was legendary. He'd offered to see much more famous and important people, then simply never showed up or sent an emissary. He even snubbed the UN. At this point he hadn't spoken to a journalist since June 1997—almost two years. The Australians kept tabs on us because they were unsure of what we were up to. I guess if they saw us in town, they felt they had nothing to worry about.

The mountain was the backdrop to Arawa. It had been raining in the mountains every day. The granite peaks pulled and tugged at the clouds as they slipped across. Waterfalls appeared between the massive rock faces, and the rivers in town were swollen and brown. Dark, misty clouds covered the tops and sides of the peak, but above us it was clear and blue.

Our contact was looking for a certain blue Hilux that would take us up to the mine, but it hadn't arrived. Our BRA friend Robinson was looking for Francis Ona's son, who drove a bus into town. I gave a copy of the letter to the BRA driver to show to the boys at the checkpoint. He said he would take it up to Francis to see if it was okay to get through. So we went back to waiting.

I went to Loholo again, the port about three miles south of town. The asphalt road went to the cutoff that led to Francis's mountain kingdom. The junction was supposed to be guarded by a group of PNGDF soldiers. I was curious to see the skull or other warnings.

The facility at Loholo was impressive, or rather used to be. The people had stripped the facilities like ants, and the jungle had taken the mining harbor back. The tin roofing on the buildings was peeled back to reveal wiring and structural remains. Millions of dollars in technology and heavy equipment had been stripped to skeletal remains and left to be reclaimed by the jungle.

Inside the cavernous tentlike building was an extraordinary collection of trucks, boats, spares, food, equipment, and military supplies. The Australians lived in thick green canvas tents with cables and electricity routed into each one. There was a medical facility for locals, and doctors tried to determine a screaming infant's problems. The mess area had complete self-contained food serving equipment, storage, and refrigeration. The menu for today offered a selection of Aussie tucker and doxycycline pills for anti-malarial protection. A soldier called Trops wore a T-shirt that said GROUND-HOG DAY. I asked why. "Because every day is the same as the last one."

Troops also discussed the latest surf spots and news from home. There was a small PX with electronics, tapes and junk food. A few feet way soldiers swam in the crystal clear water of the deep harbor. The only disturbing sound was the continuous arrival and departure of the bright orange Huey helicopters. They were orange so that the locals wouldn't think they were related to the Hueys that brought attacking soldiers to their villages.

There are large military maps in the command-and-control room along with radio transmitters, filing cabinets, and sprawling snakes of power and computer cords. It was an alien environment. The Australians were here to supervise the millions of dollars of reconstruction and to ensure the peaceful creation of a government. They weren't allowed to use weapons, but were required to negotiate their way through any problems. If a local shot at them they couldn't shoot back. They not only were unarmed, they had to go where problems occurred and work out settlements with the chiefs. The locals didn't like them here, but they had no choice in the matter. The Australians hoped that in time, the Bougainvilleans would understand that an army doesn't have to kill or threaten in order to do its job. It was a strategy that was very different from Sandline's.

An orange Huey thrupped in the distance. Careful to avoid Francis's kingdom, it curved around the imaginary no-fly zone. The silence fell when I got outside the village. All I could hear were faint, lonely birdcalls and the sound of flies buzzing around the dead toad carcasses on the road. Fast-growing trees curled and wound through structures, and razor grass split the concrete like sand.

Despite our inquiries with just about every faction and helpful soul, our most constructive angel appeared in the form of our next-door neighbor, Teresa's sister, who of course was related to Francis. Her husband was excited that we wanted to meet Francis and took a number of steps to find us a ride.

Our next-door neighbor had done a lot of talking and negotiating on our behalf. He'd spoken to Michael, who was working with Tony Croft the boatman to fix the electricity at the UN person's house. Also, Tim the New Zealander was married to the Burundian Hutu woman who accompanied David to the market. It was like a jigsaw puzzle thrown up into the air . . . except it landed with all the pieces miraculously interlocked. A clear picture had emerged. It seemed that every person we spoke to had some connection with our mission. Finally a battered blue pickup truck showed up. We bought some corned beef and loaded up. Suddenly the forbidden turnoff that led to Panguna looked inviting. When we passed the PNGDF post and headed up the hill I heard songbirds, and the clouds formed a puffy crown. Perhaps I was finally heading to the hall of the mountain king.

I had to dispel many ideas as I went up. The roadblock manned by evil gunmen didn't exist. There had been nothing to block our way except fear. We made a detour to pick up a spare tire. At the end of the rough side road, I met a man who proudly showed me his new home. He had built it completely by himself using natural materials. He wanted to make the most of this paradise by living in harmony with nature. A small puppy followed him around as he showed me his progress. Shirtless and shoeless, I would say he was a native. But he had cast off the prospect of a white-collar job in the airline industry to return to a life he loved. Once again I had to rethink things.

The first sign that we were entering a no-man's-land was the first set of massive, charred power pylons that lay across the road in a twisted mess. Originally placed to block the road, they had been ripped apart to let vehicles pass. Then we crossed trenches that had been dug four feet wide and twelve feet deep to stop the army from driving up the solid mining road. The rebels had placed steel plates over the trenches to create a temporary passage. They could be pulled away quickly in case of attack. Off in the bush along the road were the blackened ruins of buildings and villages that had been burned and abandoned. It was an apocalyptic wasteland softened by lush green jungle.

The road was built to carry multiton trucks and heavy traffic. It was in perfect shape, as if an alien had placed it here for contrast. A typhoon had created a massive landslide that sheared the road in one section, so we followed a rugged dirt track. The sides of the road scraped against the side of the truck as it fit through perfectly. Now I realized why certain trucks back in town were scraped with mud. When we passed the landslide we climbed into montane forest. Sprays of fern thirty feet tall and timber bamboo groves decorated the roadside. The air became cooler and softer as we gained altitude. But a blue hole was punched into the gray fog. The mine appeared to the left, and its scale was incomparable. It was a titanic amphitheater cut in stepped ridges that led down in ever-diminishing circles. I stopped to take pictures. I could only compare it to the Grand Canyon in scope and width. Tiny yellow specks were lined up neatly deep down on the bottom ridges. It was hard to make out what they were, which was in fact dump trucks four stories tall. The toy truck lineup was burned and abandoned. Bright green copper oxide stains dribbled down the stepped sides of the mine. As we drove closer we passed by several giant structures, all destroyed: power plants with rusting turbines the size of locomotives; repair shops, crushing conveyors, office buildings . . . all shattered and reclaimed by the jungle. The only thing that wasn't being reclaimed was the hole. There was a concrete drainage canal and an underground tunnel that pulled all the rainfall off the mine, which kept it pristine and dry. The crushed volcanic rock couldn't support the energetic plant life. One of our guides pointed to the sky. There were no clouds above the mine, yet the steep forested hills were covered in mist. The mine radiated arid heat and prevented any moisture from gathering, unlike the rest of the land. Proof that man could change the world, even if it was for the worse.

As we cruised through the main mining buildings we saw that not one structure or machine hadn't been smashed or stripped. Every electrical cable had had its copper removed; every window was smashed, every engine stripped. We circled the rim and headed even higher to the village and home of Francis Ona.

An older man with a twinkle in his eye welcomed us to Guava. He had a beard and wore a faded red Umbro sweatshirt. Philip Miriori—no relation to Martin Miriori—was happy to see me. He heard that we were leaving and was going to send us a note so we wouldn't go. But instead we were here. He had followed my quest and was proud to welcome me to the home of Francis Ona. But in his presidential way, Francis wouldn't meet me today. Possibly tomorrow. For now they would prepare our rooms.

Philip acted as my tour guide and happily provided background and context to what I saw. He was eager to talk about everything they had rather than the things they lacked. We were in the village of Guava, or rather what used to be the village of Guava. A simple wooden cross signified that this was a Christian village. About three thousand people lived in Guava, which meant "hole" in the local language. In one area steel house supports rose from the ground, but the houses were gone. This had been a killing field, the place where the Huey gunships landed PNGDF troops to kill Francis and his supporters. The fighting lasted for three weeks. The villagers ran into the jungle to hide while the boys stayed behind to fight it out with the troops. Down in Arawa they could hear the shots and mortars. It was entertainment to them. Here in the hills it was death. The soldiers stole everything, then burned their homes down to the steel supports. They came back again and again. But they never won. They only pushed the people deeper into the jungle they loved. It was hard on the children, who shivered in the cold. The women remembered the nights without food, the strong rivers they crossed, the children who died. This was where the revolution began and where it was still being fought.

Below the scenic old town site was a collection of houses built from the remnants of the mine. The entrance to the village was marked with a giant Caterpillar bulldozer. The yellow monster was inert and softened by vines that curled up through the steel tracks and into the engine. Graffiti in the native language marked it as a kill, a symbol of their fight.

They had jungle medicine, a defense force, and a government. A boys' own world of houses klieged with electricity from water-powered generators and a government of grubby, T-shirted optimists. No one could deny that at first glance this was a beautiful place, a cool perch in the center of the island that commanded a view all the way to the ocean. Clouds steamed over the hills and clear cold water flowed everywhere. Although by Western standards the people were poor and isolated, by any other standards it was paradise. A curious crowd of onlookers followed us. The small boys carried tiny slingshots around their neck for birds. When we rounded a corner and surprised people they expressed genuine shock. Outsiders had never been good news. But their frozen stares eventually broke into waves and smiles.

Philip wanted to kill some time while they made up our rooms. He had the kids carry our stuff while he took me on a tour. He said they had jungle medicines here. They had found a cure for malaria and even AIDS. When I asked how they knew it cured AIDS, he told me they invited people to send AIDS patients for treatment. I realized I was just getting a pep talk. As for the naturally occurring cure for malaria, Philip asked me later if I had any malaria tablets. He also told me there were no mosquitoes up here on the mountain as one buzzed by me. As for the giant Cat bulldozer, he told me that they could fix it anytime. I inspected the weeds growing through the stripped engine. Philip talked a good game but he was trying too hard today. Still, I enjoyed his happy patter and hospitality. He just wanted to make a good impression, so I let him. I liked his easy laugh and let his joy in showing me around rule the day.

My new home would be a two-story house constructed with items scrounged from the mine offices below. It was a mishmash of doors, paneling, and wood beams, but it was comfortable. A statue of Mary, a framed Ten Commandments, and a 3-D Jesus photo were on one wall. A grubby pile of tattered magazines and books was on the bookshelf. The only books in good condition were Bibles in pidgin. One man asked me if I could send books. They liked *National Geographics* because they could use them to teach the children about the world. They were an earnest, intelligent people who constantly apologized for the conditions they lived in. Philip apologized that they didn't have hydro in this house. The famed water-turbine-powered system was on the blink.

Philip and I chatted by the light of a kerosene lamp. He was excited that I'd made it here after two years. He told me in a fatherly way that what I published must help their cause. They weren't happy with some of the things the others printed, so they were turned back. They had turned back a lot of people, including the UN. He wanted to know what I thought of certain people and whether I'd met other factions. He only told me afterward whether they were unhappy or at odds with the others. Francis had split with his commanders and was now going it alone. But he was confident that they would come back. Although they had suffered much, they weren't angry. They were firm about going it alone. It had to be peace on their terms, independence on their terms.

They also viewed the peacekeeping force as enemies. Not the individual Australian soldier per se, but the government policy that put them there.

Not surprising when you considered the dirty tricks that had been played on them. Philip was the official secretary of foreign affairs, along with a number of other jobs. He had been a fighter and was now a diplomat.

He kept saying that Bougainville was a third-world country. I reminded him that it wasn't a third-world country but an undeveloped one, and that maybe it didn't need to be developed. They wanted to start a barter economy, and he wanted to know if that worked. I told him he would need a central clearing point. When he asked what worked, I said just keep the family strong, villages small, and respect the environment. It's not hard. Banning smoking, dirty diesels, and factories would also help. The idea of starting a new country from scratch was intriguing. He was hungry for ideas and reaction to his concepts. As for the PNG soldiers, why not go down the hill and put them on a plane back home. Independence? Just declare it again. TV? Ban it. It was easy for me to fix everything, like Alexander and the Gordian knot. I wouldn't be around to work out the details.

Philip asked about our schedule. I told him that we could catch the plane tomorrow. Phillip said that the president probably wouldn't agree to such a short interview, so I told him we'd hang out longer and he was happy. He'd found a sympathetic audience and wanted maximum impact for my troubles.

I asked Philip about Francis's elusiveness.

He played cagey. "We have three more cards to play, as you shall learn tomorrow."

Francis was working his mystique rather well. I give Philip a little grilling. Why doesn't anyone know what Me'ekamui is? What was Francis's plan for the future? Isn't there a downside to being mysterious?

There is much to do when starting a country. They had a flag. Martin Miriori's wife designed it, and they brought it out for ceremonial occasions. I asked him why they didn't fly it above the village or plaster it all over the island. "Oh, we will," he assured me. Philip was flying high when we talked about the future.

There would be a small charge for fresh bread in the morning. Their lives were frugal but they were still maintaining their dignity. They weren't simple people, but they wanted to simplify their lives after seeing the problems of modern life. It's something that Americans and Europeans dream of but never achieve. I felt it was better to judge the song, not the singer. In Bougainville the people were creating a concept that was wholesome, moral, and appealing. In Western eyes could be seen as overly optimistic, but that's how all great ideas start. I found their optimism charming.

The stars filled the sky. Frogs creaked, crickets chirped, and Ann and Maggie chattered in their singsong voices as they made bread. I was told that there was 24-hour guard, so not to worry. An armed man brushed by me with an M-16. I asked why they had been so successful so far. Philip's answer was surprising. "The government of PNG is full of our schoolmates. We had a man inside who told us everything that was going on with Sandline."

The wontok, or clan and family system, is still stronger than politics.

The evening was cool but not nearly as cool as I'd imagined. I lay on my damp foam mattress and looked at the piles of damp foolscap letters and notes. They were questions and answers on every possible subject. Such weighty questions as how they would form a national assembly took up as much space as the need for batteries for their cassette recorder. The mundane mingled with the philosophical. Like a child achieving manhood they were working through the ponderous demands of government.

But the politics were set against background of harmony. Outside my window toads sang, children cried, and showers of rain passed through with a hissing and drumming sound. The vagaries of politics are rooted in reality.

After two years of planning I was to meet Francis. No one told me how lucky I was to be meeting the man. Everybody seemed to know Francis but few had actually met him. His family took him more lightly, but to the man on the street he was viewed as a frightening and mysterious figure.

As we were taking a tour of the village a man pointed him out. "There . . . there . . . he is coming up." All I could see were two tiny specks on the path below.

A lot of expectation is built into meeting rebel leaders, even if it doesn't take years to find them. They tend to build it in themselves—delaying, being coy, holding off. In reality Francis Ona was just a short barrel of a man dressed in a fading T-shirt and shorts. His head looked like it was carved out of ebony and sat squarely on his shoulders. His curly black beard exaggerated the carved-idol effect.

We were perched on the spur of a hill with a dramatic view of the mountains and the ocean far below us. Philip brought out two red plastic chairs, and David set up the camera. A gaggle of children was sticking hibiscus flowers in a white cross. The children went to a rudimentary school but I was a curiosity, the first white person they had ever seen. A large praying mantis landed on my hand. A rust-colored eagle with a white head swooped. It didn't seem like a major event.

Francis was a little stiff on camera. He was careful to consult with Philip before answering questions. He looked stern. Then the blockbuster: He was no longer in charge of the BRA since Sam and Ishmael defected. They were bought off. He wasn't worried about this change in plans. He said that the people would come around.

Francis believed he was sitting in an independent country. How did he go from being a surveyor to founder of a new country?

His journey from workingman to rebel leader took two or three years. It began with traditional means of protest, via the Landowners' Association and his sister-in-law Perpetua. Then Perpetua died and he felt he had to take on the leadership role. The people supported him. "Around the 1980s I came into management and we used to rip stubs and get all the reports. I saw plans and I knew they were going to level off the mountain. Then I would go into operations to see how much they were really taking out. I found how many loads were actually going out. Even the Papua New Guinea government didn't know how much was going out. I had calculated that each truckload was about half a million."

He decided that since the mine was not going to benefit the majority of the people, it was time to shut it down. "We only have 160,000 people. We don't need the mine. We have cash crops, timber forest, fish. We have too much. We want people to know that the land is our lifeline. We all benefit from this land. It is like our mother and we don't want to destroy her."

"What training have you had to be president?" I asked.

"You don't need training on Bougainville as long as you have the courage and the people support you. That is all you need."

He reminded me that people in Bougainville had been demanding their independence for more than a century, but that many of their leaders were bribed to allow foreigners to run their island. He viewed the Australian military as just the latest arrivals. He didn't like the Australians here because they weren't impartial. They had the interests of Papua New Guinea at heart. "They must go. We want a neutral force."

The first thing he wanted to do was unite all Bougainville; too much outside influence had separated people. I asked why he had turned people back—from the UN to the government.

"We have a conflict of our own. We must solve our own problems before we can deal with anyone else." Ona waxed grandiloquent as he described how outsiders had aggravated the problem.

"I want to tell the world that Bougainville wants to help. We want to help the world. The world is dying. People are dying in Chicago. People are dying in Calcutta. People are dying in Australia. And in the whole world this environment has been destroyed. Bougainville will want to help. Not with guns but health, financially, and whatever way we can. We want to save the world. I think that is the main thing why we are fighting for, we are not only fighting for Bougainville, we are fighting for the rest of the world.

"Our problem is no different than the rest of the world's. People on this planet need land; whether you are building a skyscraper or up in the moon, you will always need to eat something, and that something you eat comes from the land. You don't eat copper or steel. That's why men must save this planet earth, and I am for it.

"The world must give us recognition. Well, on top of what I have said. I just want to express that my society is very unique. We got moral obligation to everybody. And I know our customs—we look at everybody. There is no dependence on Bougainville. I mean there is nobody which begs. I think this is a very strong custom. We want to extend that so we start helping other people. That is one big point that I want to express. On Bougainville there is nobody dying."

I asked him when he would come down from the mountain.

"As soon as I got recognition. As soon as I set up my government I am coming down."

What did he expect me do?

"You can help by getting my message out there. You can help by telling the world, telling the nations, telling the leaders they must give us recognition. So that we can help the world. We can save the world.

"We have been blockaded, but that that blockade was not effective because we have a strong binding. And we got a land here that supplies food and everything. We have nothing to lose now. No, there is nothing to give up because we already paid a price with blood and death. There is no turning back. Bougainville must be independent."

"Did you have gray hair before the crisis?" I asked.

Ona laughed. "No, I was all black."

Ona had seven children. I asked him if they would have a good future here.

"Well why not, I want everybody to be happy and I want everybody to have decent life. One other thing I need to mention. I must tell the world the Papua New Guinea government is incapable of running its own affairs. And it can't menace Bougainville. We don't want to be apart of that corrupt nation. People, the leaders are corrupt, you know, and you know they even can't keep law and order."

He was looking for tourism to help him out.

"When my government is all set up and given recognition we will set up stations here for visitors."

"So maybe when you come off the mountain, then that will be the signal to come and visit?"

He laughed. "Yeah."

Afterward Francis introduced me to Moses, his military commander. Moses was a tall, lean man who lived in a village about a kilometer away. Moses was credited with shooting Singirok in the arm when he landed in a chopper to collect dead bodies. Moses said he had two hundred fighters and then expanded it to a thousand just to be safe. I had seen only two men carrying M-16s, although I had seen sideways glances from a number of young fighters. I asked Francis how he dealt with killing people as a devout Catholic. He said that in combat you are just worried about protecting yourself. Philip chimed in that the Bible said it was okay to kill people.

The kids were playing. They threw a tiny sick kitten around like a rag doll and clambered up and over the abandoned mining trucks like a playground. When they saw me they played too roughly with the kitten. I was worried that they would kill it for fun. Some of the kids were thrown into the ravine but they kept smiling and waving at me. Years of isolation and war had left deep scars.

I decided to clean out my pack. I gave away things like chocolate bars, gum, and medicine. They immediately ate all the power bars and gum even though I advised them to save it. And to share. Even my hat appeared on somebody else's head after I gave it to the young boy who carried my bag. I knew that all the painkillers and decongestants would disappear by morning. Even the word Superman, as we called the tiny boy who carried Dave's bag, became a war cry as the kids wrestled and fought each other. They yelled "Superman!" as a challenge. As they walked back from the pit the boys immediately started shooting at every bird they saw with their slingshots. It was hard to figure these folks—warlike, easygoing, and deadly serious all at the same time.

Ann and Maggie were always chatty and cheerful even though they went to bed at 3 A.M. They said the women did all the work. The men were good for heavy work like cutting trees. They were here just to cook for me. The priests and missionaries taught them how to cook. I asked if they ever thought about living in town.

"The city?" said Maggie. "Oooo I don't like it. So many people, so ehhh. Once I was in Australia and things like balls fell from the sky. It was very cold. I was in Sydney. I went through a long tunnel. I thought I would die. Sooo dark. I like the sun. They put money in a machine and push the button and $70 comes out. I went to Sydney Square building, it was forty-seven floors high."

They were supposed to go to a sing sing where a man had died. They sang all night and then in the morning they killed the pigs and divided the meat. Even when the BRA were killed they had sings sings until dawn. They talked about what it was like when the fighting was here. The helicopters would come and the soldiers would burn their houses. They used to have nice houses. Now they were not so nice. They would run away into the bush and the soldiers would chase them. One of them lost a daughter when she was hit by a grenade. I asked them if they were mad when the soldiers burned their houses. Maggie laughed and said, "What do you think?"

Francis came to dinner and the talk centered on the job ahead. It was also interrupted by left-field questions: "How is buying real estate in America?" "What are Australians like to do business with?" Francis was quiet and wanted to gauge my reaction.

Philip mentioned that one villager thought I was a stockbroker when he first saw me. Philip asked if he could share in the profits of the show we were doing. He was just asking. Could they use my office as their U.S. representation? They were also trying to buy a coffee processor. Sprinkled in between were offhand jokes a journalist would commit to paper without noting the sly twinkle in Francis's eye.

"We will buy the Solomons. Give PNG their independence and send aid."

I threw in a few myself. "Provide jungle warfare training, teach the Australian army how to cook, give the aborigines their independence." The possibilities are endless when you have nothing to lose and everything to gain. Money is also easy to spend when you don't have it. Francis pointed out that the Australians spent six million kina building a schoolhouse like the one we were sitting in.

He complimented me on my story that pegged the peace treaty as a sellout. They laughed and said that they had scored a point. But Francis also apologized for it taking so long for me to get here. I asked him what his plans were for Bougainville. He said he didn't have a time frame and that he had three trump cards to play yet. But he wouldn't tell me what they were.

He wanted to make it clear that he'd split with Sam Kauona and the rest. He even said that he kicked Kauona out, but "don't worry, all the boys are coming back to me. Kauona has taken over and paid the commanders with Australian money."

The lawyers had to produce a rebel leader, so fifty-eight thousand kina was paid to Sam Kauona by the lawyers to show up at the peace talks. Francis didn't know what the other commanders were getting. Francis's basic line was that they were fighting for the land and its people, not some standard political formula. They would create a government of chiefs on the clan basis. He continually pointed out how rich the Bougainvilleans were, and pointed to the food left over on the table. "We have so much, we want to help our brothers," he said. "We don't need much. God has been helping."

He was going to start an orphanage and feed less fortunate people. He would also provide aid to the PNG to the tune of five to ten million kina. Their constitution is based on *sipungeta,* which meant wisdom, or government of the land. *Osikaian* was the people and landownership. *Me'ekamui* meant the land and the environment. "Holy Land means everything, is very sacred, people and environment," Francis explained.

Some might think it odd that I had spent so much time trying to meet Francis Ona. To me he is an example of what is right about dangerous places, a man who believes in something right and is willing to die for it. Many can talk about saving this world, but few take the dramatic steps necessary to preserve a small piece of what this world should be. And Francis is nothing special. Which is exactly what makes him special. He wasn't born to leadership or even trained. He is a local man. He has never been on an airplane, never written a book, and he doesn't own much, if anything. This very ordinariness, this lack of official dogma or sponsor, had spawned myths and legends; some say he is a crazy man mixing religion with tribal warfare, others that he is a crafty manipulator. My gut feeling is that he is just an ordinary man thrust into an extraordinary situation. More important, Francis has a lesson that could benefit us all.

In my odyssey to visit Francis I had traveled from the airy circles of wealth to the high altitudes of Panguna. I found that each person had a reason for doing what he did and in the end, although evil had been done, men were corrupted, and innocent people were killed, there was a steadying influence of morality and honest intentions. Bougainville was on its way to peace; a vote was being set up for a referendum on freedom. From that point the locals would have a few years to create their new independent homeland. As for me, I was being kicked out of paradise again.

Philip made up a bill for 250 kina, then he crossed it out to read 150 kina, about $70 U.S. I mentioned that it seemed a bit steep. "Okay," he said. "Pay what you like." Philip encourages me. We needed to leave quickly with our videotapes before the Australians could catch us. We rushed to the airport. The ticket agent, a man with a Superman T-shirt, said that he was worried about us. There was a flight that left in one hour. It might even connect to Port Moresby.

Being cautious, I told Dave to give me all the tapes, and I secreted them away. He was a little pissed about having to unpack his luggage, but he did it. He even suggested that we label some of the blank tapes PANGUNA. Then it happened.

A short man with a sheaf of rolled-up papers walked up to me and said quietly, "Are you Robert Young Pelton?" As he opened up the sheaf of papers I saw that it was a printout of my bio from my Web site. He had highlighted certain parts of the printout—"Canadian survival," a bit about meeting with Francis Ona, and the word "mercenary." He said that he wanted to have a word with us. I stayed put, and for kicks turned on a video camera in my pocket pouch to videotape him. He was backed up by a group of men that had come out of a pickup truck. He walked over to Dave and told him the same thing. Then it began.

The other men, one wearing a Tupac Shakur shirt, closed in slowly.

"Who let you in?" he asked. "Why are you here? We are going to take away all your bloody cameras and films and smash them. We will smash you."

His anger was delivered in a cold, calculated manner. He insisted that we were spies who were using journalism as a cover. I reminded him that he wouldn't want to cause a scene because a couple of tourists were nabbed as mercenaries again. He knew exactly why I was here and when I arrived.

He said that a man had come here before, Mark Felinger, and wrote a number of things only to become Julius Chan's press secretary. He was a spy. He wanted to know again how we got here.

"What did you tell the PNG customs?"

"Nothing."

"Why didn't you check in at the BRA office in Buka?"

"Didn't know it existed."

But I had made a potentially fatal mistake. I didn't realize that Francis had split from the BRA, and like an idiot, I had walked up to them and handed a copy of Francis's letter. I could only wonder how they handled their good fortune.

He had been hunting for us for a week. He was told that two white men had arrived and somehow slipped by the security in Buka. He had flown down here from Buka to "catch us" and interrogate us.

"It is the journalists who have caused the split in the first place," he said. "Now we are going to take your cameras!"

I tried to explain that we hadn't been hiding, just the opposite. We had been talking to everyone about our trip.

"What did the president say? What papers did he give you? What did you think of him?" he said. He sounded like a man who was asking about his ex-wife. He wouldn't give me his name but said he was a former BRA commander. His sidekicks seemed a little smug that they had caught us. I reminded them that I hadn't made it too hard for them find me, since we'd talked to just about everybody we met, including Robinson the BRA man.

"We are very suspicious of foreigners coming here," he said. "You have been to all these countries and you know these mercenaries. You could be creating a bridge to them."

As I argued onward, the point I was trying to make finally started to sink in: that maybe they were creating just the kind of incident they were trying to avoid. Now they wanted to know why we hadn't talked to them, why we hadn't checked in with the resistance or the BRA or BIG. By now we were going in circles and since I refused to hand over anything or give in, it was up to them to make the first move.

I told him that I thought tourists had been here. He was surprised.

"Who told you that? There are no tourists here. We don't want them here while the peace process is on. Things are too fragile now."

Frustrated by my reluctance to hand over our tapes or cameras, he conferred with a large man behind the pickup truck. We had kept our story straight and it was hard for them to really nail me as journalist or a mercenary.

He came back, tapping the rolled-up printout.

"We are going to let you go now," he said. His sidekicks lightened up a bit.

"We are suspicious of you white people," one said. "You come here to disturb us."

As if on perfect cue the aircraft showed up and drowned out our conversation. I used the diversion to shake his hand, smile, and disappear. The plane took us to Buka, and as we hung out at the airport I waited for the other shoe to drop. I took a while but a large Australian with wraparound glasses walked over and shook my hand. He wanted to know if I was David or Robert.

"You guys heading out?"

"Yep."

"We got an urgent phone call to see if you were getting on the plane." He didn't identify himself, but I didn't need to ask.

"We wanted to make sure we weren't grabbed by the BRA or something. You never know. You guys could be Sandline or something."

POSTSCRIPT

On December 6, 2000, the law firm of Hagens Berman filed a class-action suit against Rio Tinto on behalf of the people of Bougainville. The seventy-two-page document charged that the mining company entered "into this tranquil and pristine environment . . . seeking to exploit the area's resources and to do so in blatant disregard for the people and the environment."

After weathering the "Arms for Africa" affair and the debacle in Papua New Guinea, Tim Spicer no longer works for Sandline International. Spicer sued the publisher of *The World's Most Dangerous Places* for describing his incarceration in Papua New Guinea. His claim was settled out of court by the publisher.

Sandline International still does consulting and training around the world and is waiting for the phone to ring.

Jerry Singirok, the man who said "It is my professional and ethical view that it is wrong to hire Sandline to carry out the operations on Bougainville at a price which could re-equip and boost the morale of our security forces" was found to have accepted £31,000 in bribes from J&S Franklin between April 1996 and February 1997. He was removed from his position as commander of the PNGDF in March 2000. Singirok lost his appeal to regain his position as head of the PNG military in February 2001.

Sam Kauona now lives in Palmerston North on the North Island of New Zealand. He was given a scholarship to become a helicopter pilot.

The peace process is moving forward with the expectation that Bougainville will achieve autonomy.

Francis Ona is still up on his mountain.